ᒪᐤ

GIANT STEPS

Therapeutic Innovations in Child Mental Health

LEE COMBRINCK-GRAHAM

BasicBooks
A Division of HarperCollins*Publishers*

Permission to reprint figures 4.8 and 4.9 has been granted by *Family Process*

Jacket drawing by Mark Combrinck-Hertz

The author is grateful to The Guilford Press for permission to use an adaptation of figure 2-2 in *Families and Larger Systems* by Evan Imber-Black (1988).

Library of Congress Cataloging-in-Publication Data
Combrinck-Graham, Lee
      Giant steps:therapeutic innovations in child mental
health/Lee Combrinck-Graham.
          p. cm.
      Includes bibliographical references.
      Includes index.
      ISBN 0-465-02679-6
      1. Child mental health.   2. Child mental health services.
3. Child psychiatry.   I. Title.
      [DNLM: 1. Mental Disorders—in infancy & child-
hood.   2. Mental Disorders—therapy.   3. Mental Health Services   in infancy & childhood—United States.   WS 350.2
C731g]
RJ499.C595 1990
618.92'89—dc20
DNLM/DLC   90–80674
                                                                CIP

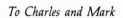

To Charles and Mark

CONTENTS

PREFACE

I must confess that this book has turned out to be much different from my original plan. I started out to preach the gospel of the systems approach to working with children, and this I have pursued. But when I started out, I had worked in a semiprivate child guidance clinic with a public mission, as a teacher and trainer of child psychiatrists and family therapists, and as an independent practitioner and consultant. I had designed and co-led an inpatient treatment unit and a day treatment program, and I had designed and been medical director of a residential treatment program for women with eating disorders. I had been a consultant to parent groups, schools, day care centers, early intervention centers for handicapped youngsters, a residential center for retarded individuals, pediatric units (specializing in oncology and bone marrow transplantation), and both public and private psychiatric hospitals. I had developed curricula and taught in university-based professional training programs, mental health centers, hospitals, and independent workshops. I thought I had been around, and I had a good picture of the field. Then I moved to Illinois and began to work for the Illinois Department of Mental Health and Developmental Disabilities (DMH).

Almost the first thing that happened was the problem of finding a suitable place and program for a young woman who was nineteen. She had "aged out" of the child and adolescent mental health system, but she was still, until age twenty-one, a ward of the Department of Children and Family Services (DCFS). Because of the paralysis of the systems—DCFS saying, "We can't find a place for her, she's too crazy," and DMH saying, "She has signed herself out; we cannot commit her, and we can't hold her"—a judge had ordered that DCFS provide a place, but that the two agencies collaborate. The moments (several weeks) that this young woman had in the spotlight resulted in the formation of a committee, led by someone from the governor's office, of providers from the two state agencies as well as some from the community who might have an advisory function about what to do with this type of youth. The young woman solved her problem by taking matters into her own hands. She ran away, found herself a place to live, and had a baby. Three years later, she is now beyond the age served by DCFS. She surfaces every once in a while. She seems to be doing okay, but people wonder when her children may become involved with DCFS. After she ran away, the spotlight moved on, and the committee never met again.

I had been catapulted into a new level and a new process. The new level was that of government and state agencies, who always have the dual role of serving those in the area represented by the agency and their political masters. The former directed sincere efforts to assess what must be done for the well-being of the clients (or "recipients," as they are called in DMH); the latter dictated the priorities and the amount of time attached to each one. The committee to work out the way DMH and DCFS could jointly care for people between eighteen and twenty-one had its time. Other interagency efforts had longer durations, but they, too, fell to other politicized priorities.

In my role as evangelist, I tried to persuade people that they needed to make children and adolescents a higher priority on the department agenda. But other problems such as those with tardive dyskinesia, recidivism, dual diagnosis, and, more recently, the new standards from the Health Care Financing Authority (HCFA) under the Omnibus Reconciliation Act (OBRA) commanded the majority of the departmental staff attention and resources. For a year or so, teen suicide got people's attention. The legislature passed bills requiring DMH to introduce education programs and to evaluate prevention programs for teen suicide. Fortunately, this was not funded, because how could we evaluate the success of programs aimed at preventing such a rare event? Children and adolescents maintained a shadowy presence in the department's agenda. The major buttons pushed by the press, the public, and the American Civil Liberties Union (ACLU) were the Individual Care Grant Program (ICG), where the department paid costs for residential treatment for eligible children, and one children's unit in a state hospital. Generally, the department was accused of depriving children of their rights through refusing to fund residential treatment for all and through maltreatment, overtreatment, or inadequate treatment in the state hospital. I, the evangelist, tried to persuade my colleagues about the right way to design a system of care for children and adolescents. But they were trying to defend themselves.

People in the department were tolerant. They read my memos, met with me at my request, and invited me to sit in meetings they were having about these issues. They allowed me to represent them at the State Mental Health Representatives for Children and Youth annual meeting (SMHRCY), where I began to compare Illinois's programs with those of other states. Illinois wasn't bad in this comparison. Some states had programs to bring children placed in out-of-state residential programs back home, and these had been successful. Other states had done needs assessments and developed model state plans that were impressing their legislatures. Through a small amount of money from the National Institute of Mental Health (NIMH), grants were given to a number of states to develop systems of care (CASSP), and this got the attention of the governors, at least during the application process. Later, the Robert Wood Johnson Foundation offered a more substantial amount of money for five years, and this too got the passing attention of the governors.

I came back from these meetings with more evangelical thoughts, stimulated by ideas and models in other states. Certain words and phrases became commonplace: *family preservation, system of care, wrap-around services, flexible dollars, interagency collaboration, severely emotionally disturbed children and youth.* Still, the total mental health budget for child and adolescent programs was less than 4 percent of the DMH budget.

Through this three-and-a-half-year period, I achieved a perspective on my previous experiences working with children and their families in the situations where they found themselves. I do not criticize the workings of DMH, because I understand its economic and political realities. One cannot focus just on a child, or on the children who need mental health assistance. One needs to get the big picture, and this includes the problems of children and their families along with all of the other demands on government.

In the three and a half years I have been in Illinois there has been considerable increase in interest and in the quality of thinking about mental health services for children. In my view this reflects the national focus on children that is forced by the enormous costs of taking care of the children who are injured, abandoned, or neglected. "Their families" is now always added on to "children" in talking about programs and legislation, and this is in response to two things: The sublime is that people do actually recognize the value and potency of the family; the mundane is that it is cheaper to maintain children in their own families. There is now a convergence of a technology that enables us to nurture, support, and even empower families to care for their children and a dire economic need to make this happen. But this means a real redefinition of what mental health is all about.

More committees, task forces, advisory groups, and work groups have formed in Illinois, and I have been privileged to attend some of them. In one gathering that included an impressive selection of leaders from the public sector agencies—mental health, juvenile corrections, children and family services, and education, as well as many interested academic and institute leaders—we discussed how to follow up on the recently completed survey and commentary about the "mental health" services for children. Who should follow up? I stated that it definitely should be mental health (i.e., DMH), for that was the overriding issue. The others stared at me. Mental health? They can't even take care of children in their own hospitals, and they don't meet their responsibilities by paying for the long-term residential treatment children need. Mental health's failure is what is creating pressure on these other agencies to perform functions we are not equipped to perform. "Mental health is not a place," I said. "Mental health is a state of mind. Mental health should be helping you accomplish what you are trying to do with the kids in your care, without your having to send them to mental health." Everyone laughed and wished it were so.

Things haven't stopped there. Our efforts in mental health have moved toward defining ourselves as more than just a place. We sponsored some special programs to evaluate and plan for the most severely disturbed youth in their catchment areas, youth who were best characterized as being on the verge of extrusion from their communities and who were involved in multiple systems. In planning how these youngsters should be assessed, we included the psychological as only one of eight areas of assessment, thus taking a firm stand that mental health concerns itself with the total child in relationship to his or her family and community and youthful tasks. Many of these developments are described through the course of this book.

I am very excited about the movement in child mental health. This book's completion and publication is occurring concurrently with changes in thinking and direction that are very positive. Yet I know that many in the field are still bogged down with some old-fashioned ways of thinking and that even though people are logging on to the new phrases—like *family preservation, system of care, wrap-around services, flexible dollars,* and *interagency collaboration*—many have not made the conceptual leaps that must be made to make these things work. Thus, I have turned my evangelism, in this book, to delineating what these steps must be; how they change the way we in the mental health profession must think and act; what are, at the level of the individual child and family, the clinical implications; and what are the implications for the overall mental health of children, adolescents, and their families. To take these steps is an exhilarating release from imprisoning paradoxes and frustrations, and it is just a little investment in what promises a big return—our children, our future. In this book, ecosystemic approaches to understanding and assisting children and their families are elaborated and explored. Chapter 1 lays the foundation by describing a crisis in child mental health. In this chapter the conceptual premises that underlie the crisis are examined and the conceptual giant steps that might lead us out of the crisis are proposed. The next three chapters elaborate important principles of the first three giant steps. Chapter 2 describes framing and reframing, processes by which information is organized into meaningful relationships. In chapter 3 conceptual levels are presented to explain some common clinical dilemmas and to propose positions that observers must take to apprehend these dilemmas. Chapter 4 discusses pattern as the general organizing principle of systems thinking and then describes the ways patterns have been used to develop understanding of systems. Chapters 5, 6, and 7 apply these principles specifically to the clinical activities of assessment and treatment of systems of children who are experiencing difficulties.

Chapters 8, 9, 10, 11, and 12 each describe a larger system in which children and families commonly interact and in which they may be confounded. Chapter 8 discusses the mental health system that competes with other child-serving systems for definition of turf. Chapter 9 deals with the child welfare system and the conundrum of the system itself, designed both to protect children and to remove children from their families. Abuse and violence within families are examined as they interface with larger systems' efforts to reduce the damaging effects of abuse and violence on children. The interaction of child, family, and legal system, with the underlying paradigm clash, is the subject of chapter 10. The varying processes of disputed custody and juvenile justice are also considered. Chapter 11 explores the patterns of fit and lack of fit between the systems of child, family, and schools, as well as the consequences and clinical implications. The circumstances of children with disabilities are also examined. Chapter 12 explores the implications of the health system as a matrix within which children and families experience physical integrity and well-being. Management of severely and chronically ill children is discussed as an example of the importance of recognizing that the child and family are part of the health care system. Chapter 13 brings everything together in a description of a comprehensive mental health approach for children and families. A definition of mental health is implicit to and naturally emerges from the discussion throughout the entire book and is elaborated in this chapter with proposals for how a mental health system should operate in order to ratify all of the systems of childhood.

These ideas did not originate with me, although I think that this particular arrangement is original. I owe debts of gratitude to my teachers and my superiors who have encouraged me, pushed me, and told me when I was full of baloney. There are many from Philadelphia, where I did all my training and spent my first eighteen years after graduating from medical school. Teachers and mentors included Braulio Montalvo, Jay Haley, and Warren Hampe. Colleagues were of invaluable support. Wayne Higley taught me how to think about education. Bernice Rosman held me in productive dialogue. Ellen Sterling set the standard for psychologists and for psychologist–psychiatrist collaboration. Diane Hunt, an art therapist, opened the door to expressiveness and creative play. There are so many others to whom I owe the debt of friendship for their generosity in sharing their ideas with me. In Chicago, I am indebted to my loyal colleagues in the family systems program at the Institute for Juvenile Research, Dick Schwartz, Doug Breunlin, Betty Karrer, and Rocco Cimmarusti, and also to a number of child psychiatry fellows who have indulged me by entering into intensive probing explorations of their own chosen field—Larry Kerns, Geri Fox, Neal Spira, John Costigan, Norman Chapman, Catherine Nageotte, and Paul Hannah. Tremendous support and tolerance has come from people in the Department of Mental Health; my boss, Ivan Pavkovic, is one of the wisest men I have ever met. The director of mental health during most of the three years was the late Ann Kiley. She and other women in the department, most notably Leigh Steiner, set leadership examples for me as well as patiently listening to my sometimes raving ideas. Joyce Farries, my secretary, has competently kept me and my daily work afloat. Jo Ann Miller, my editor at Basic Books, has been a steady guide and encouraging force. Finally, there is one person who has informed and given direction to my professional development and thinking more than anyone else. This is Salvador Minuchin—always himself, setting an example by never stagnating, always growing and changing and continuously remaining committed to children and families.

My husband, Charles, has always put his confidence and trust in my professional development, and my son, Mark, has taught me more than I could ever have learned in a professional setting. The two of them have put up with a lot of absence, while I retreated to the word processor, and I thank them for that.

PART I

Framing the Issues

CHAPTER 1

The Crisis in Child Mental Health

Daniel is an eight-year-old boy awaiting placement in a residential treatment center. He was adopted into the Johnson family after five years as their foster child. Before that he had been in two other foster homes and a Catholic residential home for children. Daniel had been taken from his birth mother at four months of age after being found abused and neglected. Information about his mother's health during pregnancy is sparse, but he was a full-term, normal birth-weight baby in good physical condition. In each foster home Daniel proved to be a difficult child—active, irritable, irregular, and aggressive. His months in the home prior to placement with the Johnsons were particularly difficult. He was sent to the Johnsons because they sought hard-to-place children. Mr. Johnson describes his wife as someone who picks up stray and injured animals and adopts them. In addition to five children, the Johnson household contains two dogs, three cats, a pigeon, a turtle, three hamsters, a rabbit, and a parakeet. Daniel is not the only child in his family with problems. An older adopted sister has diabetes, and a younger adopted brother has spina bifida with spastic paresis of the lower limbs.

Daniel's activity level has always been high, even given somewhat slow motor and language development. His overall intellectual level is in the average range, with performance test outcomes being consistently poorer than verbal ones. He has been described as impulsive, aggressive, and dangerous. Daniel has been in special education since he began school at age four. In early assessments a pediatric neurologist and the educational specialists found that his activity had a provocative quality—a demand for structure and limits. The pediatric neurologist did not make a diagnosis, nor did he place Daniel on medication. Nevertheless, shortly after Daniel

3

began school, his family pediatrician placed him on Ritalin to control his hyperactivity. By age seven, Daniel had been tried on maximum doses of Ritalin, followed by Cylert and then Dexedrine. Each drug seemed to help for several weeks, but then Daniel would get more active, and a new drug would be tried.

For about eight months the medication trial became very elaborate as other drugs were added to a foundation of Ritalin treatment. A cycle developed: a new drug in an elaborate dosage schedule was added; a few weeks of assessment led to the conclusion that he was not responding; the schedule was changed, the dosage was increased, or another drug was added; he remained very active and impulsive, or he became more active and impulsive; a new schedule, dosage, or drug was added, and so on. By the end of the eight months Daniel was on four different drugs, and everyone in Daniel's school and family was exhausted, confounded, and discouraged. He was hospitalized and withdrawn from the medication. As a consequence of withdrawal, he became lethargic and complained of hallucinations. The hospital staff assessed a psychotic process and decided that Daniel needed long-term residential placement.

At eight, then, Daniel is headed for his sixth different living environment, having been diagnosed as mentally ill. His behavior is still not under control; he has mastered only preprimer reading and only basic number skills. He tests his family members constantly, greeting their care and devotion with a mixture of affection and unpredicted attacks. Yet the Johnsons don't want Daniel placed. They have invested in him and are prepared to invest more, if necessary. The Johnsons are facing a system that has little else to offer Daniel than residential placement. The local school authorities are willing to pay for residential treatment because they cannot educate Daniel in the district. The Johnsons have visited the residences recommended by child welfare agency and by the local mental health department, however, and they don't see those as offering an improvement. Furthermore, the residences have no openings; Daniel would have to wait at least six months. If Daniel were to be placed, the Johnsons would have to give custody to the state's child welfare department. No day school will take him unless his behavior is somewhat controlled with medication. Daniel has stolen from his mother, from one of his family's neighbors, and from a local store, yet the police have not been involved. Mrs. Johnson called them once; but, knowing that Daniel is a disturbed boy, they decided not to get involved.

This illustration encapsulates the crisis in child mental health. In Daniel's case, every child-caring system—including child welfare (represented by Catholic Social Services), health, education, and legal agencies—had taken the position that the child was disturbed and must be fixed by mental health professionals. His parents did not see it this way, but without professional support for their position, they felt they had to yield to the pressures to place Daniel. Since there was no space open, however, they had to keep Daniel at home essentially without treatment, awaiting the moment when the only proper treatment would become available.

Defining the Current Crisis

When assessing the current crisis in child mental health, many people note first that the number of children and adolescents who require mental health services is increasing rapidly. Concern about these youngsters has promoted research, greater specificity of diagnosis, and a proliferation of child and adolescent inpatient psychiatric diagnostic and treatment units. Our children are calling for attention in many ways, and the general response appears to be to provide attention through mental health treatment. With more children requiring such services, there is a staffing shortage in the field of child mental health. At least there seems to be a shortage of people specifically trained to work with the children in need.

Viewed this way, the current crisis in child and adolescent mental health is one of sheer numbers: there are too many children requiring mental health services and not enough professionals to serve them. This reflects prevailing views about the risk factors for emotional disturbance, biological bases of behavior, and the nature of services required to prevent and treat emotional disturbances. These views have profound political and economic implications. But there are also many contradictions leading to another level of appreciation of crisis. At this level, the crisis is not caused by the fact of undisputed numbers, but by the perception of large numbers of children needing service that is created by the ways in which emotional disturbance is defined and treated. Daniel's case illustrates both aspects of the crisis: the fact that there are more children requiring services than there are services available, and the characterization of increasing numbers of childhood problems as due to emotional disturbance. The perception or definition of Daniel's problems as due to emotional disturbance had taken over, even though the standard fare of mental health treatment, hospitalization and medication had not ameliorated his condition. What was being proposed was more of the same kind of treatment, but more intense, more structured, over a longer period of time. And now, Daniel having been defined as emotionally disturbed, he and his family faced the other aspect of the crisis: the unavailability of services because of insufficient resources.

Let us examine the premise that the crisis in child mental health is a result of too many children and too few professionals. Then let us examine the conceptual frameworks for this premise and ask whether another way of evaluating the situation might lead to different conclusions. This process—one applied throughout this book—must be pursued to accomplish the much-needed revolution in mental health, a revolution involving a series of giant steps.

Too Many Children?

Two primary factors contribute to the overall impression of too many children needing to be served. First are the broad, vague definitions not only of *mental disturbance* and *at risk* but also of *normal* and *without risk.* Second is a documented trend toward increasing numbers of children in risk situations (e.g., abused children, those whose parents are separated or divorced, children raised in single-parent households, those in poverty). Given these factors, we must carefully evaluate what we mean by "too many children." The phrase means that too many children for whom our current service systems can respond adequately have been identified as needing mental health services or as being at risk. In what sense, then, do we have a crisis?

CHANGING DEFINITIONS

When the child guidance movement began in the early 1900s, the focus was on children who had been involved with the juvenile justice system. Advocates perceived that some antisocial behavior was repetitive and seemingly out of the rational control of the youngster. Questions were raised: Are these children suffering from mental illness? Are they mad rather than bad? Many such children came from environments of neglect, stress, poverty, and lack of opportunities for education and improvement of status. In the early 1900s, then, it was a new idea that some children committed antisocial acts because of emotional disturbance. That view has changed markedly. Recent studies of a large cohort of "seriously emotionally disturbed" children found that few were "mad," most were "bad," many were "sad," and generally they were doing poorly in school ("can't add") (Friedman et al. 1989). This large group of children, having now been classified as emotionally disturbed, will all require mental health services to resolve their problems.

6

REFINED TECHNOLOGIES AND NEW DATA

Another factor contributing to the impression of too many children is the recognition that difficult early experiences such as social deprivations and traumata cause permanent impairments. Since many children who experience life situations that place them at risk for developmental disturbance do become maladjusted, the presence of risk factors should also open doors to preventive mental health services. There are, in fact, more recognized cases of child abuse and neglect now than there were twenty years ago, and the numbers keep increasing. Consequent emotional disturbances are regarded as inevitable. Children are automatically referred for treatment upon the discovery of sexual abuse. Similarly, children who have lost parents, whose parents have separated or divorced, or who have had other traumatic experiences require mental health services.

The 1969 Joint Commission on Mental Health of Children concluded that 13.6 percent of children were emotionally disturbed, with 2 percent to 4 percent having severe disorders (including psychoses) and 8 percent to 10 percent with other disturbances requiring treatment. The 1978 President's Commission on Mental Health estimated that from 5 percent to 15 percent of all children and adolescents need some form of mental health services (Kazdin 1989). A 1983 American Academy of Child Psychiatry study of the tasks and staffing in child mental health for the 1980s concluded by defining critical problems such as the number of underserved children and the need for more trained professionals. The academy study listed nine categories of children at risk for mental health problems: children from low-income, single-parent, racial minority, and migrant worker families; children with handicaps or in foster care; the institutionalized mentally retarded; criminally detained youths; and offspring of high-risk mothers. Furthermore, it now appears that risk for emotional disturbance increases with age and that the lives of the 2 percent to 5 percent of children classified as severely emotionally disturbed are so disrupted that most are served by at least two of the four major child-serving agencies, including mental health, juvenile justice, child welfare, and special education.

In the last few decades many new problems have been identified and have added more children to the lists of those who need mental health services. Many of these have been identified as a result of the development of a more refined technology for identifying and defining disturbances in cognitive, behavioral, and affective realms. Perhaps the most prominent examples are the broad categories of learning disabilities and attention deficit disorders, to which many school difficulties are now attributed. Childhood onset affective disorder explains many other school difficulties. All children thought to have such disorders need mental health services in addition to special education.

Too Few Professionals?

There are several explanations for why there appear to be too few professionals to meet the needs of this increasing population of children who require mental health services. An overriding problem is that many services are provided in ways unsuited, either in tempo or in focus, to the expanding population of children in need of them, by a pool of professionals trained to treat children in hospital or office practice. Furthermore, most professionals believe that mental health service always requires some form of face-to-face counseling or psychotherapy. This prevalent form of practice, along with diminishing funds to support public mental health services, has led to a shortage of professionals equipped to offer the needed services.

TREATMENT TRENDS

As social changes undoubtedly underlie the mushrooming population of children at risk for and actually experiencing emotional disturbance, so social changes also contribute to the shortage of qualified professionals. In the 1960s the community mental health movement, which encouraged the active identification of populations in need of services, was richly supported. But then, after having identified so many children in need of services and having held out the promise of accessible services in the community, the community mental health movement faded away, leaving child mental health in shambles.

How service should be provided was brought into question, both by the identification of those populations of children in need of treatment and the evident need for new treatment approaches specifically tailored to address these newly identified problems. Psychotherapy had a distinguished history as an aid to self-actualization, self-education, and personal growth as well as a tool in overcoming crippling neuroses, as had been demonstrated during and after the Second World War. But views of psychopathology and its development encouraged the notion that corrective processes must be intensive and often long. For example, in one case a nine-year-old boy had been hospitalized for three months because of panic, obsessive fears of someone breaking into his house, and associated disruptive behavior. Three months of hospital treatment had failed to effect the level of im-

8

provement that would, in the professionals' opinion, permit the child to function in the home, so long-term residential treatment was recommended. The parents were told that, although there might be some interventions that could produce some behavioral change at home, it was necessary to get at the root of these problems through a process that would necessarily take a long time.

The 1983 American Academy of Child Psychiatry study reported that the shortest average length of treatment by a psychiatrist for any childhood disorder was thirty-one weeks at a rate of 1.5 visits per week (1983, 25). Such lengthy treatment has proved too expensive and possibly inappropriate for many children who require service. Treatment approaches that address problems quickly are needed to meet the urgent needs of so many children, but these generally have been regarded with suspicion. Thus, the many professionals working within the more traditional modalities have been able to treat relatively few children.

INCENTIVES FOR PROFESSIONALS

In 1982 there were only 3,000 physicians in the United States who identified themselves as child psychiatrists, and of those only 1,700 were certified in the specialty. Each year about 150 more physicians become board certified child psychiatrists. If a similarly small proportion of other mental health professionals specialized in work with children, there would appear to be a significant unmet need for mental health services for children. However, more people are entering the service professions, and service professions are gaining more prestige and commanding higher salaries. One might expect, then, that the demand for child mental health professionals might be met. If the strong support for community mental health in the 1960s had been sustained or had grown, there might be a chance of such expansion now. But it is hard to find competitive opportunities for professionals in the public sector. In the 1990s there is little glory or economic reward for trained professionals to provide services to the largest group of underserved children—those who are poor. The result is an excess of professionals competing for private patients and a shortage of those working in the public sector. In fact, if one looked only at professional competition in the private sector, one might conclude that there are too many professionals, too many hospital beds, and not enough children. Perhaps there is such an abundance of mental health professionals that their only means of economic survival is to increase the intensity and expense of the technology for evaluating and treating children and to broaden the definition of mental health morbidity, effectively increasing the population of children needing treatment. Thus, the group of "mentally disturbed children" has been inappropriately increased and the group of qualified helpers unnecessarily limited.

The Crisis Reviewed

The crisis in child mental health revolves around perceptions regarding an enormous need for services, insufficient personnel to meet the need, increasing risks to children, a prevalent pathology in our society, and inadequate resources. One obvious solution to the problem of too many children and too few professionals is to increase the number of professionals. Doing that, however, requires more money, as well as respect for the profession and expanded opportunities for professional recognition and advancement.

Another solution is to improve the conditions in which children are growing up so that there will be fewer children requiring special attention. For this, there is obviously a need to focus more resources on children's needs. But several factors militate against this solution. First, funding is more often approved for treatment of mental problems than for improvement of the conditions in which these develop, such as poor housing, inadequate medical care, and poor schooling. Second, children cannot advocate for themselves. Third, wealthy families buy services for their children, whereas poor families have few advocates and are often entangled with a variety of governmental agencies. Fourth, there are often threats of or actual cutbacks to public spending for entitlement programs.

The approach to solving the problem by increasing the resources for providing preventive and therapeutic mental health services for children follows logically from the way the problem is defined, namely, that there are vast numbers of underserved children. Yet it appears unlikely that this particular solution will be successfully implemented because of the many factors that interfere with effective service provision for children—insufficient resources and the expanding definition of the class of disturbed children within a limited technology to serve them. *This is the crisis in child mental health.*

Revolutions

A crisis arises when events occur that cannot be absorbed and mastered by the mechanisms usually employed to manage daily affairs. By its very nature, a crisis does not dissolve in response to the usual ways of dealing with problems. The crisis in child mental health cannot be resolved simply by increasing the number of mental health professionals. In fact, as I have suggested, there is a steadily increasing number of mental health professionals, but they serve a small population of children. The crisis also cannot be resolved by increasing resources and prestige for providing services for underprivileged children, because support for services to the poor is dwindling rather than increasing. New ways of examining the problems are necessary to bring fresh approaches to the field.

Science historian Thomas Kuhn has developed a model of scientific revolutions that offers a useful paradigm for new approaches to the problems. Fundamental to every revolution in scientific thought has been a major shift in perspective, so that scientific questions are formulated in a different way. The biomedical approach to child mental health is, today, what Kuhn would call "normal science" (1970). It has been pursued and practiced and has offered a powerful technology to study and treat many conditions in children. But this conceptual framework may actually be responsible for the identification of too many children in need of treatment, and of too few technicians qualified to provide what seems to be needed. Kuhn tells us that periods of normal science are followed by upheaval, challenge, debate, and elaboration of new conceptual paradigms that resolve the difficulties raised in the previous practices of normal science. These revolutions, in turn, lead to new periods of normal science practice and exploration. The challenge and debate that eventually arise revolve around developing different perspectives, organizing the data in new ways, and redefining both the problems and solutions. Kuhn has provided a model for looking, at least historically, at the evolution of points of view. From this perspective it is possible to examine not only the data of interest but also the framework we have for examining those, so that many more interpretive possibilities become available.

Giant Steps

According to Kuhn's model, revolutionary change occurs through discontinuous shifts in thinking, or logical departures from normal science. In reviewing what appear to be the makings of a necessary revolution in child mental health, I have identified some of these discontinuous shifts in what I call *giant steps.*

The game "Mother, May I?" involves the players taking a number of steps of different sizes ordered by the "mother." There are the baby steps, kangaroo hops, scissor steps, and some steps backward. One can also try to sneak forward moves without being seen. But, by far the fastest means to the goal is giant steps, which are like donning seven-league boots to traverse vast territory. At least four giant steps must be taken to transform the ways in which the crisis in child mental health is understood and to shape different solutions to the problems. These four revolutionary steps are as follows.

STEP 1: WORKING WITH DIFFERENT EXPERIENCES OF REALITY

This step is to understand different versions of reality according to the various perspectives from which they are experienced, rather than insisting on one correct interpretation. Different versions may be contradictory, but they are not mutually exclusive. The validity of different viewpoints can be acknowledged if the observer carefully examines how they came to be experienced. This conceptual appreciation for diverse experiences and interpretations of reality does not, however, hold that reality is entirely subjective. When there are multiple views of events, a multiocular perspective allows for depth and richness of the overall formulation. Chapters 2 and 3 explain the conceptual and practical implications of this step further. An example, however, would be presentation of a child at a case conference, followed by the question What is the diagnosis? The answer is that there are *several* useful maps for understanding what might be happening and what plans might be made.

STEP 2: IDENTIFYING HOW EVENTS ARE PARTS OF PATTERNS

Every event is both an outcome and a cause—and more. To identify meaningful patterns requires a level of assessment different from that required to assess the single event. Furthermore, every intervention will become a part of a pattern and will have consequences. This step allows further expansion of conceptual models away from reductionism, which often characterizes linear causality, one useful explanatory framework. Linear causality suggests that there is a simple and direct relationship between events designated as causal and those seen as effects or outcomes. Associations of ideas and events form patterns within which there may be linear relationships. An example is a cybernetic cycle, such as the home heating system, where the temperature drops, activating the thermostat (one linear relationship), which turns on the furnace (a second), which generates heat (a third), which turns off the thermostat (a fourth). Not all patterns link linear events; not all patterns are cybernetic (see chapter 4).

An example of the difference that pattern makes is in the examination of traits, such as aggression, that have been found to be remarkably stable throughout development. The question comes up, then, Does aggression represent an unmodifiable inborn trait? That is, if we have an aggressive toddler, do we have to resign ourselves to this and just learn to accommodate? Exploring the question should involve an examination of patterns in which the child's aggression appears. Who does what before and after aggressive episodes, and is there consistency to the responses to the aggression and responses to the responses? A consistent response might be found across situations. Or it may be found that there are different responses in different settings—for example, when the child is with his father, there is one set; with his mother, another; at school, a third; with peers, still another, and so on. This could lead to the conviction, first, that it is the child's aggressive nature that is stable across contexts and, second, that the patterns of *each* of these situations must be examined in order to understand what might be changed to ameliorate the difficulties.

STEP 3: A FOCUS ON COMPETENCE

This represents a major shift from seeking causes for dysfunction, identifying pathology, labeling, and cataloguing liabilities to recognizing and drawing out the values built into systems, by searching for strengths within expanding layers of systems. This step must be taken in any assessment procedure (see chapter 5) as well as in assessment of change or alteration of a system in response to interventions (see chapters 6 and 7). For example, one approach to assessment involves a family or other system evaluating itself, as described in chapters 9 and 12. The members are then in a position to examine their areas of strength and competence and also to propose those areas in which they would like to change.

STEP 4: DEFINING MENTAL HEALTH

Mental health is a state of systems, not a series of techniques or institutions. Mental health is found in a system that is organized for the benefit of its individual members. Mental health can be evaluated on the basis of the well-being of its members in relationship to each other and the systems formed by their relationships. Mental health refers, then, not simply to internal states of individuals but also to their membership and contributions to the systems within which they live. For children, these include families, schools, peer groups, and neighborhoods, as well as the larger systems of which these are a part, such as educational and governmental systems.

A Systems Perspective

In his landmark book *The Fallacy of Understanding* (1973), psychoanalyst Edgar Levenson proposed that there have been three paradigms of psychological thinking since the early 1900s. The first was the mechanistic paradigm represented by early drive theory. The second was the communication paradigm. The third is organismic, representing the complex integration of organisms, be they cells or galaxies.

To give form, pattern, and a language to the scientific movement to consider systems, thinkers in the field have borrowed from Ludwig von Bertalanffy, a biologist who described general systems theory and biological systems; Norbert Wiener, a mathematician who introduced cybernetics; Ilya Prigogine, a physicist who, through the notion of order through fluctuation, elaborated a systemic model of development; and Umberto Maturana, a biologist who described structural relationships of biological systems. Thinkers and writers in the family systems field have borrowed names from biology when talking about ecology and ecosystems; from mathematics when talking about cybernetics, both first and second order; and from physics when talking about entropy and negentropy. Thus, a certain vocabulary has evolved.

A *living system* is a coordination of subsystems structurally coupled in action. An *open system* is one whose actions and structures may be freely modified by exchange with other systems, whereas a *closed system* is more internally consistent over time. Each designation within living systems is relative. Systems evolve over time, ideally elaborating more complexity and variety. System change is called *morphogenesis*. Systems also maintain certain identities, or continuities in the face of change over time. This maintenance of identity is called *morphostasis*. Cybernetic patterns of interaction between subsystems are some systems operations that contribute both to morphostasis and morphogenesis.

Family Therapy and Family Systems

Some papers in family therapy journals have claimed that family therapy is the application of the organismic paradigm. What has emerged in the elaboration of family systems, ecosystemic epistemology, or systems thinking is a technology for assuming and integrating a variety of viewpoints and for apprehending coherent patterns in system functioning. Not all those who think family members should be seen conjointly, work with interpersonal systems, or practice family therapy, however, operate with ecosystemic epistemology or the collective conceptual frameworks that evolve out of examining systems. Many family therapists have simply translated the worldviews of the biomedical model from individuals to particular families, whether the families are viewed longitudinally over generations or vertically in their ongoing relationships.

The family therapy that is a revolutionary departure is not actually a therapy, nor is it only about families. It is about systems. Individuals are systems; so are families, schools, and governments. Its principles incorporate biomedical, developmental, behavioral, and rational methods. The revolutionary departure confronts the inevitability that some experiences in the behavioral sciences must be addressed in new ways. In this view the symptom is best understood and approached as but one element influencing and being influenced by the larger whole. Struggling for coherence, this approach has as its patriarch Milton Erickson, a psychiatrist who worked with hypnosis but was not a family therapist, and Gregory Bateson, an anthropologist who was not a therapist at all. This approach, however, offers a fresh way of evaluating children's mental health needs.

Mental Health within the Medical Model

As discussed, many people assume that the crisis in child mental health is that there are too many children requiring mental health services and too few professionals available to provide the necessary services. But if we examine how each of these conclusions has been reached, we may arrive at a different assessment of the situation and move toward a more effective set of solutions.

A first step might be to review the prevailing conceptual framework of mental health, the "normal science." This conceptual paradigm is what psychiatrist George Engel (1977) has called the "biomedical" model. The specific theories about mental health and mental illness may vary, but the outlines of the scientific method are what characterize the paradigm.

The Biomedical Paradigm

As the biomedical paradigm is applied to emotional functioning, disease is understood to be residing in some recognizable fashion within the body. It is based on Koch's principles of identifying pathogenic organisms— relating certain body conditions to the dis-eased condition or behavior, and being able to produce the diseased condition or behavior by introducing these body conditions and then reidentifying them in connection with

15

the diseased state. Once the pathogen can be identified, it can be selectively attacked. Treating malignancies with chemotherapy and radiation is a good example of these principles. The danger of malignant growth is that it occupies space, invades, and interferes with normal cell function. If one can find agents that specifically attack and kill the tumor cells, then one might have the cancer licked. Unfortunately, most such agents also kill normal cells, so technological advances are in finding agents that will kill more pathological cells but not normal ones. This linear search has yielded few developments in the past fifteen years, a situation that may presage a crisis in cancer research.

The characteristics of scientific inquiry within the biomedical model have been variously referred to as reductionistic (i.e., reducing complex phenomena to single explanatory principles) and as linear causal (i.e., finding underlying causes for observed outcomes). Such inquiry is characterized by dualities and dichotomies. The mind–body dualism leads those of the biomedical persuasion to explain everything as somatic. Dualisms lead to dichotomies, and dichotomies lead to exclusionary choices. "Nature versus nurture" is an exemplary dichotomy. Nurture predominated as the explanatory basis for mental disturbances until the 1950s when a number of observations about children confirmed that constitutional factors contributed to the outcome of emotional development. This discovery tipped the balance from nurture to nature, so the recent emphasis has been more on the biological bases of mental illnesses than on the psychosocial parts. Most agree that both nature and nurture play a role. Choosing one explanation over the other is characteristic of the dichotomous nature of biomedical thinking.

More and more behavioral disturbances are called mental illnesses and are characterized in terms of their biological bases. The principles of the biomedical paradigm subsume most behavioral, learning, cognitive, and developmental postulates, as well as many ecological ones, regarding emotions and behavior, even though these may not result in strictly "biological" explanations. The reductionistic aspects of the biomedical model focus on individuals and specific functions inside individuals that are within the parameters of known biological processes. Application of principles of biomedical technology to areas as abstract as human emotions and psychology has resulted in major advances in treatment, such as the development of psychotropic medications. Some neurobiological processes increasing understanding of the complex functioning of the brain in its relation to behavior have also been elucidated, and there is an explosion of new and clarifying information in this area.

However, many of the developments have produced problems. For example, tardive dyskinesia, a deforming involuntary movement disorder, is a hazard of psychotropic drugs that seldom occurred before widespread use of such drugs. Other social and legal issues can also be traced back to the medication "solution." Issues about the right to obtain or refuse treatment become especially heated when psychotropic medication is offered as a standard of treatment for mental illness. The effectiveness of psychotropics in controlling the unacceptable social effects of psychosis has made it possible to reduce the number of chronically hospitalized patients, but deinstitutionalization has contributed to embarrassing problems, such as homelessness and inadequate care for the chronically mentally ill. Chains of problems leading to solutions that, in turn, engender more problems are inevitable in a linear approach to problem defining and solving.

The biomedical paradigm is a deficit model, organized to explain and correct malfunction. This framework incorporates no adequate definition of health. People and processes are defined in terms of the presence or absence of deviance, malfunction, or pathology. In an article in the journal *Science,* Engel nicely summarized the biomedical paradigm's limitations: There are "only two alternatives whereby behavior and disease can be reconciled: the *reductionist,* which says that all behavioral phenomena of disease must be conceptualized in terms of physiochemical principles; and the *exclusionist,* which says that whatever is not capable of being so explained must be excluded from the category of disease" (1977, 130). Lacking methods for characterizing health or for including the interaction of many diverse factors to grasp how things happen, the biomedical paradigm, despite technical sophistication, provides only a partial framework for assessing, understanding, and interacting with complex human emotions and behaviors. It is from this conceptual framework that our crisis in child mental health has been constructed.

Too Many Children and Too Few Professionals Reviewed

From the beginning, the child mental health field encompassed children suffering from a wide range of social problems. This is because, in its broadest definition, a child's mental health involves the conditions in which the child develops. Since the post–Second World War era emphasizing the relationship between the environment and mental health, there has been an expanding demand for mental health services as solutions to a wide variety of human ills. Referred to as "the medicalization of social deviance" (Conrad 1980), this belief that social deviance was a product of biopsychological factors that could be circumscribed in a medical discipline led to the optimism that mental health as a medical subspecialty would salve some of the pains of a society struggling with the emerging awareness of issues such as racism, sexism, and poverty. Such optimism peaked during the 1960s, took form in a series of federal mental health acts, and led to the proliferation of community mental health centers. By the mid-1970s, the enthusiasm and funding for community mental health had died, but we still have the legacy of many social deviants who have been defined as mentally disturbed—and as candidates for mental health services.

I propose that because of this designation of mental health as a medical state, the vast number of factors that contribute to mental health are overlooked. Further, too many children are incorrectly identified as requiring services specifically designated as mental health. They are mistakenly either placed in mental health facilities or "deprived" of treatment because of the dearth of such resources. Think of Daniel, the boy described at the beginning of this chapter, who was waiting, without schooling or treatment, for a place in a residential treatment center. By focusing on such children's emotional lives to the exclusion of their cognitive development, their education, their social lives, their sense of interpersonal security, and their sense of being valued and prepared to make responsible contributions to their society, the system does these children an injustice and deprives them of their birthright. Birthright is represented, first, by the family as the most immediate context of socialization and values and, in wider circles, by neighbors, schools, churches, and workplaces. The contributions of these varied influences to the development of a whole child are not considered when only the child's mental state is.

Rethinking Childhood Mental Illness

What is mental illness in children? When is a child's behavior the manifestation of a psychiatric disorder (i.e., a biomedical dysfunction)? When is it simply an adaptive or competent response to a social demand? The parameters of the biomedical paradigm make it difficult to consider these questions. Yet children are more likely to be labeled as mentally ill when they are examined without consideration of the demands of the context. Developments in biomedical research on adult psychiatric disorders have refined psychiatric practice so that a thorough assessment process leads to a diagnosis, which, in turn, virtually prescribes the treatment. The reasoning is linear: The dysfunction is caused by a biochemical imbalance. One needs only to correct the imbalance by giving medications, and the patient will improve. Why not apply these successful principles to children, as well?

18

For example, the possibility that children suffer from affective disorders has led, since the mid-1970s, to the reinterpretation of a number of childhood behaviors ranging from failure to aggression to irritability to sleep disturbances. This is an example of a popular tendency to shift away from a developmental and psychodynamic understanding of children's emotional lives to a form of assessment that puts both psychodynamics and development in a secondary, almost irrelevant place. Study of these newly recognized disorders emphasizes their hereditary and biological bases and their relationship to adult disorders. The exclusionary bias of the biomedical paradigm often results in a choice of medication versus psychotherapy, rather than a combination of medication and psychotherapy. Furthermore, because of the search for consistency between childhood and adult conditions, the transformations inherent in the developmental plasticity of childhood may be ignored. Instead, some children may be sentenced to lives of affective disorder as researchers examine the plasticity of the expression of the disorders rather than of the children. There is no place in this approach for consideration of the possibility that some of those identified as ill may be victims of the medicalization of social deviance.

Thus, some of the perception of "too many children" stems from a point of view. The medicalization of social deviance is a way of defining deviant behavior as illness. When we explain conditions in this way, we must continue to ask, What treatments does medicine offer that justify our classification of so many problems as medical? The framework of the biomedical model and the adherence of the majority of clinicians to this framework actually limit mental health professionals' ability to respond to the many children who have been defined as needing their services. We can see this only if we move to a position that permits a perspective on both the problems and the framework of the problems. To solve the problems we can then propose alternative frameworks—a variety of frameworks that consider the different settings and conditions of the problems as they are presented and evaluated.

Rethinking Resources

I have already suggested that the impression of too few professionals may be due partially to maldistribution and partially to identification of too many children. But most significantly, the impression comes from targeting only a small class of specially trained professionals while ignoring the multiple personal resources in any child's relationship system, resources that are undoubtedly vital to a child's mental health.

When examining the situation in child mental health from a different perspective, one can see that the problem is not necessarily one of sheer numbers. This explanation for the problem comes from the identification of social deviance as a medical problem and the therapeutic response as a biomedical one.

Systemic Thinking in Child Mental Health

What does the systems revolution have to offer? Certainly, no final answers or ultimate solutions beckon, but there are some fruitful new ways of organizing data, viewing problems, and responding to complaints. Looking at the problems of children in a broader context than that of individual malfunction offers different ways of understanding the problems, including the possibility that they lie beyond where they are manifested.

Child mental health needs a revolution. There are too many children because the focus has become so narrowed that many professionals hardly know how to respond to children except in terms of their emotional lives. Teachers provide children with the technology of their society, literacy. If a teacher believes that a mental health professional can contribute more to a child's sense of competence and self-esteem than the teacher can by helping the child succeed, the teacher has been coopted by the mental health craze. There are not enough professionals because the natural resources of children, their parents, their friends, and their teachers have been overlooked, rejected, and undermined, or they have stepped aside in deference to mental health experts. Children's mental health is not to be found strictly in their genes, in their neurochemistry, or in the mythical realm of the psyche. It is to be found in the interaction between each child's organism (including genes, neurochemistry, and psyche) and the richness of his or her interpersonal context and the opportunities provided therein. These aspects of children's lives cannot be fully appreciated in the relative isolation of the offices of mental health professionals or in mental institutions. Child mental health has to burst out of its narrow confines into the complex lives of children. Otherwise, we simply have a mass of mentally handicapped children and an assortment of mental illness technologists.

Systems of Childhood

I have proposed that the systems approach may represent the revolutionary framework needed to resolve the crisis in child mental health. The systems approach looks at children in their own varied contexts. Thus,

20

systems thinkers ask, What is the context in which the child is being viewed as either difficult or not difficult? It is natural to begin looking at children's families because they are essential and, in the sense that most nuclear families can get to and will fit into a practitioner's office, seemingly portable human systems. Systems-oriented investigators involve families not to find fault with them but to fill out the picture and to evaluate the child's resources. Family therapy has become the practical expression of the fundamental notion that children shape themselves and are shaped within a family context. This shaping is mutual and reciprocal; thus, if the family relationship system changes, the child will change. Within the past thirty years a largely acausal body of theory for understanding children's behavior in their family context has evolved, and it emphasizes the child's own contribution to the way the family responds to him or her.

More recently, systems other than the family have also been included in the contextual assessment of children. Historical contributions from the family's extended family context have been examined since the beginnings of family therapy, but utilizing current interactions within the extended family is a more recent development in response to the better understanding of changing family relationships through the life cycle. There has been an upsurge of interest, too, in families' relationships to the various agencies and institutions with whom they interface; these are the next layers of contextual influences to be examined. Themes that have been identified in the individual child and in the nuclear family may also be played in these other spheres. Beyond the layers of systems with which the family interfaces lie a layer of sociocultural issues such as ethnos and socioeconomic factors, a layer of sociopolitical factors, and, finally, the atmosphere of life itself. These contextual spheres and their interrelationships can be understood to comprise the ecology of children. Figure 1.1 illustrates the concentric domains of child ecology, which are discussed further in chapter 3.

Systems Imply Resources

In assessing children's contexts not as causative but as involved in the definition of children's problems, one must look at systems as resourceful rather than malfunctioning. The resources of children and their systems must be sought and noted. Doing so immediately corrects for the deficit orientation of the biomedical model but alters the usual assessment procedure from a cataloguing of assets and liabilities to an examining of the richness of adaptive processes and resources. The search for resources can begin with the altered role of the mental health professional in the child's system. Moving from the traditional position of concern for individual malfunction to evaluating children in a systemic context, such as the family or school setting, marks a significant shift in the therapist's attitude about healthy change for children.

When a child psychiatrist becomes a family or systems therapist, she must shift her opinions about the family's own expertise and the family's role in healing the child. Interestingly, the realization of these differences between therapist and parent may not even dawn on therapists until they have children of their own. If their parenting begins after their training as therapists, they will discover that all of their expertise as family or child therapists does not certify them as knowing and expert parents. I discovered this, myself, when I became a parent at thirty-six. The realization that parenting and doing therapy are different emphasizes that parents always

Figure 1.1   Domains of Childhood

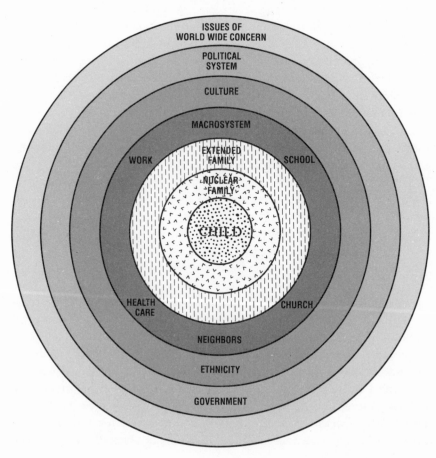

know something more about their own children than a child expert does, even though child experts know more about children in general than parents do. Similarly, teaching and doing therapy differ. For example, in a lifetime of teaching, a teacher will see a hundredfold more children than will a therapist. In systems-oriented therapy the expertise of many people will be marshaled and coordinated for the benefit of troubled children.

UTILIZING RESOURCES: A CASE STUDY

A ten-year-old boy, Kerry Jackson, was brought to my office by his divorced parents and their current spouses. They had picked him up at the hospital where he had been on the psychiatric unit for thirty days, and they were stopping at my office on their way to the state hospital where he was to be admitted. The four adults—his mother, Mrs. Brown, a large, overbearing lady; his father, a slender and mild-mannered man; his stepfather, Mr. Brown, a college football hero; and his stepmother, Mrs. Jackson, a social worker, had never been together in the same room before. Kerry was overwhelmed.

"The boy has a murderous temper," said his stepmother. "He threatened to kill us all in our sleep." A note from the hospital confirmed that Kerry suffered from poor impulse control and said he needed long-term residential treatment. Both of Kerry's parents were incredulous. They had never seen this behavior. How could this be? Were they blind to their son's outbursts? Or did he somehow manage to control his impulses around them? Kerry's mother confirmed that if he tried anything around her she'd . . . ! Kerry's eyes widened.

With prompting from me, Kerry's father asked him what he would like to do. Kerry froze in silence. Everyone looked at me. Maybe there is something wrong with him, their looks seemed to say.

"You asked him a question. Do you want his answer?" I prompted. Oh, you mean we can expect an answer from this psychiatric-patient-with-poor-impulse-control-who-is-on-his-way-to-the-state-hospital? their looks seemed to say.

To get Kerry to answer a question, they had to convince him that his answer was important. Finally Kerry mumbled that he wanted to go home. The four adults had to negotiate where home would be. Kerry had lived with his father and his stepmother. His mother thought he should go to a day camp near where she lived, and she and her husband thought he should live with them for the summer. The four adults tackled the issue of Kerry's impulse control and aggressive behavior. They were encouraged to make meaning out of their experience of the child and then to think about how they could help him stay out of trouble. Kerry did not go to

23

the state hospital that day. His parents enrolled him in day camp, instead. He had one blowup that summer, but his stepfather came down to the camp and blew up at him, and that was that for the summer. Everyone agreed it was a good summer.

Kerry had a lot of resources. He had not only parents but also stepparents who cared about him. When he went to the hospital, however, the hospital staff talked only to his stepmother because she was a mental health professional. She had framed Kerry's behavior as "sick" by taking him to the hospital, and the staff operated on the assumption that the source of the problem was inside the child. They observed him on the ward, alone, for thirty days. They never even met his mother, though they heard, from his stepmother, that she was inconsistent and, therefore, a bad influence on Kerry. They never saw Kerry together with his father and stepmother, even though he had lived with them before his hospitalization. Thus, they never had the opportunity to evaluate what might have been available to Kerry in that household. Having discounted the mother, they didn't count his stepfather either. Although Kerry was his parents' only child, he had stepsiblings on both sides. Both of his stepparents were experienced parents.

The hospital staff used their own expertise about children—an expertise based on theories about the intrapsychic life, the biological basis of poor impulse control, and behavioral management techniques. When Kerry continued to do mean things to other children despite the staff members' interventions, they decided his problems were more serious and would require longer-term treatment. That is, they felt that his failure to improve in thirty days in the hospital demonstrated that he needed more time in the hospital. The state hospital was a resource to them, but it did not occur to them that perhaps in-hospital treatment wasn't the best way to work with Kerry, because they had not assessed either Kerry's behavior in its natural context or his natural resources.

Kerry's family arrived in my office with instructions that their son needed long-term hospitalization. I encouraged them to look at the situation in their own way, to question authorities on their own terms, and to arrive at their own solutions. To the extent that they felt that their solutions were satisfactory, they worked on their own. For them, working together was new and very difficult. When they got stuck, they returned for more reflections on the situation and what could be done. Kerry's aggressive behavior flared up when Mom and Dad disagreed about plans, visits, and discipline. When school started again and Kerry moved back with his father, it was necessary to get all of the adults together with the school authorities to work out a network for troubleshooting. For the most part, they designed Kerry's treatment.

GIANT STEPS IN ACTION

Treating Kerry in such a way that he did not become an institutional child required taking four giant steps. First, everyone involved had to recognize that the reality of his mental illness and the necessity for further hospitalization were formulated in a particular context, namely, that of biopsychologically trained professionals working in a psychiatric hospital. In a different context, we were able to make a different assessment. Second, we sought patterns in which Kerry's disruptive behavior occurred. A fundamental pattern was one of competition between his parents, in which Kerry's behavior often served to reorient things and to bring them together. Third, we worked with the system's competence: the competence of the parents' knowledge of their child, of their partners' experience with children, and of Kerry's ability to manage himself when he was given clear instructions and consequences. Fourth, we believed that we had the best chance of contributing to Kerry's mental health when working with the whole system, which sometimes included the school personnel, as well as the family members. We had to recognize that Kerry's well-being depended on that of his mother which, in turn, depended on her relationship with Hank, and with his father, which involved his stepmother and her children. And their well-being related to their feeling of competence in parenting and pride in their son's success.

* * *

This summary of the approach to Kerry's treatment may suggest that taking the giant steps is relatively easy. But even in this single case one can see that the giant steps—whenever taken—require nontraditional thinking, coordination of complex systems, and careful planning for resource utilization. The complexity of these efforts is revealed further in other vignettes throughout this book. Kerry's case helps highlight a key point: the giant steps to resolving the crisis in child mental health require assessment and involvement of the natural resources in the child's ecology. There is an important role for professionals with expertise in evaluating and working with systems of childhood. Recognizing that childhood changes according to the framework in which it is studied will require that professionals take a different position than they traditionally have. They must involve crucial elements in the child's resource system in the treatment process, and, as much as possible, observe the reverberating effects of their own interventions throughout the child's ecology.

CHAPTER 2

Frames of Childhood

We all know what childhood is. Or do we? It is the life-cycle period when a person is dependent, requiring older, more experienced people to provide basics, like food, clothing, and shelter, and basic education to be a contributing member of society. Broadly defined, it covers the years between birth and age eighteen. Or does it? In earlier stages of history childhood was shorter, ending variously at thirteen or even seven. Modern adolescence is a relatively new invention as childhood dependency has been drawn out over a longer span. If childhood's limits keep changing, what is childhood, anyway? Asking such questions and developing a multiocular view of childhood are essential in taking the first giant step toward resolution of the crisis in child mental health.

The First Giant Step

Perceptions of the current crisis in child and adolescent mental health represent the outcome of prevailing points of view about childhood. The first giant step toward a resolution of the crisis is to acknowledge different shapes of reality. First, one must accept that different versions of experiences are not necessarily correct or incorrect. They represent a "framing" of available data in order to draw meaningful conclusions from them. Second, one must be able to describe realities differently according to various frameworks and to acknowledge the validity of each description within its framework. In many cases there will be many complementary realities, forming meaningful patterns.

A first step in advancing beyond the biomedical paradigm, the "normal" scientific framework for identifying and correcting emotional problems in children, is assessing how reality is defined within that framework. Biomedical diagnosticians reify specific differentiated properties of different diseases; the diseases are regarded as real processes caused by real pathogens. This is an excellent working model for many medical illnesses such as those caused by microbes or known and treatable pathogenic processes, but none of the so-called mental illnesses has reached this degree of specificity. The medicalization of social deviance comes about through the application of the biomedical paradigm to processes that occur in the metaphorical realm of the psyche. Systems epistemology, on the other hand, posits that what is experienced as reality is related to the perception and preparation of the individual who defines the reality. Multiple factors influence how a therapist and a patient, or client, in a therapeutic system appreciate each other and the experience they are having. These factors include history, expectation, and the setting of the experience, as well as the verbalized interpretation. To make meaning out of the situation, the individual "punctuates" the experience, isolating certain sequences that are assigned beginnings at a particular place and are seen to evolve in certain ways.

This viewpoint reflects a relativistic position rather than the Newtonian absolutist position characteristic of the medical model. For example, in a standard medical history, a physician asks about the presenting symptoms, then does a family history, inquiring about the presence of diabetes, heart disease, and other relevant conditions in the family. Finally, the physician asks about symptoms affecting each major physiologic system. The picture framed by this sort of inquiry is the health of the individual defined by the presence or absence of symptoms. In contrast, some family therapists ask questions only about solutions and the successful outcome of such solutions, so the inquiry develops the clients' sense of competence. A picture emerges of persons resourcefully tackling problems, evaluating their success, and redesigning their approaches. Circular questioning is still another approach to information gathering. This is a form of questioning that stimulates curiosity in those being queried, so that they may actually change their conception of themselves as the interview progresses.

Frameworks for Evaluating Children

A perspective on the present can be achieved by reviewing differences in history. The concept of childhood has been redefined throughout history and has been transformed by the historical, social, and contextual frameworks within which it is examined. Understanding the variability in contextual frameworks enables scientists and clinicians to appreciate not only a child and his problem but also the contextual frame that integrates them and the resources available. How children are evaluated depends, then, on how we look at them. What is normal for a child, and, more important, what is prescribed practice in child rearing and education change according to the way childhood is defined and the perspective on systems in which children develop.

Thus, children may be studied as individuals, as participants in mother–child interactions, as family members, as students, as peer group participants, and so on. Furthermore, the approach or topic selected also directs the data collection. For example, among those who study children, some focus on children's vulnerability whereas others focus on invulnerability, or some evaluate children within a particular theoretical framework whereas others ask children directly for their own descriptions of childhood. These varied impressions of childhood illustrate that as views of childhood are always changing, so, too, will be our definitions of adequate child care and of child mental health. Examples of these different pictures, or frames, of childhood are discussed in more detail later in this chapter.

The recognition that childhood has different meanings in different contexts requires that both the children's and the relevant caretakers' views on problems and solutions be elicited, recognizing that both the problems and the solutions are organic to the particular situation. For example, a child who constantly keeps tabs on what her classmates are doing and always notes who comes into or leaves the classroom and keeps track of all the teacher's movements may be described as distractible, whereas the same vigilance may be seen as an asset to this child when she is at home in a rough neighborhood, looking after younger siblings. In school the child has attention deficits, but at home this behavior is highly adaptive. Taking the giant step that comprehends varied experiences of reality leads to the ability to understand the meaning of particular frameworks and how they are constructed.

The Construction of Childhood

"In the morning it goes on four feet, at noon on two, and in the evening on three. Of all creatures living, it is the only one that changes the number of its feet, yet just when it walks on the most feet, its speed and strength are at their lowest ebb"—thus goes the so-called riddle of the Sphinx (cited in Schwab 1950, 234). Childhood has been recognized as a distinct epoch of the life span, at least since the time of the riddle of the Sphinx, but people in each historical era have constructed their own definition of childhood. Social historian Philippe Ariès (1962) traced some of the different ways childhood was viewed through the Middle Ages, and he offered an evolutionary view of how childhood came to be viewed as it is today. Feminist writer Deborah Leupnitz (1988) posited that the contemporary version of childhood did not evolve directly out of the Middle Ages, because the roles of children in the twentieth-century family are similar to their roles in the middle-class family during the Roman Empire. Thus, whereas Ariès saw a linear evolution of the roles of children, Leupnitz described a historical oscillation. In either case, views of childhood have varied markedly over time.

Tenth-century paintings portray the medieval picture of childhood— children looking like miniature adults, dressed in miniature adult clothing. This society, in which children apprenticed to learn the skills they would eventually practice to support themselves, experienced children as little adults, albeit weaker and less experienced. According to Ariès, childhood was not really "discovered" in Europe until the seventeenth century. Ariès posited that although children were nurtured and cared for before this time, the interest in children as different from adults, other than in size and strength, was not apparent until the seventeenth century when childish language and playthings were distinguished in paintings and literature. Prior to this, Ariès suggested, so few children lived beyond childhood that it was perhaps easier to acknowledge them only when they became old enough to give some promise of survival. Childhood in a currently recognizable form seems to have evolved through the seventeenth and eighteenth centuries and to have arrived by the mid-nineteenth century at the time of the industrial revolution. The end of the eighteenth century and the Romantic movement found the innocence of children virtually worshipped, its loss mourned.

> But trailing clouds of glory do we come
> From God, who is our home:
> Heaven lies about us in our infancy!
> Shades of the prison-house begin to close
> Upon the growing Boy
> . . . .
>
> The Youth, who daily farther from the east
> Must travel, still is Nature's Priest,
> And by the vision splendid
> Is on his way attended;
> At length the Man perceives it die away,
> And fade into the light of common day.
>
> —William Wordsworth, "Ode: Intimations of Immortality"

In the nineteenth century families became progressively more organized around their possessions, homes, relatives, and children—all considered part of men's personal wealth. At the same time, interestingly, women gradually became confined to the home and the care of these now-precious children. As children became more precious, they became more protected, and theories were developed about the fundamental innocence of children that differentiated them from adults. The laws imposed in mid-nineteenth-century England forbidding child labor contrasted sharply with the former practice of young apprenticeship. Although the child labor laws were enacted in part for economic reasons (children in the work force reduced the number of jobs available for adults), the proscription of child labor marked a different role for children. The child labor laws reflected an opinion that children were human beings with a special status.

In the Western world the perception has developed that children are innocent, dependent, corruptible, and vulnerable—a relatively new view of children, historically. This framing of childhood places responsibility on adults—particularly the child's parents—to shape the youngster, provide moral guidance, and to civilize him or her. The implications of these views about both children and adults are that children's suffering is generally held to be the responsibility of their parents, and children's failures are attributed to failures of their parents or other benevolent and responsible adults. In recent times, children's rights movements have placed even more responsibility on caretaking adults, albeit of a different nature; now adults must educate, nurture, and guide their children, but they must also stand back to allow free expression of children's individuality. Many parents experience these two directions in child rearing as contradictory; even so, the responsibility for outcome generally belongs to the parents.

Different Views of Child Rearing

Even in the twentieth century there have been major shifts of opinion on child rearing, each representing alternative pictures of childhood. Martha Wolfenstein (1972) explored changes in the authoritative infant-care manuals released by the U.S. Children's Bureau in 1914, 1921, 1929, 1938, 1942, 1945, and 1951. She found contradictory shifts in emphasis, ranging from intensive efforts to inhibit "autoerotic" activities, such as binding the thumb to stop thumb sucking, to a permissive attitude, such as encouraging the parent to let the child find his own comforts and "grow out" of thumb sucking. Similar changes were noted in attitudes about breast feeding, weaning, and toilet training. In general, the authoritative and regulated practices of the earlier era gradually gave way to more permissive and "adaptive" practices by the early 1950s. Noting these changes, two observers commented, "Many professionals make little effort to clarify for themselves—much less for their 'audience' of parents—the actual scientific bases for the changing winds of child-rearing doctrine. And they pay equally little attention to the probable consequences of pressing new recommendations upon parents who have been nurtured on diametrically opposite tenets" (Harrison and McDermott 1972, 176). Consequently, the practices and beliefs of mental health professionals may often be out of sync with those of parents. That is, the parents and professionals may be acting out of different, even contradictory, frames of childhood.

In another reflection on the evolution of attitudes toward childhood in this century, psychologist Jerome Kagan (1984) reminds us of a scientific view of childhood from the early 1900s when citing Havelock Ellis, who equated the erect nipple of nursing with the erect penis, and the hungry infant's mouth with the throbbing vagina. Kagan observes that in the 1940s Erik Erikson emphasized the elements of nursing that resemble the bond of trust between adults. Both of these descriptions involve analogies between infant and adult behavior. Clearly, emphases have changed since Ellis's and Erikson's work. In the 1980s the issues of bonding and attachment were often seen as the foundation of development, but contemporary emphasis is on the emergence of the self (Stern 1985). Even these current beliefs can be viewed in perspective, as Kagan considered contemporary concepts of attachment and bonding in light of current social preoccupations with trust and anxiety. He observed, "Every society needs some transcendental theme to which citizens can be loyal. . . . The sacredness of the parent–infant bond may be one of the last unsullied beliefs. . . . If the infant can be cared for by any concerned adult, and the biological mother is expendable (this is not yet proven), then one more moral imperative will have been destroyed" (Kagan 1984, 56–57). Thus, Kagan points out that features of childhood are defined in terms of society's most important preoccupations: with Ellis it was sexuality; now it may be, as Kagan suggests, anxiety and trust as they influence the experience of self.

What is perceived as appropriate for childhood has continued to change rapidly. In the 1950s, U.S. society was largely child centered. Men came back from the Second World War and went to work, comfortable that their wives were home taking care of the children. For wives this pattern marked a change from the very active wartime duties they had had when their husbands were away. In this period Benjamin Spock wrote the bible of child rearing. During this period, too, middle-class women developed "the problem that has no name" (feminist writer Betty Friedan 1963)—that is, many women were bored, miserable, and trapped in the image of the sappy, happy wives that they were expected to be. The consequence of the misery was the "gray syndrome," a languid state. Middle-class children were often overprotected and overindulged, and they were raised in a climate that presented growing up as a serious but unexciting affair in which they were expected to provide fulfillment to mothers whose lives were for them only. Such a predicament would understandably be followed by a backlash. It took one form in the women's liberation movement, which is associated with yet another framing of childhood—a consciousness about gender roles and the influence of early life experiences on children's perceptions of these roles. Another form of the backlash has been adults' greater preoccupation with themselves, their search for more direct gratification from their own lives rather than vicariously through their children. But such a redirection of energy and attention also places different expectations on the children. As more women enter the work force and nuclear families move farther from the child-care resources of their families of origin, more children are in day care or are so-called latchkey children.

Shifts in Parent–Child Roles

Whether they literally fend for themselves after school or not, children of the 1990s have to do a lot more emotional fending for themselves than they did in the 1950s, for they grow up with adults who are much more self-involved than 1950s adults were allowed to be. Adult self-involvement is related to higher divorce rates, more two-career families, and more children in child care. These developments and other socioeconomic factors seem to place new pressures on children that the adults in their lives are not able to relieve. One example may be the increasing number of teenagers who serve as emotional supports for one another.

On the other hand, adult entitlement is also associated with greater involvement of fathers in child care, for while many women may feel more entitled to express themselves outside the home, many men are feeling more entitled to be involved with their children. Some older fathers of children from a second marriage seize the opportunity for involvement with their children that they missed in the first, usually more traditional, marriage. A rare but fascinating twist are the "father-mothers," fathers who become the primary nurturing parents while their spouses are the major breadwinners. Child psychiatrist Kyle Pruett (1983, 1985) has studied some of these families, showing that this alternate form of child rearing can have good outcomes for parents and children.

Many of these developments, especially those that appear to leave children more on their own, are deplored by those who say that narcissistic adults have abandoned their children. But in the context of the history of childhood, such changes may signal an emerging definition of childhood with a new role for children. Cognitive psychologist David Elkind (1981, 1984) has bemoaned the prevalence of self-sufficient, pseudomature youngsters he describes as "all grown up and no place to go." However, he may be sentimentally attached to a view of childhood that is no longer relevant. Evaluating today's children in terms of yesterday's framework of childhood may not be realistic in helping children tackle contemporary stresses. Today's children are indeed in danger by the criteria of frameworks evolved through the first half of the century. But given the individualism and sophistication we have fostered in our youngsters, we must question the appropriateness of evaluating them by these older standards.

Focus on Dysfunction

Most research in child mental health is designed to investigate malfunction, as framed by the biomedical model. Research inquiry began with seeking the cause of malfunction. Children first became of interest when the sources of adult neuroses were revealed through psychoanalytic inquiry. In fact, a whole theory of childhood and child development emerged through the process of researching the causes of adult dysfunction. This framework, a picture of the emotional life of children as constructed through adult retrospection, was the original one from which childhood was understood when children entered the psychotherapeutic population.

The more current application of the biomedical model to research in child mental health produces different information, but in being primarily organized to study the causes of dysfunction, it tends to focus on losses, trauma, and disability. Life circumstances that deviate from a vague notion of normal are called risk factors. The path from risk to dysfunction is studied. For example, children of divorce are generally perceived as victims of adult selfishness, and some lines of research focus on the emotional deficits related to these children's reactions to loss and stress.

Sociocultural Frames in Perspective

Changes in child-rearing practices and ways of viewing children are now based on research and scientific observations of children. Research frameworks and topics, however, depend on prevailing attitudes. Controversial Freud archivist Jeffrey Masson's attack on Freud's "suppression" of the facts about child sexual abuse is an example. Masson (1984) asserted that what Freud's patients told him in hypnotic states and through analytic work about their abuse was true. Masson further asserted that Freud deliberately suppressed this information, explaining that these were fantasies and wishes rather than actual experiences. Psychoanalyst Alice Miller (1984) posited that Freud's alleged reinterpretation of the information given by his patients is actually characteristic of how adults (often parents) who physically or emotionally abuse children shift the blame to the victimized children. Both Masson's and Miller's positions are supported by the contemporary alarm about the incidence of child sexual abuse and by the current liberty to blame parents for children's problems. Their opinions are framed by the place that child sexual abuse has in our current concerns about childhood. These concerns, in turn, shape the attitudes we have about parents and parental responsibility.

Neither Masson nor Miller acknowledged that in turn-of-the-century Vienna, sex was a titillating but understated topic, and sexual abuse was not recognized and certainly not discussed (even though it occurred). Nor did they acknowledge the strict atmosphere of respect for elders. In that social context, it seems to me, it was remarkable that Freud brought as much attention as he did to the fact that parents do have sexual interests in their children. It seems reasonable that whether he did it consciously or unconsciously, Freud had to present what he knew in a way that was palatable enough to the scientific community of his time that he could continue to advance his work. Both Masson and Miller wrote with the assumption that in Freud's time child sexual abuse could have been recognized and discussed as openly as it is today; thus, they appear to believe that what is accepted about human nature now was accepted then. We know that the incidence of reported cases of child sexual abuse is increasing, but we do not know whether there is an actual increase in incidence or just in reporting. In either case, there is today a different moral atmosphere about the subject, an atmosphere that allows us to focus on different areas and form different opinions from those of the past. In pointing out limitations of Masson's and Miller's contentions, I do not seek to defend Freud nor to take a moral stance in favor of exploitation of children.

We must recognize, though, that strongly held opinions about how adults raise and educate children are the constructs of contemporary frames of mind.

The Current State of Childhood

As we have seen, contemporary views depict children as extremely vulnerable. The first three years of life are supposed to be critical to the formation of the personality, so the most vigorous corrective intervention efforts are developed for parents and youngsters in the early years. In contrast, programming in later years tends to reinforce the previously established status of the child. There are, for example, so-called acceleration programs such as those from the Better Baby Institute, in which infants are taught to read. The intensity of these enthusiastically undertaken programs tends to diminish as the children grow older. Particularly in the area of special education for exceptional children, the intensity, creativity, and individualization of the programs diminish progressively from the infant programs through high school. Get Set and Head Start are examples of programs that provide enriched schooling for preschool and kindergarten youngsters. However, many of the beneficial effects of these programs on children's academic progress have been found to be washed out by fourth or fifth grade, unless the enrichment continues (Haskins 1989).

The shift in intensity of intervention programs reflects the prevalent belief that after a certain age there are few opportunities to affect the formation of a healthy character and correct the "damage" of early life experience. This belief emerges from a framework about human development that sees all of the most important investments being made at the beginning. This framing of early childhood as all important, then, leads to the expectation that children whose early childhood was marked by traumata, separations, neglect, or abuse will inevitably be scarred. Consider how the following case examples reflect on the notion that the early years set the mold for the later ones.

A child who was cared for in infancy by her father, while her mother worked, saw her father shot to death by a stranger when she was two years old. At the age of six she was brought for treatment by her mother. The problems recounted by the mother were that the child would not sleep in her own bed and was isolated from peers. The evaluation of the child found her to be a healthy, curious, friendly child who was doing well in school academically and socially. The problems for treatment seemed to have become critical since the mother had started seriously dating someone. When this case was presented at a staff conference, the participants argued heatedly about the healthy assessment of the child. Those who believed that she could not have escaped such trauma unscathed declared that she necessarily had a need for treatment to overcome the early loss. Those on the other side proposed that she might be one of those resilient children who had coped well with her loss and had moved on.

Another child whose mother died when she was four, after a long illness, suffered severe symptoms at age eleven. The symptoms—inability to fall asleep for fear someone would come into the house and kill her family— followed a well-publicized tragedy where an assailant shot several children in a school yard in Stockton, California. Two different counselors related her symptoms to her loss of her mother, and they both prescribed treatment to help her work through this loss. A third evaluator explored the family's current situation and found that this youngster went to bed by herself, a situation that dramatized her exclusion from a family that now included a stepmother and a five-year-old half sister. An intervention to involve the whole family in a bedtime ritual, followed by an earnest discussion of her value in the family, resulted in a rapid and complete remission of her symptoms and a general improvement in her school and peer relationships.

Although it is clear from all that has been said so far that "childhood" is a concept and that it changes in different historical, social, political, economic, and moral climates, most child-care professionals portray childhood as a unitary phenomenon. Child advocates in the political arena, for example, base their pleas on some kind of standard for normal childhood, even though children of wealthy intellectuals, poor laborers, inner-city welfare recipients, and farmers obviously have strikingly different childhoods. Furthermore, expectations, standards for discipline, and dreams for the future differ not only with socioeconomic status but also with ethnic and cultural mores. Though many children do fit the template of normality sufficiently to grow up without major incident, large groups of children do not fit, such as those from divorced families, those with variations in temperament styles that interfere with learning in a normal mode, or those whose cultural backgrounds differ from a white middle-class norm. Children in these situations are likely to be seen not as adapting to a different set of expectations but as being deviant and, ultimately, suffering from pathology. Many of them will, in fact, exhibit signs of pathology. But whether the paranoia, hopelessness, nonconformity, and "unsocialized" behaviors are the causes or the outcomes of their failure to fit the mold should remain an open question.

A Frame of Adaptation

Consider how differently we regard the child if we seek adaptive and coping behavior rather than dysfunctional behavior. How do they manage? has profoundly different implications from What is the cause of their problem? The former question directs the inquiry into larger and larger circles of children's lives. The goals of such inquiry are to discover how children actually cope with conditions such as growing up with a mentally ill parent, surviving the loss of a parent, or poverty, all of which are generally regarded as risky. These research efforts probe not for pathogenic factors or disease but for protective factors, or resources, both within the children and within the patterns of their lives. Then identification of specific factors in adverse situations that are associated with subsequent maladaptation is in the richer context of a complex picture of multiple systems involved in the outcome. This approach raises alternatives to the more conventional assumption that these life events are pathogenic. Contrast the pessimism of the linear connection between risk and malfunction with the assertion of Adolph Meyer that "an injury leaves . . . scars, but it may also leave an experiential residue, a memory capable of serving in many additional associative possibilities as a person-function, as something . . . operative in our expectations and motives in life" (cited in Rutter 1986, 1078).

Many studies have demonstrated that chronic adversity—not any single adverse event—is associated with disturbances in children, including cognitive, behavioral, and emotional problems. Michael Rutter (1986) has pointed out that dysfunctional patterns develop in adversity. At first these patterns can be developed as adaptive responses to the stressors, but they can become problems in different ways. Some individuals maintain behavior patterns that, although once adaptive, become maladaptive. This is true, for example, of many children who have been adopted into stable homes after a few years in institutions. Other individuals may have been so mobilized to attend to unwonted stresses that other critical areas have been neglected and have failed to develop adequately. This may be a partial explanation for the kinds of cognitive deficiencies found in children coping with persistent stress. Nevertheless, Rutter stated, "the notion that adverse experiences lead to lasting damage to personality 'structure' has very little empirical support," and "longitudinal data all indicate the modifiability of human functioning provided that the environmental conditions are sufficiently good" (1986, 1081).

The biomedical approach to coping has delineated characteristics of a child who survives extreme disadvantage, termed the resilient child. As described by James Anthony (1987), this child is one who retains a constructive approach, manages to involve adults in a supportive fashion, and remains optimistic about being able to carry out future plans. Anthony also noted, however, that these children maintain distance in interpersonal relationships even after having become successful as adults. Thus, he pointed out that a sacrifice is made for the resiliency exhibited in childhood. Anthony's trade-off theory derives from searching for the sources of resilience primarily within the child, with the environment regarded as either not contributing, as providing stress that must be confronted, or at best, as offering only modest support. Rutter, who included multiple environmental factors in his inquiries, commented that two factors seem to be associated with resilience in the face of adversity: "secure, stable, affectional relationships and the experiences of success and achievement" (1986, 1082). This does not contradict Anthony's findings but expands the framework in which the phenomena are appreciated.

Children's Points of View

Again, consider how differently we regard children if they are asked for their views directly. One such inquiry was conducted by journalist Penelope Mesic, who interviewed a number of fourth-grade children in the Chicago area (1987) and reported their responses with wonderment and admiration. The children revealed much about coping with complicated families, poverty, and the adaptation to requirements of different cultures and neighborhoods. About parents, one girl commented, "They like to correct you. That's their favorite thing to do. They like to sit down and correct you," but "with me it's necessary for my mom to tell me what to do" (122). Asked if adults enjoy telling children what to do, a child said, "I hope so. Because if they don't, they're wasting their lives" (122). The children recognized that parents did have to remind them and correct them, but they said such activity was often excessive and pointless. On the other hand, most of the children had a fairly sympathetic understanding of family loyalty and the hardships and responsibilities involved in being grown up. One child said, "I would like to grow up . . . I want to work two jobs a day. You need another job, in case you have to have something to fall back on" (122). The children captivated the interviewer with their grasp of their own relationship contexts. One child referred to her relationship system in a precise, detailed way, referring to "my sister's father, my auntie's boy's brother" (122). Another girl described a frightening episode when her mother got drunk and couldn't move, and her friend commented, "They drink 'cause they think it's a good time" (123).

Children in suburban areas felt that being tough was not a good attribute, observing that "you don't get many friends . . . these tough people work so much on being tough they don't get a good start on their future. Some people, like on the South Side . . . they could turn out, well—another thing that depends on is their school" (123). Boys from the South Side of Chicago, however, disagreed. "He's not right," said one. "Even if [they] got a chauffeur or bodyguards or somebody standing up for them. We don't have to do that. We know how to fight" (123). Obviously, these children from different settings had conflicting views about important personal attributes. Looking at what they imagined the others to be like, each group judged the others in relation to their own contexts. The suburban boys would not have been admired or respected on the South Side, and the South Side boys would not have had friends in the suburban setting.

These children tell a great deal about what it takes to be healthy where they live, and it is useful to hear them in their own terms. Once again, a different picture is presented, depending on who is the reporter, who is the questioner, and what is being investigated. The Chicago children gave different versions of childhood, flavored by their own personal experiences, to a reporter who was curious without being judgmental.

The Nation's View and Children's Policy

It is inevitable that there will be national views of childhood, even in a country as varied as the United States. Unfortunately, individual children have to be measured against this national standard. Schoolchildren take standardized tests annually to measure educational progress, and whole schools and school systems are evaluated on the basis of the collective performance of their students. Groups who gather to study "the state of the child" or the mental health of children use statistics and a general value system to make their arguments, which are intended to influence policies for protecting, nurturing, and educating children. Claims that children growing up in single-parent families are at risk or that the consistency of mothering in infancy is critical to later development are examples of a belief that environment causes risk. Most would not argue that these claims are untrue, but it is important to note that these conclusions result from a set of beliefs about childhood risk.

Judith Wallerstein and associate (1989), for example, reported finding poor outcomes among children of divorce in their ten-year follow-up study. In contrast, other researchers have shown that children adapt quite well after divorce, and they have explored the conditions that contribute to both good and poor adjustment (Heatherington, Stanley-Hagan, and Anderson 1989). The fact that many children grow up in conditions others *regard* as placing them at risk must have its own effect on them. For example, children of divorce are often described as coming from "broken homes" or as being "poor fatherless children," despite ample documentation of adequate functioning and successful parenting in many such situations. As long as children hear continually that they are missing something in not having an intact family, they are likely to concentrate on what is missing rather than what is available. Many such general claims of risk are made without consideration of the wide variations in the nature of childhood in the United States today, so it is important to recognize that concentrating on the risks may actually place children at emotional risk.

Family systems theorist Evan Imber-Black (1988) suggested an additional complicating factor when describing the makeup of "larger systems." There are usually contradictions in policies at a variety of levels between departments dealing with different aspects of children's policies (e.g., maternal–child health and mental health), between federal and state legislation, and between historical attitudes and current statutes. Imber-Black observed that social policies are often dictated by a standard of normalcy in which a healthy family has two parents and two children, with the father working outside the home and the mother caring for the children—even though only 10 percent of American families fit this description. She noted that most policy is built on standards of middle-class white families, standards that may denigrate the conditions and customs of minority families, which, in turn, contributes to the often unsurmountable barriers to minority families achieving recognized status. She also commented on the complications of well-intentioned movements such as deinstitutionalization and education for all handicapped individuals. When implemented without adequate preparation, as these were, such social developments tended to place further burdens and further blame on families for inadequacies inherent in the larger systems.

Today's definitions of childhood—which, of course, are not static—have emerged out of a tension between prevailing beliefs about society's obligation to the vulnerable vehicles of the future and about the realities of adult life that necessitate more attention to personal survival and well-being. The standard-bearers for the former are social agents such as child welfare, child protective, and child mental health personnel, whereas parents represent the latter view. Thus, defense of childhood has increasingly become the responsibility of institutions, which in the zealous effort to meet this responsibility, have both defined the tasks of parents (i.e., told them what to do) and have developed the framework within which many parents fail their children.

Policy-making and the Public Sector

Within the public sector, which influences children's policy, varied pictures of childhood exist. Many juvenile court judges believe that the children who appear before them come from bad families. They advocate for the provision of more residential treatment, so these children can be removed from the bad influence and then be given a chance to grow up in a consistent environment with good values. Bureaucrats from public agencies are aware of the enormous cost of residential treatment, which concentrates scarce financial resources on the treatment of relatively few children while the majority go untreated. The bureaucrats have the larger picture.

The current trend in mental health policy for children is to keep the children at home. This is not a continuation of deinstitutionalization policy. It is a movement based on the notion that children belong with their families and that many children don't do well when taken away from them. It is also based on the increasing experience and expertise in working with families to provide a more nurturing and safe environment for their children. This trend in mental health offers the possibility that there will be a wider distribution of services to the children and families who need them. But without general professional commitment and experience with these objectives, keeping the children at home does not improve the situation, and the judges are vindicated in their belief that these children should be removed from home.

For most child mental health professionals to make this commitment, they will also have to take the first giant step: to evaluate their own beliefs and the framework in which they developed these beliefs, so that they may develop new approaches in response to the changing needs of children and families and the changing points of view about them. If not, they will continue to operate within the conundrum that currently binds so many child welfare workers: history and public attitude say they should serve children by removing them from harmful families, whereas federal law and current trends say that they should do everything possible to keep children and families together (see chapter 9). These two unreconcilable points of view can only be resolved when recognizing that there are two different

41

frameworks operating. The public sector picture of children is a hodge-podge with often chaotic outcomes in individual cases, as the following example illustrates.

THE CASE OF ROBERT

Robert is a youngster from a middle-class family whose drug and alcohol abuse at age twelve led him to become a truant from school and to break into houses to steal. To protect him from having a record in the courts, Robert's parents took him to a psychiatrist who arranged to hospitalize him. From there he was transferred to a residential treatment facility. After eighteen months he was returned to the community, where he quickly resumed his substance abuse and antisocial behavior. He was again picked up by the police and charged with breaking and entering, but because of his history as a mental patient, he was once again allowed to enter a hospital and then a residential treatment program. This time Robert returned to the community after three years, now age seventeen. Shortly thereafter he resumed his old behaviors and was picked up by the police. While in the holding facility, Robert attempted suicide by overdosing on prescribed medication. His suicidal behavior, together with his history as a mental patient, led to rehospitalization. But his insurance had finally run out, so he had to enter the state hospital system.

Authorities at the state hospital wondered why this boy had never been held legally accountable for his acts. On examining Robert, they found that he was not mentally ill and that his suicidal intentions were strictly related to his panic about being in jail. They saw the last five to six years of psychiatric treatment, which had failed to produce the desired changes, as demonstrating that this was probably not the avenue to pursue in the future. Perhaps a different approach should be undertaken, they concluded. They offered these observations to the boy's parents and furthermore offered to provide services to the family to help them work with their boy in a different way.

The case was heard in court in a small community where everyone knew this youngster, his ravages in the community, and his psychiatric history. The judge ordered Robert to be committed to the state hospital. In the hospital, he demonstrated the full measure of his lack of social responsibility. He refused to follow rules, lied, incited other youngsters to various forms of asocial behavior, smuggled drugs into the unit, and set fires. When the staff attempted to set limits, he viciously attacked them. These behaviors could be framed as evidence of his severe disturbance or as evidence of his delinquency. Here is a clash of frameworks, and the clash is perpetuated by differentiated responsibilities for children reflected in separate agencies for mental health and juvenile justice, as well as the very different frames of childhood from which they work.

Children's Policy and the Giant Steps

It is necessary to have some policy for children in a state or a country, but how can such a policy recognize these wide variations between subcultures in the way childhood is experienced? To assess children in the different realms of their experience and to study children as they are embedded in their ecologies are the answers proposed by the systems revolution. Having taken the first giant step—recognition that reality is experienced differently according to the different frameworks that generate and organize information—it is apparent that childhood has grown and been shaped by social forces throughout history. Therefore, it is important to remember that when children are examined or evaluated, the perspective of the observer changes what has been seen and what will be concluded. The assessment, the context of the location of the assessment, the expectations and beliefs of those being assessed, and the personal and professional context of those doing the assessment all contribute to the framework in which the facts are selected and organized, and a formulation is made.

Throughout history and throughout our current culture, childhood has had different manifestations, accompanied or framed by adults' beliefs about children. It is important to recognize this fact, because so many actions that affect children are based on generalizations that may not adequately comprehend what children are about or what tasks they have to perform now or in the future. We may try to put our current views into historical perspective, but we cannot do that until time has passed. We can, however, recognize that we have views with scientific validity, but that both the views and the scientific validity occur in a historical and cultural framework that will be altered in the future. Accepting this fact enables us not only to examine our assumptions and question them when they lead to a dead end but also to reevaluate them in multifaceted ways. The various frameworks described in this chapter derive from personal experience, historical overview, normal science, religion, sociology, anthropology, economics, and political science. A systems orientation to child mental health involves identifying the connections between these different approaches to understanding children, studying the relationships between them, and appreciating patterns that connect them and utilize resources available to the child.

CHAPTER 3

Levels of Clinical Experience

How children are nurtured and educated varies with the prevailing conceptual frameworks about childhood. When the framework is primarily
biomedical, problems and risks are emphasized, and resources tend to be
overlooked. A single parsimonious explanation is sought—one that best
explains the observed phenomena and thus is correct. Taking the first giant
step changes this. The frames within which information is gathered shape
perception and the interpretation of information. Because of the many
caretaking systems in a child's life, a child mental health clinician is likely
to be confronted with many interpretations of events. Furthermore, the
curious clinician will actively seek out the varieties of interpretations offered by the child, the child's parents, teachers, siblings, and other concerned individuals. Then the clinician has to deal with the question, Which
interpretation most correctly or usefully comprehends the data?

Having recognized that each opinion arises out of a framing of the data,
the clinician taking giant steps will have to recognize that each might be
true and useful, and each permits an understanding of events most suitable
to the situation within which they have been experienced. But if the
clinician feels compelled to choose one interpretation, she will encounter
a quandary that is at the heart of most controversies about models of child
mental health: Which view is most valid? This is what I call the dilemma
of clinical experience. This dilemma may be confronted best by recognizing that there are not only different frames but also different levels of
experience of the same events. To observe these different levels, one has
to take a position from which one can observe them—a metaposition.
Having comprehended these levels of experience, one can then integrate
them into a meaningful whole and apprehend a pattern.

Thus, in order to take the second giant step of identifying how events are parts of patterns, it is necessary to have taken the first step—to understand that there are different frameworks for organizing reality and that these frameworks have different levels of organization and logic. In the worlds of children, different levels of experience may be referred to as "domains."

Domains of Childhood

In chapter 1 the ecology of a child was introduced as a series of concentric spheres (figure 1.1), which I call an *ecogram.* Examining the various spheres of influences on the child is another way of appreciating the variety of frames of childhood. These frameworks are not, however, mutually exclusive but are linked by hierarchical patterns of inclusiveness. Expanding out from the center, the spheres represent contexts that define and shape the inner ones, while the inner spheres also influence the shape of the outer ones. The outer spheres include the inner ones, but because they are at a different level of organization, they are more than the sum of individual parts contributing to them. The spheres also represent different domains of childhood experience and influence. Each sphere provides a framework within which a child's functioning has meaning; each sphere is related to each other sphere, so that the frames are interdependent and must also be understood as a whole series.

The Child in the Ecosystem

The child is the innermost sphere of the ecosystem. Particular areas of functioning serve as frameworks for describing the child as a biological, psychological, and psychosocial organism. Within these frameworks the developmental stage, emotional state, cognitive ability, and socialization of individual children are evaluated, from inside the child outward. The child's physical condition, as well as biological details that affect these psychological variables, are also brought into focus within this frame. Biophysiology is a sphere of observation within the child.

A child's constitution is also part of this sphere. *Constitution* refers to the endowments that become the individual's contribution to interaction with the environment or to the individual's way of being in his or her environment. The term may refer to the child's state of health, resistance to illness, or resilience. It may be described as temperament—a constellation of patterns of reactivity that when combined with relationship and environmental factors, produce other patterns, often referred to as "fit." The sphere of the individual child, then, is a whole, as well as a part of the spheres outside of it. Through the child's particular biological and constitutional states, patterns are evolved at other levels or domains that involve and ultimately also shape the individual child.

To organize experiences and events in this sphere, one must consider the child's constitution, history, and current situation along with an assessment of his feelings, thoughts, and behavior. This is consistent with the usual way that child mental health clinicians have been trained, but the integration of all of these data is complex. Many clinicians choose an exclusionary route, emphasizing either biological disease, psychodynamic explanation, or reactive versus adaptive responses. Children who have been physically and/or sexually abused present an excellent example of the challenge for coordinating a complexity of information.

Melanie is a thirteen-year-old only child raised variously by her paternal grandmother, her mother in conjunction with a series of husbands, and, recently, her father. All of her caretakers have been heavy substance abusers, and the mother's drug use during pregnancy probably has had some ongoing effects on Melanie. Her early history is confused because the caretakers competed in describing what happened. However, as soon as she entered first grade, Melanie was identified as a hyperactive, aggressive behavior problem. She was referred to a psychiatrist and was placed in a special class for children with behavior disturbances.

As she grew older, she became more dramatic in her displays of temper and what were seen, by some, as bids for attention. In fact, she openly complained that with all of her mother's exchanging of husbands and her caretakers' attendance at self-help groups for substance users, she got too little attention. Melanie began to write suicide notes in the journal she kept for school and to make threats. She was hospitalized four times in a two-year period. After each hospitalization, her behavior escalated, with physical attacks on adults and more serious self-destructive and self-mutilating acts. She claims that she loses whole periods of recent time from memory.

With Melanie a number of internal issues must be considered. First, there is a strong suggestion that she is constitutionally vulnerable, because of the in utero exposure to a variety of toxic substances. Second, her symptoms suggest the possibility of a major affective disorder, possibly of the bipolar type. Third, she has experienced confusion, neglect, and possible abuse from her multiple caretakers, and she may have trained herself to react through dissociation. Fourth, she has been exposed to patients in four different hospital settings from whom she may have learned an expanded repertoire of behavior. To understand Melanie, all of these personal experiences and adaptations must be considered and included in the formulation. It should be clear, however, that the child sphere is not sufficient to understand the child, because it is embedded in the other domains of childhood.

The Family in the Ecosystem

The next sphere around the individual child is the nuclear family, or household, system. Here the primary framework of explanation is the interpersonal system. Individual behavior viewed from the frame of the nuclear family becomes a part of patterns of interpersonal behavior, patterns that evolve with the history and experiences of the family and function in a way that cannot be understood or explained at an individual level. To understand how something might look different from this framework, consider the way a behavioral phenomenon such as adolescent suicide looks when the explanation for suicidal intention is sought only within the individual rather than explored in the context of the whole family. Careful post hoc studies of youngsters who complete suicide usually fail to distinguish between those children and others who are emotionally disturbed. That is, the factors that induce an adolescent to make a suicide attempt are not evident beyond the general factors relating to disturbance, such as depression, stress, or isolation. An assertion in a speech by Carl Whitaker that suicide is really a family murder adds new dimensions to the study of this devastating problem. In addition to the psychological state of the youngsters, there may be factors relating to the number of people in a family or to issues about inclusion and exclusion of family members that offer further distinctions and clarification. Most studies of adolescent suicide have not included inquiries about these kinds of issues in the family. It is important to emphasize that this level of inquiry does not blame the family for the problems experienced by the child; rather, it looks to the interpersonal milieu for patterns in which the behavior, such as the suicide, may have some meaning.

Richard, a seventeen-year-old boy, shot himself with his deceased father's gun. Richard had experienced many problems in school and had dropped out. He had gotten a job that he didn't like, and he had a girlfriend. Hours before he committed suicide, he gave her a diamond engagement ring, exhausting his savings. When his actions prior to the suicide were reviewed, it seemed obvious that he had burned all of his bridges and probably saw suicide as his only option. But examining Richard in advance, it was difficult to distinguish him, psychologically, from other youngsters who dropped out of school due to poor performance and lack of interest. His discouragement, sense of having no future, and lack of self-esteem were typical for the group. How could one understand his suicide in the face of many more young men like him who do not take such action? Personal psychological variables were not sufficient to explain this choice.

When the family is examined, more information comes to light. Richard's father had died in the previous year. An alcoholic, he had abused Richard and his mother. Richard was the youngest of three children; his older siblings had moved out of the house. Shortly after their father died, his sister had married her boyfriend, the father of her infant, a person whom her father had insulted and forbidden her to see. In short, it appeared that the father's death was a relief for many of the family members. Richard's mother had worked most of his life, and she continued to do so; consequently, the family finances were secure. She began to date a man whom everyone liked and who was kind to the children. In fact, he gave Richard's sister away at her wedding. On the surface, it appeared that the changes in the family had brought greater comfort and satisfaction. But the changes also posed problems for Richard. Everyone else was settled, both in occupations and relationships. Richard wanted to marry his girlfriend, but she was only sixteen, and he did not make enough money to support them both. His mother was planning to move in with, and ultimately to marry, her new boyfriend. Richard must have felt that he did not fit in the plans. In addition to his psychological difficulties, he appeared to be an impediment to the completion of rearrangements in the family precipitated by his father's death. His suicide provided a solution to what might be formulated as the family's problems of inclusion.

Thus, the nuclear family, of which the individual child is also a member, is essential not only as a shaping context for the individual child but also as a context of explanation, beyond individual psychology. The nuclear family has been variously described as an envelope or container of emotions, the primary mediator of reality, and the medium of acculturation and civilization. If the nuclear family is a frame through which children are assessed, additional layers of information at a different level of complexity will be gained by viewing the whole family.

The Extended Family in the Ecosystem

In the next sphere of the child's ecosystem is the extended family. This variously includes relatives such as grandparents, aunts, uncles, and cousins, as well as close friends involved with the child, such as "playmamas", and "aunties." Here the genealogical context of the nuclear family is studied. The extended family is important in shaping the nuclear family context, both historically and in the present. Several important schools of family therapy use the genogram, or family tree as a basis for therapeutic training and practice because they recognize that patterns of family behavior tend to repeat themselves from generation to generation. Psychiatrist and family theorist Murray Bowen's explanation for this phenomenon of recapitulation of family patterns is that children, representing the new generation, become involved in triangles with their parents, who were involved in similar triangles with their own parents. The triangles developed in an emotional climate (within the family) in which differentiated connectedness is associated with health, whereas lack of emotional differentiation is associated with personal and relational dysfunction. A Bowenian multigenerational framework would always see individual child behavior in terms of the triangular patterns already manifested in the family's history (1978).

For example, the mother of a six-year-old boy is told by his first-grade teacher that he pays no attention in class and is constantly getting into trouble with other children both in class and on the playgrounds, where he is usually in the middle of a fight. The boy's father, an alcoholic who abused his wife, recently deserted the family. Consequently, the boy's mother has moved, with her four young children, into her mother's home. Her father died several years ago from complications of alcoholism. In light of this family history, the boy's behavior can be seen as an early version of behaviors of his father and maternal grandfather. Furthermore, one could expect that interactions between the mother and her son might be similar to interactions between the mother and her husband, as well as between the mother and her father. This formulation would provide a map for changing relationship patterns so that the child does not have to recapitulate the history of his male forebears.

Another psychiatrist and family theorist who deals with the multigenerational extended family, Ivan Boszormenyi-Nagy, proposes the transmission of legacies of justice, representing an exchange of fairness between parents and children. Each generation works with inherited legacies, building on them as best they can or attempting to extract caring from others in return for suffered neglect. The sum of these inherited and ongoing exchanges is transmitted to future generations. In the example of the six-year-old just described, the maternal grandfather always favored his daughter (the child's mother) in such a way that his wife resented her own daughter and was very harsh with her. The child's mother's victimization by her husband would be an example of negative entitlement, where she suffers because she owes so much because of the privileged relationship with her father. On the other hand, when she harshly punishes her son for his transgressions at school, she demonstrates destructive entitlement, the right to expect that the child will satisfy her in a way that she has not achieved satisfaction in relationships with either her mother or her husband. The child also demonstrates entitlement when he fights with other children, showing that he cannot participate in a fair exchange with his peers because of the lopsided burdens that have been passed on to him. This picture, again, can lead to a formulation of treatment.

Extended family patterns are also important in the present. Many children are involved with grandparents, and there are often issues of confusion of parenting function when other relatives are caretakers of children. Furthermore, there is an ethos of the extended family that may explain otherwise puzzling phenomena. For example, George, a ten-year-old boy, lived in a house with his sister, mother, two aunts and their three children, his maternal grandmother, and his maternal great-grandmother. His mother's other two sisters and three brothers lived in the neighborhood or visited frequently, and they each had several children. Furthermore, his grandmother was one of fourteen children, most of whom lived in the neighborhood with their myriad children and grandchildren.

George was referred for psychiatric evaluation because he had refused to participate in school through fourth grade. He went every day, but he did no homework and did not talk at all. George's family believed that he was a bright boy, and they had evidence. George had developed a very elaborate animated story on his home computer. Furthermore, in his neighborhood, George was an active and sociable fellow, often a leader in athletic events, and greatly admired by his cousins and other youngsters. When various of George's aunts and cousins and his grandmother assembled to help with George's problem, they were surprised to hear how serious it was. In fact, they tended to deny that it was serious. It appeared that George's world was complete within the microsociety of his family and neighborhood. He had no need to participate in the larger world represented by his school; and his family did not encourage him to do so. Rather, they explained his behavior within the ethos of the family and allowed it to continue.

On the other hand, extended family networks are often significant resources, helping out when there is a need. Indeed, the extended family is often overlooked as an important resource, as when a parent or parents are not able to care for their children and children need to be placed out of the home. Often, children are removed from the family altogether because this important resource is not adequately considered. The power of family myths and stories within the extended family domain is often overlooked, too. Some of these myths and stories are common to many families, such as "males in the family do poorly in school, dating back to your great-great-grandfather" or "the women in the family are not good in math and science." Others are very particular stories describing patterns of falling in love, experiencing early death, being late bloomers, and so on. Such family stories may be used to explain personal choices and family traditions.

Institutions Involving Family Members

In the next spheres of the ecosystem—those involving institutions and agencies in which the family members are participants, such as schools, churches, and businesses—the character of the family and, therefore, the child is intimately interwoven with the kinds of experiences family members have in these other areas. Child psychologist and social scientist Uri Bronfenbrenner (1979) has called this level of system, including the child and family, the "exosystem level." Bronfenbrenner defined exosystems as those that have a bearing on the child's development but in which the child does not play a direct role. Departing somewhat from his definition, I have included the child's school because, though the child does play a direct role in it, it is a system, itself organized by larger systems, in which the school-aged child and his family are embedded. I would also include any health clinic or psychotherapist at this level, although each system might provide its own unique framing of a particular problem.

Like every other system level, the exosystem is immensely important in defining how the family experiences itself and the child. The way a child performs in school and is perceived by the school often affects the way a child defines and perceives herself, as well as the way the family views her (see chapter 11). Health care and therapeutic systems also provide a distinctive framework within which a child may be characterized (see chapter 12). Children with problems are very often defined by those problems—an asthmatic child, a learning disabled child, a hyperactive child, and so on. Such characterizations may prescribe important ways in which the child is understood as well as educated, guided, and allowed to interact with his environment. Further, systems in which the parents interact, exclusive of the child, such as work or social settings also provide defining experiences for the child. Many children's problems are seen as related to parents' unemployment or as defined by their parents' stress at work or in social settings.

Agencies Impinging on the Family

In the next sphere of influence, institutions that impinge on the family have a shaping force, such as welfare, city government, and sanitation management. For some middle- and upper-class families the relationships with this level of the ecosystem may not ordinarily seem important, whereas economically deprived families with very serious problems may be strongly influenced by these institutions. Yet powerful indirect influences do come from the administrative and bureaucratic structures of these institutions, influencing many families. An example is the typical agency response to child abuse. Since the turn of the century, child protective services have had the authority to remove an abused child from the family and then place her in a group home or foster family. This remains the most widely practiced approach throughout the United States. In contrast, some states, such as Illinois, have laws requiring that family preservation services be available to all eligible families to help them address and possibly recover from the conditions in which child abuse has occurred. The child welfare workers have a mandate: with allotted time and some discretionary funds, go into families' households with the goal of keeping the family together. Clearly, the operations of these different approaches to child abuse have profound implications for the definition of the problem, the family's experience of itself, and the child's ultimate experience (see chapter 9).

Sociocultural Influences

Sociocultural attitudes are in the next sphere. Bronfenbrenner (1979) calls these levels the "macrosystem." The macrosystem includes the broad ideological and institutional patterns of the culture or subculture, referred to by Bronfenbrenner as the "blueprints for human ecology." Sociocultural patterns determine the ceremonies and rituals of family life as well as mores and values. The cultures of some countries are homogeneous, but there are many intermixed cultures in the United States. This situation is particularly problematic when a subculture's values clash with the majority culture's. For example, the prevailing teen culture encourages youngsters to prefer their friends' company to their family's. Consequently, teenagers from many immigrant families—especially ones that retain a strong ethnic identity—struggle with their families, whose values differ from those of the adopted society.

Such differences in child-rearing values may be very troublesome for professionals, because these usually affect discipline and expectations for education. They also affect each family's degree of openness about personal matters and parents' ways of dealing with their children about sensitive matters such as sex, illness, death, and money. All of these areas are likely to be ones in which professionals have strong personal opinions, so that it is hard to accept cultural variances.

Matters of Universal Concern

Finally, the ecosystem involves issues of world concern that shape current attitudes and views of the future. In the fifteenth century the Western world pursued expansion, exploration, and annexation of new territories. In the modern world, exploration of outer space, increasing technical sophistication, and worry about the potential destruction of unleashed nuclear power seem to be overarching issues. For example, several studies have demonstrated that concern about nuclear destruction is an issue that unites Russian and American children, who express resentment that they are facing an uncertain future because adults have mismanaged this extraordinary power (Greenwald 1989). Additionally, problems associated with drugs, pollution, and acquired immunodeficiency syndrome (AIDS) have deeply affected human experience across sociopolitical boundaries.

All Domains

Together these domains of childhood reflect the different levels of experience both of the children and of the observers. One could define more domains or differentiate them differently, but the step to be taken is to recognize that the child's persona in each of these domains is a valid description of that child. Ideally, there will be some consistency from one domain to the next; unfortunately, this is sometimes not true. In some cases, in fact, problems arise because a child must confront different perceptions and behavioral expectations across the domains. The evaluation of a child therefore must take into consideration the context in which the child is being evaluated as well as the child's own contextual experience. That is, the child must be assessed through understanding how he fits into the systems at each level of the ecogram.

Without including multiple systems levels in the total assessment of children and families, an observer is likely to misunderstand many events. The cultural environment of the family in which the father storms into an adolescent party and drags his daughter home needs to be assessed along with the reactions of both father and daughter to the event. If a parent who yells at the children every evening is under pressure at work and has been yelled at by her boss, trying to rescue the child from the frustrated parent probably will not alleviate, and may well aggravate, the situation. If the parent who is punitive with his children is being accused of being a Milquetoast by his father-in-law, trying to teach him a new way to parent will not work. Each domain of childhood represents a framework and a particular set of information and observation. Each domain relates to the other domains, not in a continuous or linearly connected fashion, but through levels of inclusion. Thus, to grasp the systems of childhood fully, one must reconcile and integrate information generated at all levels.

The Clinical Dilemma

Most complicated clinical situations with children involve significant interactions among a variety of levels, making it impossible to intervene at only one level. These situations create what I call *dilemmas of levels of clinical experience.* Psychologists Phinney and Rotheram (1986), for instance, have observed that a black or Hispanic child might function very well in her family but fail to accommodate to the expectations of her school, or vice versa. The differences in expectations place the child in a dilemma.

George, whose extended family relationships were described earlier in this chapter, was such a child. His family thought he was a good child. In school, however, he manifested what his teacher considered to be behavior, learning, or emotional disturbances. The school personnel referred the family to a mental health professional for help for George. The mental health professional naturally evaluated George on the basis of the concerns articulated in the school's referral and initially accepted the school's description of how George functioned. If the mental health professional had taken the school's side in assessing the problem, George would have been assessed as suffering from some form of emotional or learning disability. The family's surprise that George had trouble in school would have been explained as some form of ignorance or neglect, such as the family's failure to encourage the child's learning. The school counselor, learning that George's parents were divorced, described his home as "broken" and hypothesized that this must be his problem. The evaluators defined George's family as responsible for his problems: if they didn't actually cause the problems, they certainly weren't helping much.

Another child in this cultural bind between home and school might refuse to attend school or manifest other difficulties that would induce the family to seek help. When such situations arise and it is the family, rather than the school, who first identifies a problem, the involved parties typically seek explanations within the child. They focus on possible phobias, separation anxiety, learning or attentional disabilities, or social immaturity. Families may also blame the school environment: the child is okay; the school is not. When the search for the causes of the problem shifts from the child to the school, it is often because the child's parents have more influence and self-assurance; either they will not accept blame for the problem, or they do not want to acknowledge difficulties within the child. Instead, they help establish the blame elsewhere. A young and inexperienced teacher or an old and uncaring one might be blamed for the child's problem. Blame is then placed outside of the family, as the parents protect their child from the scrutiny and labeling that may be involved. Sometimes this is functional, and sometimes it is not. Kerry, the youngster described in chapter 1, often got into trouble in school. His father would race down to the school and chew out teachers and principal alike, accusing them of mistreating his son. Considerable work had to be done to help him to see that although the school had responsibility for Kerry's behavior there, both he and his son also had responsibilities for eliminating these problems.

I have pointed out that consultants who look inside the child for the problem will look in a particular way, depending on how the problem came to their attention. Consultants can also be so influenced by either the school's or the family's version of the problem that they join one side against the other. If, for instance, consultants testify for one side at a due process hearing, they contribute to a process of polarization, with the family pitted against the school system. Another example of this clinical dilemma is that of Robert in chapter 2. The legal system defined Robert's behavior as a consequence of mental illness and remanded him for treatment, whereas the mental health system found Robert to be delinquent and demanded that he be held accountable for his acts under the law. Thoughtful and caring professionals became coopted to one position or the other, finally neglecting to integrate these two significant areas of Robert's dysfunction. The clinical dilemma experienced at this level of state agency interaction turns into a turf battle. Funds and resources are at stake, and the child's specific needs may ultimately be disregarded.

Working from a Metalevel

An outside consultant has to integrate several levels in recognizing the disparity in acculturation between the family and the school or between the legal system and the mental health system. In order to grasp that problems at other levels of the system in addition to and possibly contributing to the problems manifested by the child, the consultant will have to move to yet another level of the ecosystem, a level from which she could assess the relationship between the school and the family. This is called a metalevel. From this vantage point a consultant to George, his family, and his school would recognize that he experiences a different set of expectations at home and in school. Troubles in school may reflect his greater loyalty to the family's way of doing things. Such a consultant would try to bring the family and school personnel together to reconcile the differences.

In George's case it appeared that the situation might be ameliorated if George could be reenrolled in a regular class in the neighborhood school. When George had started kindergarten, the school integration plan had required him to be bussed to another school. George knew most of the children in his neighborhood school, and he promised to participate in class if he was allowed to go there. His family supported this idea, and they told George that they expected him to work in school. Also, they developed a plan that his grandmother would leave work, when called, and come down to the school to talk to him if he didn't cooperate. It seemed like a good plan, and the school was willing to consider it.

Although the school and the family honestly tried to accommodate to each other, they found themselves in another dilemma. George had been classified as emotionally disturbed, and it was impossible to implement even a trial plan without a complete reassessment, which required an evaluation of George's in-school participation. George adamantly refused to participate unless his class was changed. The system was unbending. This posed a dilemma very similar to the one George originally experienced, when he could not reconcile his family's values and demands with those of the school. But this new dilemma arose from differences determined at yet another level of the ecosystem, one that could not be resolved by George, his family, or the schools involved. This dilemma needed a level of assessment and intervention that recognized factors affecting the status of minority families and standards for public education.

In Robert's case a consultant would need to recognize that Robert's difficulties persisted partly because of the adversarial relationships generated around him. Psychiatrists were engaged in the battle from both sides. The integrative solution would involve the observation that controversy was a process perpetuating, rather than resolving, the problems and interfering with collaboration. Both sides were using the biomedical paradigm to describe Robert and to buttress their arguments. In truth, Robert was obviously both emotionally disturbed and delinquent, and a joint enterprise would be needed to provide adequate treatment for him. Making this happen would, of course, require tackling the issues of funding, resources, and turf at the larger agency levels. If, for example, a case manager were to be appointed, from which agency would the case manager come? And what kind of authority would that person have over resources from both agencies? These are the sorts of dilemmas of clinical experience that pervade child mental health.

Hierarchies and Levels of Logic

The quest to organize experiences in levels has long fascinated people, and hierarchies are one way of organizing levels. In systems conventions, hierarchies refer both to ranking levels of power, logical types, and hierarchies of description. An abstract principle of hierarchies is articulated in philosophers Russell and Whitehead's theory of logical types. Paraphrased by systems theorists Paul Watzlawick, Janet Beavin, and Don Jackson (1967), the theory postulates that "whatever involves all of a collection must not be one of the collection" (192). This can be useful as a basis for forming conceptual and real hierarchies. For example, the domains of childhood just discussed may be seen as hierarchically expanding out from the center, the individual child. The child may be a member of the family, but the family is not a member of the child. Similarly, the nuclear family is a member of the extended family, but not vice versa. What this means is that each level of the hierarchy has a different logical or conceptual significance. The family, for example, is not just a collection of individuals but a system with its own characteristics.

In discussing the implications of the theory of logical types, Watzlawick and colleagues (1967) described Russell's assertion that there are hierarchies of language; that is, every language has a structure about which nothing can be said in the language itself, but another language deals with the structure, and so forth. Thus, the statement "I am a liar" is paradoxical and a confusion of levels of language, containing a statement at the object level (the individual, I), and another that comments on the statement at the object level—that it is not true. This second statement is said to be on a metalevel. For, if "I am" a liar, then a statement that I make is not true; thus, the statement that "I am a liar" is not true; or if it is true, then I am not a liar. Such an analysis is another illustration of the metalevel. As discussed earlier in this chapter, the metalevel is the level from which one can integrate information at other levels; it provides a perspective. Here the metalevel is the structure that defines the statement, the class that defines the members, and the context that defines the behavior.

An illustration of these conceptual levels in a clinical situation involves seven-year-old David, who had been vomiting and eating very little for about two months, during which he had lost twenty pounds. He came to the attention of a psychiatrist who was consulted by the pediatrician. On the basis of these facts, a physician would ordinarily believe that David had an illness involving his gastrointestinal tract or the innervation to the gastrointestinal tract. But in this case, for some reason, the pediatrician called a psychiatrist to request that David be hospitalized on a psychiatric unit. When the psychiatrist met David and his family, he was impressed with the facts of the vomiting (which was not obviously self-induced or secretive, as in bulimia); the poor food intake, associated with nausea and vomiting; and the weight loss. He was also impressed with the child's healthy, somewhat chubby, and cheerful appearance. He found himself laughing and joking with David and his family. Before the psychiatrist considered hospitalization, he asked the parents to let David try bed rest at home, hoping that with this total care David might settle down. But when he checked in with the family two days later, they had not done this.

A second level of facts was emerging to give a second message. The first message was that David was ill. The second message was that this was not a real illness. This message was conveyed by the pediatrician's interest in hospitalization on a psychiatric, not a pediatric, unit. The message was conveyed by the parents' unwillingness to take the illness seriously enough to insist on their son's bed rest. And it was conveyed by David's cheerful, chubby presentation. The symptoms of serious illness were wrapped in behaviors that said it was not serious. It was a living example of the sign that said "Ignore this sign." It was a paradox.

Hierarchies and Power

Hierarchy is often equated with levels of power, and is often conceptualized in the shape of a pyramid, where progressively higher levels have a broader level of inclusion but less specificity. There is some argument about whether power is intrinsic to hierarchical relationships or is an evaluation or weighting of the importance of elements in the relationships. In the abstract, an observer given the task of evaluating (that is, giving values to) the different levels in a hierarchy relative to one another, may feel that one level is more powerful than another. In this case, power is placed into the system by the observer's evaluation; power is a metaconcept, not intrinsic to the system, but a framework used for defining it. Also in the abstract it might be said that the relative power of one level of the hierarchy is given to it by the lesser power of another. In real human systems, however, physical strength, status, and money convey power. Whether this power is abstract or not, our interpersonal systems usually respond to this as power, even though there are some actions, such as civil disobedience, that do not invest in these trappings of power and disarm them.

It might be said that higher levels of a hierarchy have the "power" to define lower levels. The Great Pyramid of Cheops is crowned by a single point but supported by thousands of massive stones at the bottom. Who is to say which is the more powerful level in this structure? Since the powerful upper levels are built on the lower levels, the concept of hierarchy is useful for differentiating between levels of the system, and moving to a metalevel allows one to see the conceptual and actual interdependence between the various levels. No hierarchical level would be as it is without either the higher or lower contiguous levels. The interrelationship itself creates the balance and harmony of the whole hierarchical design. The structure as a whole is powerful because of the integration and harmony of the levels of construction.

In presenting a theory of "mind–body patterns," family psychiatrist James Griffith and colleagues (1989) note that different levels in a hierarchy are distinct domains, having their own characteristic language and interactions. Furthermore, they observe, action and communication within each domain is greater than between domains. They also observe that communication between domains tends to be greater in one direction than another. For example, disturbances in the brain more readily affect psychological functions than the other way around (although both occur). In childhood domains, the family has much greater influence on a child than the child has on the family, although both influences occur. The school has greater influence on the family than the other way around, and so on.

The hierarchy is an approximate model for describing the domains of childhood, for it should be obvious that while any larger system is more than the sum of its parts, any smaller system is more than just a part. For example, a family is more than an aggregate of family members, and each family member is more than just a part of a family.

The Biopsychosocial Model: Hierarchies in Human Systems

When George Engel (1977) proposed the biopsychosocial model, he pointed out that thinking in the biomedical model is confined to a few levels of the system, ignoring the others. Explanation of a particular observation or experience is restricted to causes for effects seen at one level of the system or one level of explanation. Koch's principles, mentioned in chapter 1, operate on the basis of parsimony—for example, the notion that a single pathogen in an individual organism causes the disease. The treatment is to eliminate the organism. These principles do not consider other factors in illness such as those called "host factors." Host factors include the condition of the host—the age, gender, life style, immune competence, and other conditions that affect resistance, some of which can be found only by looking at the host's own context. Research on links between life stress and accidents or illness has shown a relationship between the emotional environment of the host and the host's resistance. These are contextual factors. In what context does an organism survive, multiply, and infect a host? In what context does the host effectively resist or, on the other hand, provide a hospitable environment for the organism? For the pathogenic organism to infect the host, the host must be vulnerable. In order to understand the interaction between the host and organism, one must go to another level of observation, a metaposition from which one can see both host and organism and their interaction.

The biopsychosocial model takes these contextual factors into consideration. Engel depicted biopsychosocial relationships in a hierarchy, but in a way in which, once again, no level of the hierarchy has more power—indeed, no level of the hierarchy could exist without the others. He proposed a continuing relationship from the smallest particle contributing to the integrity of an organism to the largest societal system in which the organism lives. My presentation of the domains of childhood is conceptually similar. These are presented as spheres, each one having an encompassing relationship with the ones inside while their integrity is dependent on the ones outside. This model emphasizes not only the levels themselves but the interrelationships between different levels of the system.

Obstacles to Adoption of a Systems Framework

What keeps mental health professionals from taking the giant steps that would expand appreciation of relevant information to include different frames of childhood experience as well as the different domains? One explanation is in the prevailing biomedical framework. Engel says that the problem exists because the biomedical model considers only one level of a system in assessing dysfunction and planning treatment. This is a problem that plagues child mental health.

David, the seven-year-old with the vomiting and weight loss, is a good example of such a problem, because at the level of his symptoms he appears to have a medical illness. But when the parsimonious explanations for those symptoms have been ruled out through tests, then medical illness is abandoned, at least by the pediatrician, for psychiatric disturbance. Some form of hysterical dissociation becomes an explanation, as the cheerfulness is now explained as the *belle indifférence* (a state of unconcern in the face of symptoms) classically associated with hysterical symptoms. But this is not a simple case of hysteria, because it has already been observed that David's parents and his pediatrician are also expressing *belle indifférence.* Choosing psyche as the level of explanation is not an improvement over considering the physiological, psychological, and contextual factors in examining the problem.

Several concurrent circumstances in David's family seem to be relevant. First, David's older sister is due to deliver her first child soon. Second, his maternal grandmother died several months ago. Third, several weeks ago, his maternal grandfather, suffering from Alzheimer's disease, moved in with them. Fourth, the family has experienced some belt-tightening because, although his mother works, his father was recently laid off. Each of these circumstances could be a cause of David's upset. David's expressed enthusiasm about the anticipated baby could be dismissed as reaction formation. He is sad about his grandmother's death, and his happiness about the grandfather living with them may not compensate for his loss of her. Also, he doesn't know much about the economic situation, except that his father stays home instead of going to work, but he may unconsciously pick up on his parents' worries. Even taking the domain of the family into consideration, there is a case to be made that the problem is psychogenic.

Conflicts between Therapeutic Modalities

Family therapy has added a level of observation and intervention to the individual domain. In response, many people have expressed concern about the family being substituted for the child in treatment approaches. Child psychiatrists worry that family therapists are insufficiently trained to properly attend to the developmental issues of the children, and they feel that children are neglected in family therapy. On the other hand, family therapists who insist that seeing the family is the only way to work with children (thus confining their attention to the family domain) have become as limited in their conceptualizations as the individual-child approaches they claimed to better. The "war" between child and family therapists described by child psychiatrists John F. McDermott and Walter Char (1974) is a conflict based on mutually exclusive points of view. Both points of view are valid and necessary to the proper treatment of children. In order to bring both the individual child and the family into focus, it is necessary to take a metaperspective, one from which the interaction between the two can be evaluated.

In more traditional biomedically oriented mental health circles, family therapy has been thought of as a modality of psychotherapy, that is, an approach to therapy chosen because it was the most effective way to eliminate the causes of a patient's problem. Viewed in this way, family therapy is another way to treat an individual: the individual can't improve until the unsavory environment has been cleaned up. When family therapy is used as a therapeutic modality, it has the problems intrinsic to any modality. It is either confined to one domain of ecosystem functioning—in this case, the family—or it becomes just another approach to treating an individual. As noted in chapter 1, family systems theory opens levels of experience and expands options of observation and intervention beyond those possible with family therapy.

The Need for Metaintegration

In a pioneering article entitled "Technique or Theory?" Salvador Minuchin (1969) showed the value of family observation by contrasting the views of the same fourteen-year-old boy in individual and family therapy. To his individual therapist the boy described his antipathy to his father and his ambivalent relationship with his mother, to whom he was also strongly attracted. The individual therapist noted the repetitive nature of this process through the boy's developmental history and interpreted "the material as an oedipal conflict with paratactic distortion of the present situation" (183). In this analysis, the "cause" of the problem is the boy's Oedipal conflict, which must be worked through and resolved in order for the boy to improve. In family sessions it was observed that the same youngster concentrated on his mother. Even his conversations with his father went through his mother. Minuchin observed that these are two ways of seeing and describing an Oedipal conflict. He commented that the individual therapist would "build up an explanation" of the youngster's behavior, including internalization of parent figures and the development of conflict that then intrudes in his extrafamilial life. The family therapist, on the other hand, would "necessarily be impressed with the *actuality* [my emphasis] of the phenomena and their transactional nature" (183). He would not have to postulate the introjection of other characters, since they would be present, and he could see them.

These two perspectives on the same situation are not mutually exclusive. The boy's experience of himself, as he describes himself, is integrated with what the clinician observes when the boy is interacting with his family. Minuchin, of course, was arguing that the therapist who can see the transactional patterns between the actual characters involved has an advantage over the one who has to postulate the patterns from one individual's reports, because the therapist seeing the family is experiencing the material in more than one domain of the youngster's experience. When the therapist sees both the individual and the family, and assesses data at both levels of experience, she can understand how an individual's behavior both contributes to and is encouraged by the interaction with others, even when the behavior is not generated by those interactions. Given this metaintegration of these two levels of behaviors—both those of the boy and of his family members—the therapist can recognize the threats to the individual boy as a part of the family system to which he contributes by playing his own role in the actual family transactions which represent the Oedipal conflict.

What Is Wrong Depends on Where You Look

Clinicians have a particular professional perspective that serves as a frame for apprehending data. Listening to participants' comments in a psychiatric grand rounds, one can appreciate their differing views on the clinical material as reflecting the differences in frameworks. Each professional's frame can be thought of as polarized to screen out certain data so that other data are more clearly apprehended. Similar differences exist between psychiatrists and psychologists or between psychiatrists who work in hospitals and those who never hospitalize patients.

How does a psychiatrist (Dr. A) who rarely hospitalizes patients work? The hospital psychiatrist (Dr. B) assumes that Dr. A either doesn't see difficult patients, refers the difficult ones to other psychiatrists, or loses interest in patients when they become too disturbed, so that they leave treatment with Dr. A. In fact, many of Dr. A's patients are quite disturbed, but Dr. A does not see hospitalization as a solution. Some years ago, when anorexia nervosa was thought to be an illness with only a 25 percent recovery rate, Minuchin's group published treatment results indicating a greater than 80 percent recovery rate. The response was amazing: skepticism far outweighed rejoicing. People whose careers involved researching the incurable protested that Minuchin's definition of recovery was not clear—there wasn't real recovery, and it wasn't really anorexia nervosa. Above all, Minuchin's critics insisted that anorexia was incurable.

Returning to David and his vomiting, there are now three levels of understanding of his problems. The first is that he has an illness, such as a chronic salmonella infection or an ulcer. The second level is that his symptoms are psychogenic; in his distress over the changes in his life, he is imitating the morning sickness of his sister and unconsciously drawing caretaking attention to himself. The third is that there are problems in the family to which he is reacting symptomatically. For example, David's symptoms could function to take his parents' minds off their other problems (called "detouring," a concept that is explained further in chapter 4).

It is tempting to choose one of these explanations; instead, we need to choose all of them and figure out how they go together rather than mutually exclude each other. To take care of the first two problems, David could be admitted to a pediatric unit where he would be given thorough medical evaluation and treatment. Minimal intervention would prescribe bed rest with intravenous nutrition until he was able to take in and keep down some nourishment. This would focus on the seriousness of the physical condition, thus addressing the child's and the family's apparent indifference to it. Involving the parents in nursing David in the hospital, reviewing the menu, consulting with the dietician, and feeding him would make an unusual demand on the family, which will require that they reassess their relationships, particularly to David.

Integrating Levels

In a discussion of the different levels of a system being assessed (Combrinck-Graham, 1987), I once used the illustration of a two-dimensional holograph representing a pair of lips opening and closing. Viewed at one moment, the lips are open; viewed at another, the lips are closed. The overall impression of the holograph, however, is the integration of these two views, the motion of the lips opening and closing, suggesting a kiss. Different levels of a system being assessed will include the individual, the family, the therapeutic system, the school environment, and so on, to acknowledge the contributions of all of the domains of childhood. Each level of investigation will yield valuable information. Integrating the information from all of the levels will yield the meaningful whole from which the systems therapist will work. Thus, systems assessment includes as many domains of the ecosystem as possible so that an intervention can address as many of the levels of meaning as possible. It is the coordination and integration of these subsystem levels that also represents the fourth giant step: recognizing mental health as the effect of a system organized for the benefit of all its members, at all levels.

Resolving Clinical Dilemmas

In *The Brothers Karamazov,* Fyodor Dostoyevski described a familiar phenomenon:

> It's just the same story as a doctor once told me . . . he spoke as frankly as you, though in jest, in bitter jest. "I love humanity," he said, "but I wonder at myself. The more I love humanity in general, the less I love man in particular. In my dreams," he said, "I have often come to making enthusiastic schemes for the service of humanity, . . . and yet I am incapable of living in the same room with any one for two days together." ([1880] 1950, 64)

To love humanity and not be able to endure people is a dilemma of levels of experience. The good doctor sees how his intolerance for individuals is inconsistent with his desire to serve humanity, but he is at a loss to solve this dilemma. The doctor's dilemma seems to be that he sees these two levels of experience as discrete and fails to see how his ambitions for humanity actually contribute to his intolerance for individuals.

Two major obstacles hinder adoption of a systemic framework: (1) the dilemma of levels of experience and (2) the belief that if the family or any other system is addressed, the individual child will be abandoned. In fact, when an evaluation of a child includes other levels of his or her system, more information is available, more options for change are apparent, and one is less likely to get stuck in the kinds of either/or dilemmas that Dostoyevski's doctor described. The greater danger to the child occurs when professionals focus so much on his internal emotional life that the child is invested with psychopathology and the rest of his system is abandoned. When either the child or the family or another level of the system is the exclusive focus of clinical attention, other significant areas are bound to be neglected, to the ultimate detriment of the system as a whole.

CHAPTER 4

Systems Patterns

The behavioral science revolution borrowed phrases, concepts, and organizing perceptions from the revolutions in the physical sciences. From the theory of relativity, behavioral scientists appreciated that what one sees depends on how one observes (giant step 1). Quantum theory introduced concepts of discontinuities in form, space, and time. Chaos studies provided an organizing framework of patterns, because chaos scientists have discovered that phenomena beyond explanation or prediction with traditional mathematics do form recognizable, describable patterns. Identifying how events are parts of patterns is the second giant step, and it requires a level of assessment different from that required to assess only the event. Furthermore, every intervention will become a part of a pattern and will have consequences.

Patterns and Systems Theory

Patterns are the basis of biological science, which has always been, first, a descriptive process and then—rather unsuccessfully—a mathematically based science. Morphology, the study of biological form and structure, is the basis of gross anatomy, microanatomy, and pathology. Taxonomy, the morphology of biological relatedness, has led to the description of patterns of evolution; "families" of organisms form patterns. In biological medicine there are systems whose operative processes form patterns of different sorts, such as complex cybernetic patterns in the endocrine and cardiovascular systems, which then interact with other systems in patterned ways. The challenge of neurobiology—such a popular development in mental health—is to apprehend the patterned network of neuron types, neuron connections, and neural transmitters, in all their intricacy, and relate these phenomena to psychological and behavioral outputs that occur at an entirely different level of observation and experience from the underlying events. As psychiatrist Albert Scheflin articulated,

> Previously, the focus in neurophysiology was on the activity of the single neuron, but now . . . [it is on] neural conductivity across the synaptic junction. In former years . . . [it was on] the neuronal composition of grey nuclei, while now . . . [it is on] the relation between nuclei and tracts. . . . Whereas we used to focus on the ascending sensory and the descending motor pathways of the nervous system, we now visualize the relation of many other neural subsystems (1981, 125).

Neuroscience includes identification of particular transmitters, composition, and descriptive anatomy, but these findings are connected by the understanding of patterns of relationships between these discrete elements.

Pattern has been a vital concept in the evolution of systems epistemology stemming back at least as far as anthropologist Gregory Bateson's challenge upon exhibiting a boiled crab to a group of art students: "How are you related to this creature? What pattern connects you to it?" (1979, 9). Bateson went on with his students to examine the question in terms of functional biology. The crab's pattern of bilateral symmetry is meaningful at two levels: it reflects serial development of its parts, a first-order connection called serial homology; and it is similar to that of other crustaceans, a second-order connection called phylogenetic homology. One can see that bilateral symmetry connects crustaceans to a significant portion of the animal world, including humans. This represents an even higher order connection, a pattern of patterns, or a metapattern.

Bateson also presented his students with a conch shell and asked for their observations about patterns that connect. He elaborated, "A spiral is a figure that *retains its shape (i.e., its proportions) as it grows* in one dimension by addition at the open end" (13). Second-order connections of the conch are obviously to other mollusks, such as snails and clams, but the pattern also connects the conch to whirlpools, cyclones, and galaxies. Observed patterns also tell the history of the being, Bateson suggested. Serial homology is the story of the development of bilateral symmetry and can be seen within the individual organism as well as in the collection of organisms who have bilateral symmetrical patterns as they are arranged phylogenetically. The spiral, he proposes, carries *"prochronism*—the record of how, *in its own past,* it successively solved a formal problem in pattern formation" (13).

These exercises provide a mechanism for integrating and connecting events and experiences that occur in different places and in different domains. What are the patterns that connect a child's behavior to the social context, the family experience, and all the other domains of childhood? What are the patterns that connect the child's current behavior and experience to her past? Are there records of the past in current patterns? How does one translate from the shapes of creatures to complex behaviors? Here, Bateson identified patterns of social evolution and of societies' ways of handling developmental revolutions (1958). Most societies, he observed, differentiate serially, evolving new segments, each of which more or less replicates the previous one. This is particularly obvious with family structure, where, within a particular society, successive generations of families are organized in similar patterns.

Families in American society appear to differentiate serially. The new segment looks similar morphologically to the old one—parents, children, and a generational structure. But pattern isomorphisms go beyond gross structure to characteristics of relating, as well. These similarities from generation to generation include physical and behavioral resemblances, traditions and cultural mores, and child rearing and routine family functions. It is this recognition that underlies both Bowen's and Boszormenyi-Nagy's theories of transgenerational patterns, described in chapter 3. Bowen concentrates on patterns of handling emotions, and Nagy concentrates on patterns of justice and ethical relating. Both demonstrate that apprehending these patterns is essential for changing them.

Structural Conventions

Morphology and patterns should underlie processes of assessment and provide the means of comprehending data at a variety of levels of experience. Patterns that recur frequently may be referred to as syndromes, patterns that describe events evolving over time and appearing to occur universally are called development, and patterns that form the framework within which hypotheses are developed and tested are called models. Patterns come under many labels—myths, maps, games, rituals, or rules—and they may describe regularity and repetition as well as novelty and reorganization. There have been a number of ways that family systems theorists and practitioners have described patterns and have used them to assess and intervene in systems. These form the elements of the second giant step that must be taken: recognizing that all events and shapes are parts of patterns.

Triads

The triad is a fundamental structure of interpersonal relating featured in two prominent family therapy schools: the structural family therapy of Minuchin, and the Bowen systems model. Some observers (e.g., Gerald Zuk 1971) have said that it is the appreciation of the triad that first set family therapy apart from other therapies. The significance of the triad as a structure must be appreciated against the background of the dyad and dyadic processes. Psychotherapy had always involved a dyad (therapist and patient) reflecting on dyadic relationships, such as mother and child, or husband and wife. The universal patterns of bilateral symmetry or complementarity can be evoked to characterize dyadic interaction; philosophical and religious dualities were based on these principles: self and other, good and evil, heaven and hell. Yet even as these dualities are written, the qualifier slips into the mind: *between* I and thou; *between* good and evil; *between* heaven and hell. Triads are immanent in dualities.

Triads, or trinities, have as long and distinguished a history as dyads. The ancient Taoist symbol of yin and yang in a circle is a paragon of triadic organization: the yin and yang would have no relationship at all if not bound by the circle. The notion of the Holy Trinity is relatively recent but widely recognized. One function of the third element in a triad is to provide a context for a connection between two others. Triads are fundamental patterns in family systems because nothing occurs between two people without a defining context. This third element is usually represented by other people or systems represented by other people. Bowen describes the triad as the explicit building block of patterned human relating. He speaks of the instability of dyadic relating, describing "triangling" as the natural tendency to involve a third in any dyad. Bowen reflects that triangling is common and, in itself, not pathological. In his popular book *Games People Play,* transactional analysis theorist Eric Berne (1964) described a triadic game called "Let's you and him fight," which dynamically illustrates Bowen's concept of triangling. The innocent curbside consultation often has this quality: "Excuse me, could you help us out? My friend and I were just discussing . . . and he said . . . , but I thought . . . What do you think?" A common defense used by a schoolchild called to task for some misbehavior is to involve a third: "But she made me do it."

In families, triadic sequences have many manifestations. Minuchin and his group (1978) characterized several "rigid" triads to describe parents interacting with a child with a psychosomatic illness. Three major patterns were described. In each case, conflict between the parents was regulated and resolution aborted by the involvement of the child. The three patterns are as follows:

1. Triangulation (like strangulation), where parents make equally strong, but different, demands on the child, and the child responds with paralysis, unable to choose.
2. Detouring, where parental conflict is put aside to attend to a child, either to care for her, because she is ill or needy, or to attack her, because she is misbehaving.
3. Stable coalition between one parent and a child.

Children with psychosomatic disturbances, the Minuchin group proposed, tended to have their symptoms in the contexts of unresolved parental conflict, that is, in the contexts of the triadic patterns just described. The children's symptoms, then, were not caused by the parents but were part of the family interactions. They could be seen as protective, maintaining the system, or as contributing to family homeostasis. Others, such as Zuk (1971), have described a "go-between" process in family triads, which often involves the symptomatic individual. Child psychiatrist John Byng-Hall (1980), for example, explained how a symptomatic child "goes between" his troubled parents.

COALITIONS AND ALLIANCES

Triadic functioning, however, is characterized not by symmetry and complementarity but by coalitions and alliances. Theodore Caplow, in *Two Against One* (1968), proposed some rules of triadic arrangement. One is that coalitions within functional systems are always formed with the minimum amount of strength to maintain the system. This is characteristic of all kinds of systems, such as coalition governments. In these kinds of organizations, when one system becomes too powerful, coalitions shift and re-form. The forces that hold the organization together require a relative balance of power, and coalition formation in triads makes this possible. Understanding this is essential to understanding how families with an authoritarian or physically abusive parent may stay together as a system.

Coalitions may be covert or overt, meaning that those involved may admit to or deny the existence of these coalitions. It is generally agreed that denied patterns are more confounding to both the participants and the observers. Evan Imber-Black (Imber Coppersmith 1985) developed an exercise to assist students in appreciating triads. There were several versions, each involving two parents and a child. Each "family member" is given instructions, such as "you are a child; you are in a coalition with your father; this coalition is secret and denied." Those playing the roles of mother and father are given similar instructions, and the three are instructed to enact scenes of family life. Those playing the scene, as well as those observing, experience how each member of the triad modifies the relationship between the two others. When the coalitions are denied, all three participate in the denial. For example, a parents–child triad has a denied coalition between the mother and child. The father wants to take the family on an outing—to spend Sunday afternoon together as a family. Both mother and child express enthusiasm for the idea, but each remembers that the other had some prior commitment for Sunday afternoon. The child remembers that the mother promised to sew his patches on his Cub Scout vest; the mother remembers that he has to work on his science project for school. The father protests that there are other times that these can be done, but both assure him that this is really the only time.

A second rule in triads suggested by Theodore Caplow (1968) has to do with the saying "My friend's friend is my friend; my friend's enemy is my enemy." What this adds up to is a principle that there is always an uneven number of positive relationships in a triad. Either all three are friends, or there are two friends and a common enemy (one common bond and two inimical relationships) (see figure 4.1). These two rules can be employed in constructing maps of interlocking triads in families. In a family of three, there is one triad; in a family of four, there are four triads (figure 4.2). And with each additional person, there are many more triadic possibilities. To sort one's way through a large relationship system, application of the second rule may help. In the family of four or in a system of any size, there are two possibilities: either there are two subsystems or a system in which all are apparently united against a scapegoat (figure 4.3).

A clinical example of the usefulness of this pattern was in the assessment of the Sanders family, in which there were ten children. As the family poured into the therapist's office, the logistics of finding places for everyone to sit down seemed relatively easy to solve compared to the overwhelming tasks of sorting through the names and people and discerning the patterns in this large system. Using the "friend's friend, friend's enemy" rule enabled the therapist to distinguish a meaningful pattern. Affiliations were first defined by observing who were the overweight and who were the normal weight people in the family. Those who were obese also formed a group of individuals who stayed at home, whereas the normal weight ones were employed outside the home. The focus of the

71

Figure 4.1

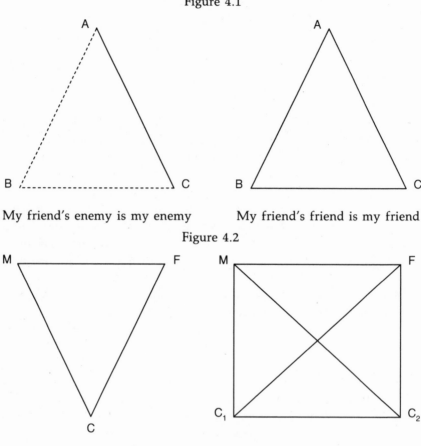

My friend's enemy is my enemy   My friend's friend is my friend

Figure 4.2

A family of three has one triad.
Add one member: A family of four
has four triads

family's involvement in treatment was one child who was obese and refused to attend school (figure 4.4).

The Sanders family further illustrates another important principle of
triadic mapping of living systems: they are not static structures that follow
rules exactly. Three family members who appeared to be moderately overweight were considered to be straddling these two subsystems in the
family. In a sense, the family subsystems formed a "metatriad" where the
obese-homebound subsystem and the normal weight–outgoing subsystem
coexisted in the context of these three nonobese, overweight, domestic
outgoers (figure 4.5). In fact, these three go-betweens formed the basis of

Figure 4.3

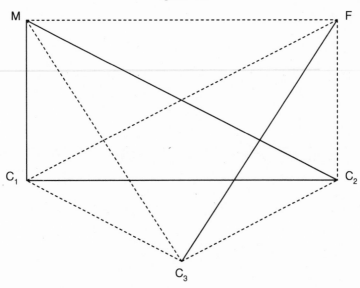

Two Subsystems

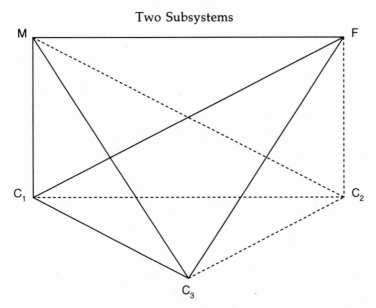

A Scapegoating Configuration

Figure 4.4

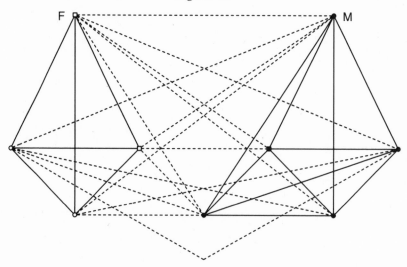

F   M

The Sanders Family
9 of 12 members

☐   NORMAL WEIGHT

■   OBESE

the therapeutic plan, as the therapist involved them in moving homebound people out and assisting them in exercising and losing weight.

TRIADIC PATTERNS INVOLVING LARGER SYSTEMS

Caplow and Bowen, among others, also applied triadic concepts to organizations other than the family. Bowen proposed that an individual's relationships to individuals in systems outside the family might have similar patterns to those within the family. Thus, a man with an authoritarian father and protective mother might have an authoritarian boss with a protective secretary. These isomorphic patterns at different system levels provide a useful way of evaluating larger system functioning with respect to a specific child, family, and problem.

There are several ways that triadic patterns involving larger systems can be manifested. One sees the larger systems forming alliances with family members in the conflicts experienced at the level of the family. Imber-

74

Figure 4.5

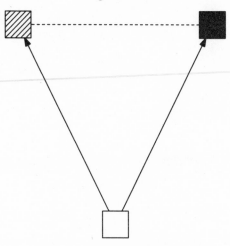

Metatriad in the Sanders Family

◨ NORMAL WEIGHT OUTGOING

■ OBESE HOMEBOUND

☐ OVERWEIGHT DOMESTIC OUTGOERS

Black (1988) described one such pattern when parents of a girl who would not eat disagreed on how to react. The extended family members and professionals who told the worried mother not to worry replicated the father's side of the conflict; those who supported her anxiety by offering advice and treatment replicated her side of the conflict. The daughter remained at the apex of this triad, which grew as more and more helping professionals involved themselves on one side or the other. This triadic pattern can be depicted as in figure 4.6. Another manifestation of triadic patterns in larger systems occurs when the systems collapse to points in other triads as the larger systems become involved. In this pattern, parents who disagree about discipline may be lumped together by school authorities who disagree with parents about discipline. By the same token, differences between school personnel about a particular child may disappear in the context of the differences between the school's position and the parents'. Figure 4.7 shows some of these variations.

Figure 4.6

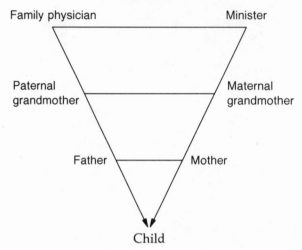

The triad maintains its shape
as more parties join the sides

Adapted from Imber-Black 1988

Figure 4.7

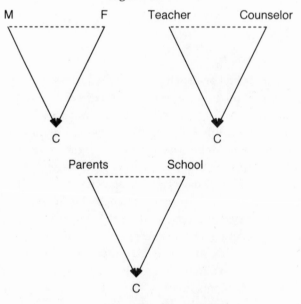

In each instance, the child is the focus of conflict
between the other two parties

Boundaries

The boundary is another structural convention. "Boundary" is a familiar concept of metapsychology, as one talks of ego boundaries and distinctions between psychic functions of id, ego, and superego. It is a concrete abstraction that originated to describe clarity of delineation of functions, and as it is used in systems theory, to distinguish between systems and between subsystems. In early applications of structural family therapy the most significant boundary in the nuclear family was the "generational boundary" (Minuchin 1974). The effectiveness of the differentiation of function between the parental subsystem and the child subsystem was represented in the quality of this hypothetical boundary. In problem families generational boundaries could be either too permeable, failing to differentiate parents and children, or too rigid, failing to make use of the exchange between generations that underlies the evolution of the family. Healthy generational boundaries distinguish the functions of parents and children, permitting the parents to nurture and guide the children, and the children to respond by accepting nurturance and guidance.

As the concept of boundaries was found useful, they were examined between the family and the outside systems, and, ultimately, between the various domains of childhood. How effectively these domains are delineated is described by the condition of the boundaries between them. If, for example, a grandmother who is not a part of the household has significant influence about child discipline, it may be said that there is a permeable boundary between the nuclear family and this part of the extended family. A variety of outside systems impinge on the family and may be closely involved with families in very special situations. In families where someone is ill, has developmental disabilities, or is otherwise exceptionally demanding, a variety of outside systems may become involved, changing the way the familial boundaries are defined and maintained.

Boundaries were further defined within families—that is, between subsystems that might be divided up in a number of ways. At times there might be subsystems differentiated according to gender, specific activities, secrets, or age and privilege. In the object relations school of family therapy, boundaries are less like fences between areas and more like the walls of containers. Here, boundaries define a relational envelope in which emotions are developed and exchanged. Family boundaries are effective to the extent that they can contain and manage emotional tensions.

Research on boundaries has led to a refinement of the concept into two areas, proximity and hierarchy (Wood and Talmon 1983; Wood 1985). Proximity is defined in terms of space and time: How close do people get? How much time do they spend together? Hierarchy is defined in terms of power, but it seems also to represent clarity of differentiation of function. This two-dimensional aspect of the boundary concept leads to the following distinctions:

1. Caring for an infant requires a high degree of proximity in terms of both time and space.
2. Caring for an infant also requires a high degree of differentiation of functions between those of the parents to nurture and comfort, and those of the infant, the recipient.
3. The interaction between parents and adolescent children requires considerable distance (i.e., low proximity) in both time and space. Adolescents close doors, become modest, are embarrassed about hugging and kissing, and don't want their families hanging around.
4. However, adolescent children may share many tasks with their parents (diminished hierarchical distinction). They may be expected to participate in the care and maintenance of the household and younger children, and they may be invited to participate in decisions about family issues.

Thus, within the life of the nuclear family, the boundaries shift from high proximity with high hierarchical clarity to low proximity with less differentiation. In the first instance, the boundary facet of proximity is permeable, whereas that of hierarchy is well defined. In the second, the facet of proximity is strongly defined, whereas the hierarchy facet is more permeable.

It is generally believed that cross-generational coalitions—coalitions across a boundary that should differentiate subsystems hierarchically—are among the most dysfunctional structures in human systems because they confuse hierarchy and proximity. With the young child this confusion blurs appropriate hierarchic distinctions; with the adolescent, distance issues are blurred. These are the kinds of boundary problems experienced in any form of parent–child incest. It is also true that when this kind of coalition takes place across any major subsystem boundaries—for example, between school authorities and one parent, between the welfare department and a child, or between a child advocate and her client (a child)—

it is a sign of serious dysfunction. Thus, the concept of boundaries as pattern markers points to the important regulation of proximity and function (hierarchy) in systems.

Process Conventions

While triads represent relatively static structural patterns, there are also patterns which describe processes which evolve over time. These processes are cyclical and incorporate cybernetic principles of feedback and recursion.

Cycles

Cycles describe processes that can be perceived as patterns because either there are repetitive elements or there are similarities in shape—isomorphisms within the cycles. In describing cycles, the simple cybernetic feedback loop is most often presented, and the example of the house thermostat is used to illustrate the notion. A negative feedback loop involves a set point and switching positions that turn the system on or off (structurally, a basic triad). A simple cybernetic loop in a family could be described by the nighttime activity of parents and an infant: the infant cries, the parents awaken, they comfort the infant, the infant stops crying, they go back to sleep. To call this a cycle is obvious and basically uninteresting. It is also clear that given two parents and many reasons for an infant to cry, much more elaborate patterns can occur.

For example, the parents may have agreed that since the mother cares for the baby all day, the father will get up when the infant cries at night. The cycle may go like this: the baby cries; the mother awakens and wakes up the father, who gets up and comforts the baby; the baby stops crying, so the parents go back to sleep. Or another cycle may occur: The baby cries, and the mother awakens and tries to decide whether this is a routine cry or a different sort of cry. For a routine cry she wakes up the father; for a different sort of cry, she gets up. Now there are two sorts of cycles: a regular cycle involving the mother and the father, and an irregular cycle involving only the mother. Each exception to the regular cycle may be different, one time stimulated by the baby's fever, another time by the mother's perception that her husband is too exhausted, a third by difficulty in arousing the husband. If the exceptions occur frequently, however, a pattern may be established, which may become the regular pattern as all three participate in a new setting for the cycle: the father likes to sleep; the baby likes to have his mother comfort him; the mother likes to feel competent.

RECURSION

The underlying principle of the meaningful cycle is recursion. This means that the evolution of the pattern is affected by the evolution of the pattern. An observer affects that which is observed, which in turn affects the observations and subsequent behavior of the observer. As discussed in chapter 5, it is important to recognize the recursiveness of observation in assessing systems. Even in a closed system, no occurrence of a pattern will ever be exactly the same as any other occurrence, because it is constantly self-modifying through recursion. This is why the concept of pattern is so important. It is morphology and relational similarity that are captured in pattern, not exact reproduction. This is the discovery of the development in physical sciences called chaos (Gleick 1987). Recursive processes are those in which the outcome of a particular chain of events affects the events themselves. The snake holding its tail is the symbol of recursion. Recursive patterns are such that it is not possible to tell whether things begin with "the chicken or the egg"; thus, it is agreed that events are "punctuated" by the observer in order to describe them.

Recursive loops may have a turning-off or negative feedback function, or they may have a facilitating, positive feedback effect that turns the system on. As noted earlier, negative feedback systems tend to maintain an equilibrium within a given setting, whereas positive feedback systems tend to propel the system forward. The beneficial aspects of this kind of systemic process occur in development, such as the development of competence in a certain area. A child learning to tie her shoes will receive positive feedback both from her coaches and from her success. The positive feedback will induce her to make more and more efforts until she has mastered this skill. However, positive feedback systems may also foster an escalating or runaway process. The nuclear arms race is an excellent example, as is almost any situation in which violence erupts. In the nuclear arms race, measures taken to ensure security by one superpower have resulted in the other superpower's production of more nuclear weapons to increase its own security, and so forth. In outbursts of violence among hospitalized adolescents, or domestic violence, there are similar positive feedback loops that turn on aggression. These patterns appear to be linear escalation, but each step represents a positive feedback loop.

A common recursive cycle often appears when apparently well conceived efforts to solve a problem are unsuccessful. A meta-analysis of such situations often leads to an occurrence systems theorists John Weakland

and colleagues (1974) labeled: "the solution becomes the problem." This may be understood in one of two ways. Either the proposed solution actually contributes to the perpetuation of the problem, as has been proposed in certain instances of depressive or violent transactions; or the interaction of problem expression and problem solving creates a new system whose maintenance depends on the persistence of the cycle.

At points in the history of systems theory, families were seen as cybernetic systems where symptoms were maintained within, and participated in maintaining, feedback loops. Clinicians sought out self-perpetuating repetitive (recursive) sequences in which the symptom functioned. The rigid triads previously described as structures are examples of such recursive sequences. In one instance, for example, a conflict between parents about how to handle a paternal grandmother was associated with their son's asthma. It was hypothesized that the conflict was detoured through and turned on the boy's asthma, which then turned off the conflict when the parents came together in their concern for him. In other instances, however, the boy's asthma could turn on parent conflict, as they fought about the aspects of the treatment. In these instances, the conflict about the asthma seemed to be more acceptable than other irritations suffered by this couple.

Thus, many kinds of dysfunction could be understood using a cybernetic model. First, the symptoms appeared to be turned on and off by the negative feedback loops in the system. Second, positive feedback loops could lead to a runaway system, also called schizmogenesis or deviance amplification (Hoffman 1981). Third, an entire system could be described to exist in a dynamic equilibrium, called homeostasis, in which the symptoms play a part. Some postulated that the symptomatic behavior served homeostatic functions. This was thought to be the basis of resistance to change; that is, the system's homeostatic mechanisms, in which the symptom serves a function, protect it from changing. But others have argued that there is no such thing as homeostasis or resistance. Systems theorist Paul Dell, for example, proposed that systems are coherent, they are as they are; in nature, each system makes sense (1982). Thus, the therapist must ascertain how the system makes sense, rather than to describe apparent resistance to change as due to homeostasis. Dell's argument is important particularly because he sees the attribution of homeostasis to a family system as anthropomorphizing and as a way of fixing pathology at the level of the family system, thus being as focal and reductionistic as fixing pathology at the individual level.

A current systemic model of depression builds on the "the solution that becomes the problem" idea. Two researchers, Kraus and Redman (1986), proposed a pattern of the development of postpartum depression in a series of steps that involve positive feedback loops amplifying an initially minor insecurity into a major illness. They begin with the observation that childbearing is a developmental crisis to which all family members are vulnerable. A natural response is to worry and feel uncertain about the health of the baby or the adequacy of one's actions as a parent. As one expresses these doubts, people probably will respond with hearty reassurance, such as, "Don't be silly; she's a wonderful baby! And you're a perfect mother." The mother is not obtaining validation of her experience; quite the contrary. Instead, her experience is being invalidated by the well-meant responses she receives. She is thrown into greater doubt which, when expressed, will elicit even heartier assurances that she is just being silly. Later levels of reassurance, however, might also have an edge of irritation that she is persisting in this folly, and efforts to persuade her differently seem to be failing. Having failed, her would-be comforters will redouble their efforts, which will increase doubt and alienation, finally leading to isolation and hopelessness about one's own perceptions. That the mother becomes more despondent when others attempt to cheer her up and that this, in turn, stimulates more cheering up is called positive feedback. This system may continue until the mother manifests a full-blown clinical depression, at which point she will be admitted to a sick role, and her experience will be validated, only as sick. In the sick role her child rearing will be recognized as inadequate, and she will be relieved of child-care responsibilities unless under supervision. This will perpetuate her perceptions of her inadequacy, these perceptions will be transmitted to the infant in her handling of him, and so on. This is a runaway system that could continue for generations.

Undoubtedly, most cyclical patterns do not represent simple recursive processes, although it is often useful to define them that way. It will be useful to find positive and negative feedback loops in many cycles in human systems, with the positive loops facilitating change, or morphogenesis, and the negative loops facilitating equilibrium, or morphostasis.

SYMPTOMATIC CYCLES

It is possible to assess many symptomatic expressions in terms of cycles that may be identified at several levels of analysis. Bateson (1972) presented an analysis of alcoholism ("the cybernetics of self") at several of these levels. Beginning with the individual, there is the complicated cycle of beliefs the individual holds about self-control, particularly regarding drinking. The alcoholic tells himself that he can give up drinking at any moment. To prove it, he does; but then, because he is persuaded that he has control, he drinks again. This process of internal struggle becomes a symmetrical escalation, as in the arms race, but it occurs within the alcoholic between two parts, which might be referred to as the sober part and the intoxicated part or the dry part and the wet part. The alcoholic's parts are on center stage, but others in his life are enlisted or enlist themselves on behalf of one side or another. When the wife, for example, strengthens the sobriety resolve, the alcoholic's other side responds in a defiant, escalating fashion.

At least two other domains of alcoholism have been thoroughly studied: the family and the helping system. The family relationship system of the alcoholic has been clearly implicated in the perpetuation of cycles of drinking. Alcoholic spouses have been referred to as "enablers." They suffer when their spouse is drinking and may demand, threaten, and plead with the individual to stop drinking. They may also provide excuses and offer forgiveness. Children and extended families are similarly involved in alcoholic cycles. Patterns of the alcoholic's internal struggle become reflected in family transactions with him and around the whole issue of drinking. Furthermore, alcoholics' families have been observed to take on different configurations depending upon whether the alcoholic is drinking or not. The "wet" phase family is described as closer and warmer emotionally, albeit fragile, disorganized, and chaotic. The "dry" phase family is more distant (Steinglass 1981). The helping system participates in perpetuation of alcoholic cycles by its confounding definition of the problem. Is the condition an illness or willful misconduct? In either case, the individual struggle goes on. When an individual successfully engages in Alcoholics Anonymous, however, she may move out of the recursive alcoholic cycles into a new relationship with alcohol, self, and others.

LIFE CYCLES

The life cycle is an important example of a cycle. The pattern of individual life is called development, and as described in an individual, takes on the shape of a line or a set of stairs representing stages in the acquisition of maturity. Patterns of development are discerned as they are followed by the lives of individuals and as these individuals' developments are similar to those of other individuals: in the same family, the same generation, the same culture, and across cultures. Jerome Kagan (Kagan and Klein 1973), for example, claims that although not all children have the sequence of cognitive development described by Piaget, all children do demonstrate the development of "stranger anxiety" at about eight months and the appearance of an awareness of satisfaction or dissatisfaction with personal accomplishment toward the end of the second year. He regards these as two major markers of human development. While developmental researchers try to tease apart lines of development to trace their paths, all are aware that there is a complex interaction of emotional, cognitive, and sensorimotor development within the individual in interaction with variables in the other domains of childhood. The word *cycle* as applied in the phrase *life cycle* suggests the universality of these developmental patterns as they describe the evolution of individuals in past, present, and future generations. An individual swallowtail butterfly begins life as a larva who feeds on parsley, spins itself into a cocoon, emerges as a butterfly, lays its eggs, and dies. The swallowtail butterfly captures the recursion in the pattern of the life cycle. When the family as an organization of individuals is studied, one needs to discern individual developmental issues (as lines of development are discriminated in the study of individual development) as well as patterns that characterize the evolution of family relationship groups. Family systems theorists have attempted to characterize the family life cycle. Problems in describing the patterned evolution of family shapes involve such questions as, Where or when does the family begin? and What is the meaningful family of description? The latter question requires framing in order to delineate which group's life span is being represented. The former question requires punctuation, in order to choose a beginning place. When framed as a nuclear family and punctuated to begin with the joining of a couple through marriage, the family life cycle is not a cycle at all but a line extending from courtship or marriage (whichever is chosen as the beginning) until some chosen endpoint, such as the death of the parents. Patterns discerned in this kind of model characterize the family's tasks at each stage of its evolution and are assumed to be similar both across families of similar type and across generations. This stage model approximates the pattern of serial homology discussed at the beginning of this chapter.

If a family is framed, however, as the multigenerational context of family relatedness, and punctuation marks life events of individual generations without signifying beginnings or endings of family periods, a cycle emerges with characteristic patterns that approximate each other in successive generations. One such model (Combrinck-Graham 1983, 1985) permits the observations of issues described in the stage models but also observes some characteristic changes in family morphology over generations of life cycles, which can be described as a metapattern in the life cycle. Figure 4.8 illustrates a family life cycle pattern arranged by stacking coinciding personal events at each generation on top of one another. The deformation of the spiral is explained in figure 4.9, which illustrates the metapattern of changing family shape: oscillating from centripetal to centrifugal, changing the internal family environment from close and intimate to more differentiated and back and forth again.

Temporal Conventions

A third approach to recognizing patterns involves observing the evolution of events over time and relating these events to ones with similar evolutionary patterns at other points in time and/or other levels of the system.

Figure 4.8 Family Life Spiral

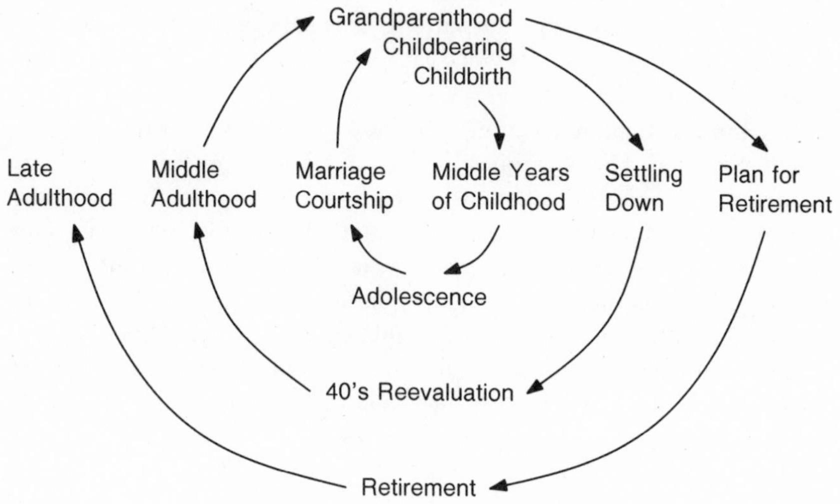

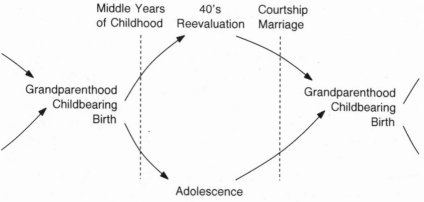

Figure 4.9 System Oscillation

Sequences

The search for patterns requires identification of events that appear to recur in similar form and sequence around the behaviors of interest. A sequence is a linear chain of events, punctuated by the observers marking the appearance of symptoms. In many instances it is possible to say that the preceding events produced the symptoms, but it is not always necessary to imply causality. Relevant sequences are associated with symptomatic behavior without necessarily being causal. The importance of the sequence is the idea that sequences are like habit patterns; they may be repetitive, whether or not they have cybernetic feedback qualities. Sequences have become important pattern concepts, because, like triads, they can be appreciated at different levels of the ecosystem, both in the hierarchy and in time. Identifying such patterns opens the opportunity to change the sequence or otherwise intervene earlier in the process before the symptomatic behavior occurs.

Most inquiries about a problem include a question: What led to the current problem? This is a question about a sequence. Add to the one instance under scrutiny other instances in the course of the particular problems being investigated, and one might find repetitive sequences. This forms the basis for some of the psychoeducational work with families of mentally ill individuals, where a collaborative effort to delineate the sequence of events preceding the psychotic episode becomes the basis by which a family anticipates the evolution of a similar pattern in the future and then plans how to interrupt the sequence to avoid further psychotic outcomes. The first two principles of sequences as relevant patterns are as follows:

1. There may be an identifiable, relevant sequence of events around a particular behavior or symptom.
2. This sequence may be repetitive in time.

Two other ways of examining sequences involve the unfolding of sequences over time and the multisystem participation in the unfolding of sequences. In proposing sequences as patterns that unify systems theory, systems theorists Douglas Breunlin and Richard Schwartz (1986) direct attention to the pacing of sequences, observing that some may occur in short time spans, from minutes to hours, or from days to weeks; others, such as anniversary reactions or seasonal disruptions, in years; and still others, over generations. These are named S1, S2, S3, and S4, respectively. The S1 sequence can be directly experienced in a course of therapy and may be observed to occur several times within one session. The S2 sequence can be inferred from data given in response to inquiries about recurring events over days and weeks and their relationship to observed symptoms. Examples of S3 sequences are the annual Christmas Eve fight, the vacation depression, the children whose problems with hyperactivity are associated with summer break from school, and the child whose asthma flares up around paternal grandmother's annual Thanksgiving visit. Repetitive behaviors over generations characterize S4 sequences. Bowen describes S4 sequences as interlocking triangles reproducing themselves across generations, and Boszormenyi-Nagy refers to the "revolving slate" of justice, the recurring ways of managing burdens passed from one generation to the next. It is often the case that child abusers were abused as children, and when this is found, it may be possible to describe an S4 pattern that links the past abuse with the present.

The multisystem or multiperson involvement in the sequence characterizes the ecosystems approach. The sequence is not simply a list of events unfolding or a repetitive pattern in time; it involves interactions among relevant subsystems. Although the term *sequence* implies an order—first this happened, and then that—the events in the sequence may be patterns, such as cycles or triads. The temporal aspect of the sequence puts dynamics into the static triad and locates cyclical processes in relevant space.

An S1 sequence was identified by Braulio Montalvo (1972) who analysed the process in one family therapy session. The sequence began when the therapist talked with a teenage daughter and appeared to be ignoring her parents. The girl's mother reached for a tissue; the girl asked to move away from the air conditioner, complaining that she was cold. By highlighting these events on videotape, Montalvo punctuated the sequence by choosing to begin when the therapist talked to the daughter, excluding the parents. He then related the other events to the first: the distressed father looked at the mother, who began an obtrusive search into her handbag for the tissue, thus attracting the daughter's attention. The daughter made a request to move away from the air conditioner, also away from the therapist, and in the direction of her parents. As punctuated by Montalvo, the therapist's approach to the girl appeared to provoke discomfort of all the family members, who then responded in what appeared to be a gracefully executed dance to get the girl away from the therapist and back into the safety and familiarity of her family.

Several things are important about this example. First, the sequence was recognized by Montalvo, who punctuated a beginning and end, thus also giving meaning to the events. Second, although the girl's symptoms—her anorexialike eating habits—were not directly involved in the sequence,

Montalvo proposed that the sequence was relevant to the underlying problem, namely, that the girl's strong attachment to her family interfered with her efforts to establish greater personal autonomy. Third, in this case, the sequence manifested itself in response to an action by the therapist, and it had the potential effect of deflecting the therapeutic intervention, thereby maintaining the family's dysfunctional interaction. This sequence can also be described in terms of triadic interactions: parents triangling in the daughter so that the therapeutic system (involving four individuals) took on the structure of excluding, or scapegoating, the therapist. In terms of cycles, one could see the facilitating, or positive feedback, effects of the father's distress, expressed by his looking at his wife. This turned on her display behavior (searching in her purse for a tissue), which turned on the daughter's loyalty behavior (asking to move away from the therapist and toward her parents). The daughter's behavior would have completed a negative feedback loop, turning off the distress display behaviors and reestablishing family security.

It is possible, now, to see how this pattern might have characterized family activity around the daughter's symptomatic behavior. On the surface, it was clear that the daughter's problems with eating involved both her parents, that is, brought her closer to them and vice versa. One could hypothesize that interpersonal events involving a bid for autonomy and parental distress displays occurred at every conflictual meal. Given this delineation of a pattern relevant to the serious symptoms of the daughter, there were several opportunities for intervention. In this case the therapist chose to block the negative feedback loop of the daughter becoming closely involved with the parents to turn off their distress display behavior. In the sequence in the therapy room, he changed chairs with her, dealing with her manifest discomfort with the air conditioner but requiring that she continue her conversation with him. In relationship to the symptoms about eating, he required her to discuss all of her decisions with him, since he was a physician, thus not permitting the symptom to involve the parents. Consistently interfering with this one aspect of the repetitive sequence obviously necessitated a change in the pattern. Another opportunity presented by the identified sequence could be to address the distress of either parent directly, suggesting an alteration of the sequence. For example, the therapist could have the parents go off alone to discuss plans for their life after their daughter leaves for college. This would also interrupt the sequence and force a change in the pattern. Such an approach, however, addresses a part of the sequence that is not explicit and is not acknowledged by the family members, and thus it has the danger either of mystifying them or of stimulating their resistance.

Narrative Patterns

Each system that has a history also has a story line, a description of itself. In chapter 5 I examine the effect of the process of taking a history of an individual or system and explore how the form of the questions interacts with the form of the system's own story to create a hybrid representing the intersection of the two narrative patterns. Folktales, fairy tales, and myths have some universal themes, such as how the world was created, how fire was discovered, how knowledge evolved, how the seasons were created, and so forth. These universal themes are elaborated in specific ways in different cultures and become increasingly distinctive and refined as they are interpreted through smaller and smaller groups. Whole nations have successfully changed their stories. We who watch the Chinese government retell the story of Tiananmen Square may be less aware of how our own nations' stories are told by our governments and news media.

Families also have their own stories, as do individuals within families.

Often these stories take the form of scripts that guide an individual or family's life and explain the past. Using a story line assists one in making meaning, connecting events and experiences. For a family whose child dies of leukemia, for example, the loss becomes tolerable through the creation of a story about the child and her place in the family, her relationship to forebears, and her example to future generations. The child's story, in turn, may become a family story that features loss as a form of redemption, a theme that might be played out in many forms through future generations.

Some universal stories for children are found among fairy tales: unfortunate children find a fairy godmother; kind children are assisted by their resourcefulness and guardian angels or spirits; children are haunted by evil forces, such as witches and sorcerers, but saved by innocence. Several popular children's stories have even been described as syndromes for adults: the Peter Pan syndrome in men who won't grow up, or the Cinderella syndrome in women who accept degraded positions at the hands of others who exploit them. As discussed in later chapters on treatment, these meaningful stories of children, families, or larger systems describe patterns that these systems experience. As narrative representations of familiar patterns, they can be examined and reconsidered, and ultimately rewritten, if so desired.

Metapatterns

One way of analyzing patterns at different levels of systems has already been suggested in the concept of isomorphisms, or the tendency of systems at different levels to manifest similar patterns. Stepping back from identified patterns may permit another level of analysis and the emergence of new patterns. Patterns at this additional level of analysis add to the richness of appreciation of system dynamics, the specificity of understanding of a particular system, and the complexity of blending events occurring at several conceptual levels of systems being examined.

One example of a metapattern has already been described in this chapter—the conceptual pattern of the family life cycle as a deformed spiral representing periods of centripetal family shape involving each of three generations in the family and periods of centrifugal shape, which also involve three generations. The metapattern suggested by this is the oscillation of family shape between centripetal and centrifugal (figure 4.9). Oscillation is an important metapattern that can be viewed as a shorthand way of describing negative feedback cycles—the thermostat pattern oscillates from on to off, while the room temperature oscillates from warmer to cooler. Family arguments oscillate between intensity and calm; individuals oscillate between autonomy and involvement; the alcoholic oscillates between wet and dry. Microanalysis of an apparently smooth progression or a steady state always demonstrates the dynamic adjustments of morphogenesis and morphostasis, which reflect the metapattern of oscillation. Douglas Breunlin (1988) has proposed that system development might be understood as a series of widening oscillations, moving from close to the state from which the system is developing to the state toward which it is moving. He observes that the system oscillates madly between the two widely different states until it settles on a new equilibrium. This observation explains the kind of inconsistency that is always experienced in the course of a system's evolution.

Another sort of metapattern is created by overlapping several patterns to form a distinctive metapattern. Family systems psychiatrist John Rolland (1984) proposed one example by presenting, first, a typology of chronic illness; second, a life span of chronic illness; and third, a pattern of the family life cycle. In order to comprehend a pattern particularly relevant to a particular family group in which an individual is suffering from a chronic illness, it is useful to superimpose these three patterns. For example, a six-year-old child has a leukemia that is an ultimately fatal condition but is in remission and that, because of hair loss due to the chemotherapy, is disfiguring. The typology (pattern level 1) of the child's illness is characterized as relapsing, ultimately fatal, and nonincapacitating but disfiguring. The illness is in what Rolland terms the "chronic" phase (pattern level 2), in that at this hypothetical point the child is neither in crisis nor terminal. The family should be in the phase of the life cycle (pattern level 3) of opening up from the centripetal period, becoming differentiated. One should add an additional pattern level that characterizes the interactions among the family members (pattern level 4). Once all four have been considered, it will become immediately evident that each is influenced by the other. This is most obvious in thinking about the family's movement through the life cycle (level 3), which will be affected by the child's illness. Specifically, the family will be more likely to remain close-knit and centripetal in responding to the illness. Furthermore, specific patterns of interaction (level 4) will evolve through the caretaking by the family as well as by the child's health care providers. A characteristic pattern with a child of six is that the mother takes the child for treatment, gets all the information, performs most of the home care, and keeps the father informed. In triadic terms, the mother will have a coalition with the child, with the father being in a peripheral position to this and other involved dyads. That is, the mother has relationships with the oncologists, nurses, and social workers, whereas the father is peripheral. It should be clear that these triadic patterns are accentuated by the child's illness and the care system. The patterns might change when the child enters a different phase of the illness (level 2), for example, by having a crisis through a relapse and infection. At this point, the father may take time from work and stay with his child in the hospital. Now the father has direct access to child care and to information from all the child's caretakers. Triadic relationships would change, ideally to include all relevant parties, but could move the mother into a peripheral position as the father steps into a role with authority.

Generic Patterns

Throughout this chapter I have briefly presented descriptions of patterns associated with certain symptomatic behaviors. Each symptom evaluated reveals patterns that may be distinct and unique to the system within which it occurs or quite like the patterns found with similar symptoms in other systems. The latter may be called generic patterns. Violence, for example, is almost always the outcome of symmetrical escalations both within and between individuals. Escalation of this sort overwhelms ordinary barriers and controls of overt aggression. Within the individual these controls are a delicate balance of neuron pathways, and within a society the controls are posed by boundaries and definitions of role that establish the status of individuals vis-à-vis each other. In the process of escalation, definition of status is either ignored or rejected. For example, an outraged teenager may reject the commandment to respect his mother and may strike her. Or a parent may ignore his status by pleading with an outraged eight-year-old to "be reasonable." As the eight-year-old accelerates "unreasonable" behavior, both she and the parent are likely to escalate to violence, which might be manifested by a tantrum by the girl or a spanking from the parent, or both. Similar patterns have been described in riots, where symmetrical exchanges escalated into violence, which was usually attributed to only one party.

Another generic pattern is deviance amplification. This pattern is found in most individuals and groups who function outside the norm. The pattern begins when a party is seen as somewhat different. This may be a child who is not at the same developmental level of accomplishment as his peers, a child who does not dress like his clothes-conscious peer group, or a child of a minority race or ethnic group. If the dominant group experiences the child as strange, they will move away from him. Any efforts that he makes to join will be scrutinized and rejected. The child may withdraw and actually become more strange, thus stimulating further distancing from the dominant group. This process is similar to that described earlier in this chapter for postpartum depression. It can also be discerned in the lives of children with a variety of symptoms and can lead to extreme deviance, including psychosis, depression, and suicide. Deviance maintenance is a variant. Here, as often happens in the education system, a child is identified as a genius or backward, and the system tends to perpetuate this view of the child.

Finding patterns throughout systems is the foundation of assessment. This serves the diagnostician, the consultant, and the therapist as she plans her interventions and evaluates the changes in the system. Examining events, expressions, symptoms, reactions, and actions as parts of patterns that occur not only at any level (or within any domain) of the system, but also across levels, is the second giant step. The pattern conventions described in this chapter assist with the complexity of integrating observations in this way.

PART II

Practical Innovations

CHAPTER 5

Diagnosing

In the mental health field, diagnosing has usually meant making a diagnosis or establishing a label according to a standardized diagnostic system. Generally, the label characterizes what is diseased. But when the systemic giant steps are taken, diagnosing also requires assessing strengths and competence. The process of identifying both what is wrong and what is working well, if it involves the system being assessed, can lead to steps taken by the system in the direction of its own healing.

Diagnosing as a Process

The word diagnosis comes from the Greek *gnosis,* meaning "knowledge," and *dia,* meaning "all through." I prefer to use a gerund, *diagnosing,* when referring to the process of knowing all through a system in order to think about what is going on and what to do. Diagnosing is a process, an activity. Diagnosing modifies itself while under way—that is, the experience of diagnosing continues as long as a clinician is involved with a system in treatment. For this reason, there is no diagnostic phase of treatment, nor is there a final diagnosis. When trying to understand fully, that is "know all through" a system being assessed, a clinician will want to examine the function of the symptoms or behaviors under consideration at each level of the system, and these questions will enrich the diagnosing. Diagnosing shifts the inquiry from What is it? to How does it work? and from Why? to How?

Three terms are used nearly interchangeably when describing the process of getting one's bearings with a patient or patient system: *diagnosing, assessing,* and *evaluating.* These terms are derived from different roots and literally refer to very different processes. Diagnosing has just been discussed. *Assessing* literally means "taking apart," or "partitioning for more detailed examination." The taking apart is in the form of reducing the system to some knowable piece, such as is sought in the biomedical model, according to Engel (1977). A literal example of assessment is the multiple impact assessment (MIA) developed by family therapy pioneers Robert MacGregor and colleagues (1964). In this process the family system is seen as a whole and taken apart into smaller subsystems—individuals, parents, siblings—and then brought back together. The term *evaluating* means "drawing value out of," and it identifies the inevitable placing of values on behaviors and feelings being observed. Evaluation always involves the values of the examiner and the values of those being examined. It is necessary, therefore, to recognize that the report of an evaluation is a statement of the personal values of the examiner as they have been activated in contact with those evaluated. This is seldom recognized in applications of the biomedical model.

Diagnosis and the Biomedical Model

Diagnoses in the medical model serve as a means for gathering data for research on phenomenology, treatment, and outcome and provide a basis for collecting third-party payments for psychotherapy. The primary guideline for diagnoses is the American Psychiatric Association's (APA) *Diagnostic and Statistical Manual of Mental Disorders,* third edition, revised (1987)—commonly called *DSM-III-R*—in which characteristics of recognized syndromes are delineated. Through such a system, clinicians have a common reference point regarding syndromes, and the collective experiences of many individuals studying and treating patients with these syndromes can be made available to everyone. Thus, establishing a diagnosis ideally enables a clinician to embark on a consensually validated course of treatment with the patient. As suggested earlier, however, the problem with "making a diagnosis" is that it is usually focused on only one level of a system, the individual. In fact, the *DSM-III-R* explicitly states this. Furthermore, most diagnoses identify deficits and deviances, but not health, strengths, or resources.

Recognizing that all conditions occur in a context, the APA in 1980 added two contextual axes to the *DSM-III* diagnostic system. Axis IV rates the severity of psychosocial stress that may have precipitated or exacerbated the problem, and axis V rates the highest level of functioning of the individual in the year prior to the time the diagnosis is being made. A relationship between psychosocial stressors (assessed on axis IV) and critical features of onset, course, and severity of conditions has not been established, so axis IV will probably be changed in future versions of the *DSM*. Axis V was changed in *DSM-III-R* to a global assessment of level of functioning, for the purpose of estimating how impaired the individual may be.

Integrating information from axes IV and V with the observations of the named syndromes in axes I and II, in the context of medical conditions designated in axis III, requires a recognition of the importance of different levels of system functioning, and it requires some integration of these levels in diagnosing and in planning for treatment. For axis IV to be meaningful, both stressors *and resources* should be identified. Resources might be considered host factors that protect the host from pathogens, such as psychosocial stressors. For example, it is possible to list a number of risk factors for teen suicide; but if one were to inventory all teenagers for the presence of such stressors, one would clearly find many more youngsters reporting the stressors than ones reporting a suicide attempt. There must be factors that "protect" a youngster from giving up on life when one or more of the stressors occur. Such factors are known to include relationships in which teenagers see their parents or other reliable adults as resources. Such resources have not yet been included in the *DSM*. Finally, since each axis reports a different level of information about an individual (but not of an individual's relational context or, more importantly, contextual resources), clinicians must take a metaposition in order to integrate information from the five axes to a total picture of the individual's health. This is rarely done, and more often than not, only conditions on the first two axes are rated.

Psychopathology

Clinicians using the *DSM-III-R* usually work at only one level of a system—the individual level. At this level findings are designated as psychopathology, meaning what is thought to be the matter with someone whose behavior is aberrant and who shows no evidence of somatic pathology. *Pathology* comes from the Greek *pathos*, meaning something which elicits sympathy. The science of pathology is the study of disease. In its unabridged sense, *patho*sology is the study of deviance from "normal" conditions that elicit sympathy. Characteristically in medicine, pathology involves the study of dead organisms or organs, such as at the postmortem examination; fixed tissue, as in a histopathological exam; or frozen tissue that has been removed from the body, as in a biopsy examination. It is this quality of fixedness that makes *psychopathology* an unsatisfactory term for explaining human behavior. The idea is that disturbed behavior comes from a disease, and in medicine disease is associated with abnormality of tissues or an imbalance of substances that regulate normal physiology.

It is possible to study behavior from this point of view, that is, seeking the sources of pathology. Psychiatry's roots in the biomedical tradition explain why its terminology is medical. Yet from Freud's time until the mid-1950s the primary level of explanation of emotional or psychological dysfunction dealt with environmental and experiential factors affecting an individual's psyche. Only since the mid-1950s have a number of explorations of genetics and neurophysiology converged to strengthen the understanding of the biological bases of behavior, many of which were postulated by Freud, but not substantiated. Biological developments in psychiatry have, in fact, had to deal with complicated interactions and patterns at a variety of levels. For example, it is now generally recognized that a human infant is not a tabula rasa upon which experience is etched but an organism with shape and substance both before and at birth, with a powerful ability to affect his environment.

Inborn characteristics—when they are not the obvious vulnerabilities and differences brought about by accidents, toxins, or transforming genetic events—are referred to as constitution or temperament. It is also known that some individuals are more prone to develop syndromes called mental illnesses, and such individuals are significantly clustered in families in such a way that it seems likely that there is a genetic component underlying these conditions. These findings should lead, however, to the exploration of why some genetically vulnerable individuals develop the syndrome and others do not. Again, it is necessary to look at interactions and resources. There is hope that the technology of neuropharmacology will ultimately reveal the mechanism of action of all pharmacologic agents, but will it also reveal why these mechanisms produce desired effects in some individuals and not in others? Wouldn't it also be necessary to study host factors, which would include environmental and relational factors as well as neuropharmacological ones? In fact, evidence abounds that medication is more effective among patients who believe that the medication will help, and among those whose families are constructively involved with the medication plan. In short, the discoveries regarding the genetic and neurobiological bases of emotional disturbances are exciting and promising, but the models of brain functioning and behavior that underlie these studies are closed individual models. They do not give information about how the parameters studied respond to the milieu in which the individual operates.

The Role of Doctors

The classical medical model identifies the doctor-diagnostician as a sleuth, one who uncovers clues and fits them together into a picture of the crime—in this case, the disease. My own favorite sleuth is Peter Sellers's character, Inspector Clouseau, who stumbles over, scrambles, and misinterprets clues, thus changing the evidence and reaching the wrong conclusions. His happy outcomes are purely by chance. Pathologists and psychopathologists are not as obviously blundering as Inspector Clouseau, but the fact of exploring inevitably changes the field being explored. The sleuth alters the data being investigated, notices only those data that can fit within her frame of reality, and organizes those data for coherence within these frameworks.

A role for a doctor besides that of sleuth is that of healer, and this role is implicit in the term *therapist.* Healing is quite different from treatment that derives from the diagnostic sleuthing just described. Healing involves all levels of the system, most particularly the patient. To be a healer, the professional must assess the healthy, working, living resources of the organism as well as the dysfunctional aspects. Thus, diagnosing necessitates a description of how the organism is functioning, which may include psychopathology but will encompass more aspects of individual functioning than malfunction and more levels of the system than the individual whose behavior has attracted attention. For example, currently there is considerable attention devoted to stress management and adaptation, which reflects the recognition of these other important levels of functioning.

Clinicians' Changing Evaluative Role

The past few decades have seen a great refinement in the technology and techniques for examining children. Ranging from laboratory methods for evaluating the infant–mother relationship, such as the Ainsworth Strange Situation used to measure attachment, to computer-assisted brain function scans, such as with positron emission tomography (PET), recent approaches have focused the investigator on bits of information that, in themselves, form only parts of ever-expanding contexts of understanding. It is tempting to see each bit of information as a potential explanation;

thus, a brain lesion may be designated as the cause of a certain behavior. But, as a classic experiment by José Delgado (1969) shows, the social context of the individual with the lesion will have an important effect on the behavioral expression. A monkey with a lesion in the limbic lobe would show aggression if he were top monkey, and submission, if he were lower on the monkey hierarchy. It is tempting to look deeper and deeper into the functioning of individual children, seeking in the psychopathology the explanation for bits of behavior. But strange things happen when we do this. First, we have explanation but no map for correction or compensation for the dysfunction. Second, we have not examined the context of the dysfunction, failing, therefore, to understand how it operates at different levels of the system, how the system maintains it, and how we, as evaluating clinicians, may be a part of the system that maintains it.

For diagnosing to develop a useful understanding of troubling processes that can form a map for intervention, the adaptive functions of the system and its resources need to be addressed, as well as those areas in a system that also need adjusting. This means that for effective diagnosing, clinicians will have to take the third giant step to focus on competence. This represents a major shift from seeking causes for dysfunction, identifying pathology, labeling, and cataloguing liabilities to recognizing the values built into systems and searching for strengths within expanding layers of systems.

Labeling

Labeling can be one of the more unfortunate outcomes of attribution of psychopathology or admission to the sick role. Beginning as a shorthand in communication, labeling can be dehumanizing. An example is the identification of a patient by her ailment. When a nurse on a pediatric ward says, "Could you take a glass of water to the 'wrist' in bed four?" she means, "to the child with a broken wrist." This may be harmless, but psychiatric labeling can be stigmatizing. For example, in a videotape titled *Leaving Home,* the narrator, Jay Haley, reports that the young person had been hospitalized and had been diagnosed as a paranoid schizophrenic, "which means they didn't like him very well." Sometimes the label applied reflects more about the therapist's views than about any objective conclusion drawn from carefully ordered data. This idea was suggested by Haley's irreverent comment. What does it mean to give someone the diagnosis of paranoid schizophrenia? In addition to the precise descriptive meaning, this label indicates that the person has a very poor prognosis. If he doesn't deteriorate from his illness, he'll probably succumb to the effects of his treatment—dulling of consciousness followed by tardive dyskinesia, or the leveling effects of chronic institutionalization.

This kind of labeling can often become a way in which a patient is identified and identifies himself. Psychiatrists often refer to schizophrenics, borderlines, manics, and bulimics. Schizophrenia is usually a chronic, handicapping condition. People with borderline personality disorders often have dramatic self-destructive behavior, are difficult to deal with, and take a long time to treat. One must consider the power of self-fulfilling prophecies and ask, To what extent might the label itself produce some of the symptoms predicted by it? I have heard children introduce themselves with, "I'm a hyperactive child." Often they do not even pronounce it properly, and they could not explain what it means, but in their behavior one can see that this identity has given them license to be hyperactive. Fortunately, this self-perception can be flexible, as the following examples illustrate.

One day a mother brought one of her children who was feeling sad for a consultation. She brought another one of her children along, too, because he was home that day. He was supposed to be hyperactive. As she came into the consulting room with the two children, she said, somewhat defiantly, "I brought Ernie; he's hyperactive." Ernie obliged by moving rapidly around the room, twirling all the chairs, writing on the blackboard, and rifling through my papers. After a short time, I turned to Ernie and said, "Hyperactive or not, you'll have to sit down and be quiet so I can talk to your sister." Ernie stopped, and as the session went on with no further explicit attention to him, he took out his homework and began to do it.

Years ago I worked with a woman who had multiple sclerosis (MS). When she began treatment, she practically introduced herself as Ms. MS. The therapy was directed at recognizing other aspects of her current and future identity, so that at the end of treatment she met her future husband. Ms. MS, who was fated to spend her invalid life in a wheelchair, initially felt she should not impose herself on someone in marriage. But my patient, quite ambitious, an excellent lawyer, and a good friend, eventually married and became a good wife.

SOCIAL EXPLANATION AND CONTROL

A final difficulty with labeling is in the aspect of social explanation and control inherent in the labeling process. An example of this is the story of an eight-year-old girl, Lottie, whose great-grandmother was described as a manic-depressive. The singular example of her manic behavior was that she had run off with a circus performer, leaving her husband and small children. The possibilities that she couldn't stand her husband or that he was an intolerable bore were ignored when she was labeled. The label explained the behavior and exonerated others in her context from any responsibility for her departure. The less benign aspect of having designated the great-grandmother as manic-depressive, however, was that this became a family legacy. Her children's behaviors were explained in terms of their mother's illness. Future generations would have the opportunity of characterizing their behavior as manic-depressive, and they, too, would not have the opportunity of being held accountable for their behavior or holding others accountable for their responses to them.

This case came to my attention because Lottie was hospitalized on a psychiatric unit. She had been staying home from school and telling her mother she was going to kill herself. Her mother, too, had threatened suicide in the past; thus, she was in treatment. When her mother told the therapist about Lottie's behavior, the therapist assumed that Lottie, too, was suffering from an affective disorder, and he placed her on antidepressants. Lottie refused to take the medication. Her refusal was understood as a confirmation that she was ill and not able to conduct herself in a healthy fashion.

As it turned out, Lottie's mother left the house for work before Lottie got up in the morning. Thus, Lottie's "refusal" to go to school could be better understood by recognizing that no one was sending her to school. Solving the problem of making arrangements to have someone get Lottie off to school in the morning was not easy. Furthermore, after many months of erratic school attendance, Lottie resisted the efforts to get her to school. But the struggle to normalize her school behavior without the burden of affective illness would have lasting beneficial effects for her and for her mother, who would experience her own success in providing for her child, practically for the first time in Lottie's life. The legacy from her great-grandmother, however, had led everyone to see Lottie, like her relatives, as suffering from a psychiatric illness and to treat her accordingly.

SOME PEOPLE NEED LABELS

One of the most effective treatments of chronic schizophrenia today is based on labeling. This treatment is actually a combination of a variety of interventions based on family psychoeducation. The first step in this process is to make a correct diagnosis of the patient, thus clarifying that the patient has a disease that is not caused by the family. Having released the family from the responsibility that families inevitably feel for the terrible condition of their family member, the psychoeducational treatments teach family members what is known about schizophrenia's etiology, manifestations, and treatment.

The practice of labeling the patient and then working with the family in this way is in keeping with two important movements in the mental health field. The first is biological psychiatry, which emphasizes nature over nurture in studying genealogies, genetics, neurosynapses, neuroendocrinology, and the particular neurophysiology and neuropsychology of mentally ill people. The second is the family advocate movement, represented by the National Alliance for the Mentally Ill (NAMI), which denounces the tendency of mental health professionals, particularly family therapists, to blame families of the mentally ill. Although focused on the individual level, both of these movements have led to a broadening of research efforts. Albert Scheflin's 1981 assessment of several levels of schizophrenia illustrates how the persuasive findings of biological vulnerability and deviance derived from studying the individual can be integrated with information derived from studying each domain of the schizophrenic's system.

ANOTHER APPROACH: METAPHORS

Problems can be assessed in a way that is more tailored to the particular system experiencing difficulties. This can be thought of as developing a shared metaphor, a description that derives from the patient system but also gives the system a way of thinking about itself and what must be done. For example, a young woman who had tried several professions (she had the dubious good fortune to be proficient at all of them) and several diagnostic identities, all without any satisfaction, was described as "a character in search of a story." This label explained her lack of satisfaction and gave her some sense of what had to be done in order to achieve the satisfaction she sought. In another example, a family with six children tumbled into the office with many stories and people interrupting each other and finishing each other's sentences. At the end of the session, the therapist, seizing on one theme that had been raised, remarked that this was a family that seemed to have trouble getting people's socks in the right drawer. Delighted with this description of themselves, the family set upon the task of sorting out the laundry. Another patient who was constantly intruding emotionally on her children and being intruded upon by her husband and parents was told that she was borderline. She was delighted with the metaphor, because it suggested that she needed to get her borders and boundaries straightened out. In fantasy, she began to design and describe her boundaries, and the next time she began to tangle with her daughter, she imagined a thick windbreak of pines coming between them, allowing her to stay on her side and keep her daughter on the other.

A Diagnosing Dilemma

A child psychiatry fellow presented the case of Ahmed at a grand rounds. She framed the presentation with the following question about her patient: "How does one make a differential diagnosis of conduct disorder, oppositional disorder, or attention deficit hyperactivity disorder (ADHD), and differentiate these from normal conflicts of adolescence?"

Ahmed is a thirteen-year-old only child of a brief union between his father, whose parents emigrated from Africa, and his African-American mother. He has been referred because of repeated problems in school, resulting most recently in his being required to repeat seventh grade. He is assessed to be of superior intelligence, with verbal scores substantially higher than performance scores. His behavior at school is reported to be rebellious and contentious, and he neither does homework nor studies. Ahmed lives with his paternal aunt, his paternal grandmother, and his paternal great-grandfather, all of whom came from Africa after a civil war in which they were among the ousted old guard. His mother lives in another state, and he has no contact with her. His father is remarried and lives nearby, but he has little contact with Ahmed except when he is called in to discipline him. Everyone in the family is very upset with Ahmed's failure.

I was one of the discussants for the presentation, and I first responded to the fellow's question about differential diagnosis, "Indeed, how does one differentiate between those different labels?" I then asked myself, What earthly good would differentiating do? I understood that if the child had a conduct disorder, a behavior modification program might be the best treatment. And if he was aggressive and impulsive, some form of medication might be helpful. If he had ADHD, a stimulant could substantially improve his perceived success in school through greater attention. And if he had an oppositional disorder, his prognosis would be better. If he was just going through the normal throes of adolescence, we needed not to worry nearly as much.

So issues of treatment and outcome are immanent in the names one chooses for the patient, the way psychopathology is described, the diagnoses that are made. In Ahmed's case, I wondered in my discussion, Why not select all of the choices offered? I would have been happy, too, to include identity disorder and the possibility of depression (probably of the dysthymic disorder type) as well. In choosing all of these, I would expect that the youngster might benefit from the behavior modification and the stimulants. Further, he would benefit from the relationships formed to address his identity issues and his persistent dysphoria in the face of chronic school failure (which was due to misbehavior; Ahmed performed very well on a standardized intelligence test, but did not conform to expectations in school). Recognition that many of the problems with which he was struggling were normative for young adolescents might encourage him not to give up on himself. Settling on *the* diagnosis seemed unnecessarily limiting. Narrowing down to one might generate other problems because doing so excludes many possibilities. In Ahmed's case I favored choosing all of the possible diagnoses, thereby keeping the field as open as possible. As Scheflin (1980) once said about his own epistemological shift away from Augustinian dichotomies, "When confronted with a dichotomy, choose both; when confronted with a trichotomy, choose all three!"

Of course, none of the diagnoses proposed for Ahmed would be sufficient, nor the interventions effective, unless Ahmed's difficulties were understood in the context of his family and the family's contextual relationships in their country of adoption, the United States. In Ahmed's case the family displayed three generations of revolutionary behavior, and they retained their cultural identity in their new country. The descendants of an African chief of state who had been forced to leave his country were now living among black Americans. The race was the same, but the culture, educational goals, and ambitions were utterly foreign to the child's family. Always keeping alive the hope of a return, the family deliberately did not assimilate. Even given that his family sent him to private schools, how was such a child to thrive in the American education system? Diagnosing at the family level would have to include a recognition of the family's revolutionary stance and its message about this to the child. Any of the diagnoses suggested for Ahmed would be acceptable, as I mentioned, but none would lead to an effective treatment plan without the recognition of the family's culture, that in which the child was thriving. A behavior program, methylphenidate for his attention deficit, and intensive work with him on clarifying his identity could be extremely effective in the context of working with the family.

As it happened in Ahmed's family, the paternal aunt had made her own adjustment to this country. She had completed graduate education and was a professional. She had invested her income wisely and was financially well established. It was hardly surprising, then, that Ahmed and his aunt had a particularly aggravated relationship. As the holdout for the family's old revolutionary values, Ahmed constantly challenged his aunt, whom he saw as having sold out to the new country. Nor was it surprising that he usually won the arguments and that his aunt typically gave in. But a thirteen-year-old boy on the brink of puberty doesn't have the power to defeat a highly educated adult unless he gets help. Furthermore, he doesn't have the power to defy school system after school system without help. Ahmed's paternal grandmother was the survivor, the daughter of the revolutionary, who maintained the family's dream and status. In Ahmed's household she drew back when the boy fought with his aunt, as if deliberately refusing to press the boy to settle down. Thus, the function of Ahmed's battle with his aunt and his failure in school could be understood both as his effort to uphold the family's revolutionary stance and as actions supported by his grandmother, whose own role in upholding the family's stance was being supported by Ahmed.

Where were the boy's parents? His mother had been discarded early in his life, as if she were simply a surrogate to perpetuate the noble line. She was in another state, to be contacted only occasionally. The boy's father, as described by his relatives, was a brilliant man but a ne'er-do-well who repeatedly copped out in one way or another. He, too, was a revolutionary, a sometime follower and fellow exile of Malcolm X. Ahmed was being raised by his grandmother, who lived with the aunt. The family system could be described as revolutionary, as a way of being in this country that prohibited the child from conforming by doing well in school and getting along socially. This label of the family leads to a treatment plan that integrates the various levels of the system involving difficulties.

A way to begin with Ahmed's treatment might have been to meet with the family to examine their views of the child's difficulties. Capitalizing on their distress at a recent school failure, one might have been able to engage the grandmother to help Ahmed settle down in school. Each piece of the child psychiatrist's diagnosis could have been explained to her. She could have visited the school, looked over his homework, and seen the results of his psychological tests. With these assessments of her grandson's trouble, she might have been willing to participate in a variety of treatments on his behalf. She might have overseen a trial of methylphenidate, thereby having her own way of evaluating its effects. She might have administered a behavior modification program. She might have looked over his homework and visited his school, collaborating with his teacher. She might, through the transformations of her own life in this process, have been able to confer on the youngster permission to form an identity in this country that would permit him to be a successful student preparing to be a successful American adult.

Unfortunately, someone had evaluated Ahmed's grandmother and had concluded that she clung too tenaciously to the dream of restoring her family's power in Africa to be of any assistance. She, too, was evaluated according to traditional diagnostic conventions and consequently was dismissed as a resource to Ahmed. This made the professionals' jobs much more difficult, because it meant they were the only ones who could treat Ahmed, and that they would have to do this in spite of his grandmother and her aspirations for this special grandson. With the grandmother's help, this child could yet become the major link to his family's new country, the one to make the adoption official. But this could not happen at all unless the family was involved not only in the treatment but in the conceptualization of the problem, in the process of diagnosing.

Contextual Diagnosing

Contextual diagnosing should accomplish the goals of knowing all through the system (and therefore involve multiple system levels), searching for strengths and competence, identifying patterns of interaction in which behaviors function, and evaluating the problems in such a way that the system's values are elicited and incorporated into the process. The process should involve assessment—but not in the usual sense where someone outside the system, a clinician or researcher, evaluates some things or some people. Contextual diagnosing involves a mutual assessment by all involved parties of the life situation in which the system being assessed finds itself.

The outcome of the assessment should be formulated in terms that reflect the language of the system being assessed and should include a critique of the situation under examination. Formulations should include what is going well and should continue, and what is not going well and should be changed. The outcome of any change that would be undertaken for the better should be predicted, and those involved should present a general map of how to get from their current situation to their desired one. Finally, some specific steps about how to initiate these changes should also come out of the assessment. Clearly, the system being evaluated has an active role in this kind of assessment, and in order to achieve such a collaboration, members of the system need to be recruited into the process through experiencing the respect, curiosity, and empathy of the clinicians.

An Example: The Bruszkowskis

In the Bruszkowski family, Stella, the oldest daughter, was diagnosed at age thirteen as having acute lymphoblastic leukemia (ALL). Ordinarily, the prognosis for ALL is quite good, but Stella relapsed within a year after she went into remission. A bone marrow transplant, killing her own marrow with radiation and chemotherapy and rescuing her with human leukocyte antigen (HLA) matched marrow, was her best chance for a cure, and her seven-year-old brother, Alex, the only boy in the family, was the best match. There was a legal requirement to assess Alex in order to determine that he understood what was being asked of him and that he was agreeing to it of his own free will. But there was a practical demand to involve the family in this assessment as they anticipated a long and complicated course of preparing for a transplant and the care of Stella afterwards.

Shortly after marrying, Stella's parents had emigrated from Poland. In the United States they lived in a Polish neighborhood and had their children. Mr. Bruszkowski was a cabinetmaker, and his trade had involved him widely around the city. He was fluent in English. The children, of course, were all fluent in English, but Mrs. Bruszkowski, who stayed in the neighborhood, spoke no English and understood very little. Thus, all of the conversations about Stella's illness, the blood samples taken from the children for HLA testing, and the plans for a transplant had to be translated to her by either her husband or her children. As the hospital personnel were proceeding with the plans, Mr. Bruszkowski came for a conference without his family to say that they had decided not to go through with the transplant. His wife, he said, did not want to sacrifice Alex for Stella, even though Stella was her oldest and favorite daughter. Further, he said all of their relatives and in-laws were agreeing with his wife. He asked us how they could make such a decision, and if something happened to Alex, or if Stella died, how they could face their families.

We decided to begin with a meeting that would include as many of the Bruszkowski relatives as possible. Stella's parents brought Mr. Bruszkowski's sister and brother-in-law and his sister-in-law, and Mrs. Bruszkowski's mother. The hospital staff included the social worker, the attending oncologist, a child psychiatrist, and a visiting child psychiatrist from Warsaw who served as an expert interpreter. The meeting was set up to involve the most significant resources to the Bruszkowski household, their extended family, and their trusted doctors. Its objective was to provide information so the family could be empowered to make a decision they could live with.

We talked for two hours, with all of the adults asking many questions. At the end of the session, the doctor from Warsaw reported that Mr. Bruszkowski's brother had said, "We cannot make such a decision for you. We understand that this is a very difficult decision, and we will support you, whatever you decide to do." Subsequently, the Bruszkowskis decided to go through with the transplant. Alex was in the hospital for twenty-four hours for the marrow harvest and was fine. The graft never took, however, and Stella died. Several months later the family agreed to allow Alex to come for another interview. This interview, and the follow-up by the social worker indicated that the family deeply grieved the loss of Stella, but the extended family, true to their word, stood by them. Alex did not regret having served as a donor, and the family did not regret their choice.

Questions of Inclusion in Assessment

The system to be assembled in this form of assessment can include any collection of individuals involved in the issues under consideration. It may involve only an individual child, but usually such an interview alone would not complete a process. The assembled system often should include a child and his parents and, at best, those actively involved with one another within a household. Relevant others may include some members of the extended family, as in the instance of the Bruszkowskis, as well as those from involved systems, such as the school, welfare, legal, and health care systems (as in the Bruszkowski story). Anderson, Goolishian, and Winderman (1986) have advocated including all who worry that there is a problem needing to be addressed, all of whom constitute the "problem-defined system." Including in the assessment all of those involved in the problem offers a special opportunity for expression and appreciation of competence in children and their families. The usual approaches to assessment offer a static view of an individual's or system's level of functioning, but they do not provide any picture of the range of adaptive responses. The process of inviting relevant members of the system to assess the situation together is a first step. But certain techniques in the conduct of the interview itself are also necessary to make the interview(s) highly effective in stimulating the system's creativity and curiosity, and, finally, in solving problems.

Other Positive Interviewing Techniques

Some special approaches to interviewing enhance a system's positive view of itself, stimulate curiosity, and promote a process of self-examination in the interviewees. Some of these techniques are positive connotation, eliciting prevailing beliefs and mythology, circular questioning, and solution defining.

Positive connotation refers to the reframing of events, acts, or feelings that have been seen as problems in positive terms. For example, a woman who is a compulsive runner has a disorganized son, Jon, who almost daily forgets things he needs for school. So almost every day she runs up to the school to take him the forgotten items. The boy's father complains of his distractibility and disorganization, and the mother agrees. A clinician positively connotes the child's disorganization as providing his mother a necessary opportunity for exercise.

In some systems there are governing myths or superstitions, and in families these may be carried through generations. A prevailing belief in Jon's family is that boys are less organized than girls, because they are more intellectual. When the school personnel becomes concerned about Jon's persistent forgetting, certain beliefs operate in that system, too. For example, a counselor believes that Jon's mother doesn't wake him up early enough in the morning for him to get organized before school. She (being a proponent of a nutritional breakfast) also believes that he does not eat properly. The teacher thinks that Jon has attention deficit hyperactivity disorder and his forgetting is due to his distractibility, which she sees as part of a larger picture of his work and social interaction. In light of these views Jon's behavior is seen as problematic and incompetent, but the positive connotation proposes a way in which the behavior is competently involving his mother in her favorite pastime, running.

Circular questioning involves both the content and way in which systemic probes are made. Formally, circular questions are asked of one person about the interactions between others. This stimulates the observing aspects of the system. The questions are structured in order to raise possibilities about relationships that may not have been considered. This can be done by asking comparison questions, like, "Who gets more upset about Jon's disorganization, Dad, Mom, or Grandma? And who is least upset?" It can also be done by asking about the past: "If this had happened five years ago, when Dad was away in the merchant marines, what would Mom have done?" And there are also questions about the future: "When Jon is away at camp, will his little sister increase her demands on Mom? If she does, how will she do it?" Unlike the usual questions in an assessment interview—questions such as, "What is the problem? When did it start? How long have you been married?" which are designed to gather information for the record—circular questions stimulate thinking but not specific or final answers.

Solution definition contrasts with problem definition. Rather than focus on the repeated failures represented by an intensive account of symptoms and failed efforts to resolve them, solution definition focuses on the stimulation of problem solving. And in the process of solution finding there is an emphasis on solutions that might work, rather than a review of failed solutions. Some approaches to this include inquiring about a desired outcome, exploring how this outcome differs from the current situation, and plotting some of the steps to be taken.

The interview itself needs to be focused not on gaining a wide spectrum of information but on raising questions in spheres related to the issues at hand. Generally, this is not an information-gathering session in the ordinary sense. Information is to be *generated* by the process of the interview and is, in fact, the goal of the assessment. For each area of inquiry it is important that the interviewer stay focused and assist family members in doing so as well. This will reduce the possibility of the process disintegrating into a judgmental or blaming situation.

To be properly focused, the clinician needs to be clear with the family at the outset about the agenda. For example, if there is an issue about protection of a child, the clinician should make that a part of the introductory comments. In Jon's case, the interview would start out with the clinician's review of what he or she has been told of the problem—that Jon forgets things he needs in school—and most important, what the purpose of the interview is—to find out what everyone thinks and to see what can be done. All of this must be transacted in language the family understands so that a genuine conversation can be had. It is through assembling the involved individuals from different domains of a child's ecosystem; stimulating curiosity, creativity, and competence to break out of old frames into new possibilities; and integrating information derived from these many levels of experience that diagnosing is most effective and beneficial.

Impacts of Contextual Diagnosing

In describing the diagnosing dilemma of Ahmed, I illustrated how to build successive domains of a child's experience into the diagnosing process. It was done this way in his case because that was how the information was presented. Indeed, the need to collect and integrate many specific reports on one case is common and unavoidable. It is one important task of diagnosing. In addition to the specific reports on Ahmed, such as his school achievement and psychological testing, a whole system session such as has just been described could have been immensely helpful. This session would have brought together school personnel and various members of the family, including the grandmother, the aunt, other children in the household, and the father and stepmother.

The purpose of the meeting would have been to review the situation in which the participants found themselves. The therapist would have invited them, one by one, to describe the situation in their own words and state what they would like to see happen. Each person would also have been invited to describe the strengths of the family, of Ahmed, and of the relationships involved with the school. From this point, they would have assessed themselves, and they might then have been able to consider what to do. The clinicians conducting the interview might have offered some stimulating questions, using positive connotation, circular questioning, and solution finding. They might also have offered suggestions about such things as the specific treatments recommended.

Diagnosing is a process to which the first three giant steps apply. Many different viewpoints must be obtained and integrated at multiple levels to identify meaningful patterns which can form maps for intervention. The system's competence must be identified and stimulated through the diagnosing. When diagnosing is conducted in this fashion, both the mental health professional and the system are acting interactively in a healthy fashion as defined in the fourth giant step.

CHAPTER 6

Therapy Principles

Therapy, like diagnosing, should be directed at the biological and psychological functioning of the individual child as well as the function of the other levels of the biopsychosocial continuum, or domains of childhood. The principles of therapeutic intervention should embody the conceptual giant steps. Therapy should invite participants to examine their situation from many different points of view; people should learn how their behaviors form parts of patterns that can be altered, if desired; therapy should build on systems' competencies and incorporate systems' resources; and therapy must lead to a healthy system that is organized for the well-being of its members.

Systems Therapy Versus Traditional Child Therapy

In proposing these principles of therapy, I am aware of a departure from common practice—a departure that requires taking giant steps. As noted earlier, the usual procedure of formulating a problem and embarking on therapy requires imposing constraints, narrowing the focus, discarding irrelevant information, organizing data into parsimonious explanations, and selecting diagnostic labels. Ordinarily, a client asks a therapist simple questions: "What is the matter? What shall I do about it?" The questions are constraining. The answers, which come after suitable evaluation, are also constrained: "Your son has attention deficit hyperactivity disorder. You should give him this medication." The exchange sustains the hierarchy of the therapist who directs and clients who bring complaints and follow instructions. What would happen if the therapist chose instead to introduce variety rather than constraint? If, instead of answering the questions by giving his opinion, the therapist had the client observe herself, thus generating curiosity, what would the consequences be? If therapist and patient were encouraged to describe and discuss together the perceived reality of the situation being addressed, even changing the way they view it as they work, what would happen to the therapeutic relationship?

There are two key aspects of these proposed changes. The first is in the nature of exploration and how the therapist and client engage in it. Circular questioning, described in chapter 5, is a technique that sparks clients' inquisitiveness about themselves. The therapist either remains neutral or reflects back to the clients her perception of their questions and their struggle for answers. In either case, however, the roles of therapist and clients may remain in the traditional, therapist one-up, client one-down structure of traditional psychotherapeutic relationships, if the therapist sustains the patients' expectations that she is drawing conclusions from the data and will act according to her conclusions, even if they are not articulated. On the other hand, the roles may change the traditional hierarchical ones, and this has important implications for how the treatment will unfold.

The second aspect of the proposed change, then, is the working relationship of therapist and clients. Who is responsible for what will unfold? Can anyone predict how things will turn out? The therapist can direct the treatment, or the therapist and clients can continue with the exploration, generating more possibilities and exposing more choices. Change takes place as a consequence of the self-conscious experience of a wider range of possibilities, which inevitably reframes the original situation. The therapist may become incidental to the real work of change, or the therapist may change along with the clients, as they change in relationship to him. Is it correct to call this therapy or to call a professional a therapist if he truly directs no therapy? Hierarchical dependence might be sustained merely by calling it therapy. Perhaps work with systems, including individuals, families, and organizations, should be called "consultation." Consultations are done between colleagues with equal status but differentiated knowledge and experience. Consultation implies an exchange. To be involved fully in this exchange, the mental health professional has to be open to change. Carl Whitaker has referred to this phenomenon as "the growing edge" of therapy and has often said that when he stops growing in therapy, he will stop seeing clients. I will continue to use the terms *therapy* and *therapist,* attempting, by description of the principles, to illustrate the elimination of a one-up/one-down hierarchical relationship between them, and I will refer to this overall approach as *systems therapy.*

Mental Health Professional as Consultant

There are some important implications for practice if this new position of mental health professional—consultant or facilitator—is adopted. First, assessment must begin with the current patterns in which troublesome experiences occur, because this is directly relevant to the reasons a consultation is being sought. Without established reference points in the present, questions about history can mystify the clients rather than involve them. Patterns should be assessed at all the levels possible, including patterns of interaction between therapist and patient and, of course, historical ones. It behooves the therapist to observe, catalogue, and reflect patients' strengths and competencies. Further, the therapist needs to inquire about and discover the patients' resources. This is essential for therapy to proceed, for patients don't recover in therapy; they recover only within the system in which they live. A therapist who works with a child without careful assessment and inclusion of these resources in the therapeutic plan risks imposing herself into a system in which she ultimately doesn't belong. Finally, it is very difficult to affect the outcome of a healthy system organized to support the well-being of all of its members through working with one member or only a subsystem. Ivan Boszormenyi-Nagy observed, "A therapist is ethically responsible for the effects of the therapy on all members of the relationship system" (conversation, 1982).

Clearly, I advocate such an orientation to therapy, but this approach is beyond particular frameworks or techniques. To teach specific techniques would be logically confusing. Having taken the position that the professional should have an exchange with the client about the problems and the changes, I would also encourage supervisors and teachers to have similar exchanges with their students. I have taught, supervised, or consulted with many different professionals working with children, including all of the mental health disciplines as well as pastoral counselors, teachers, health care professionals, mediators, attorneys, and judges. When people have to be told how to do therapy, they exhibit the behavior of Epaminandas, the little boy in the children's story, who always spoiled his grandmother's gifts by doing literally what his mother had just told him to do, whether the situation called for it or not. Good therapists do what makes sense and is comfortable for them. All of the techniques that have been derived through working with individuals, such as play, behavior therapy, cognitive restructuring, exploration of intrapsychic constructs, and medication, are used within a systemic framework. What must change in systems therapy is not the techniques but the formulation of the problems and therapeutic goals, which should include as many levels of systems functioning as can be usefully apprehended by the therapist and clients. Having all of these arenas available for assessment and intervention offers the systemic therapist many opportunities for activating resources in the patient system, finding unused repertoires within the system, and restructuring relationships.

Having been a family therapy training director in a pluralistic setting, with teachers from many systems backgrounds, I have developed greater respect for a variety of schools of family therapy, taking a metaposition about systems of treatment, as I am recommending should be taken with every practice system within which one works. Having seen scores of students struggle with the apparently conflicting viewpoints presented by their different teachers, I asked myself, What goes into a student's choice of styles? Some students adopt one orientation and ignore the others; others, however, seem to take a little bit here and a little bit there. The three factors that seem most influential in the student's choice of a therapeutic approach in a given situation are the student's personal style and worldview, his supervisor's interests, and the particular client system with which he is dealing. The most interesting students could be quite experimental, using, for example, a practice based on restructuring roles in a family within a philosophical approach that considers issues of loyalties and the balance of fairness. I call this "scrambling," mixing ingredients to come up with a product particularly suited to the therapist. Learning that students could, and do, scramble, I became more confident about providing them with a smorgasbord of ingredients from which to choose for their scrambling. With this in mind, I am presenting a skeleton of therapy practice in order to maximize the flexibility of the practitioner.

Traditional Child Therapy

Child therapy began with the technique of psychoanalysis, derived from psychoanalysis for adults. Children's conscious and unconscious thoughts and feelings were elicited through free association in play. Through similar processes in the facilitating relationship with the therapist, the children could work through their anxieties and conflicts. Analytic sessions might be held several times a week, and for adolescents the verbal free association of the adult models substituted for play. Classical child analyses are fairly rare, but child analysis has remained the major exemplar upon which most approaches to child therapy are based. The style I advocate for the systems therapist, like that of the analyst, involves not being overtly judgmental and not attempting to constrain the child's expressions through explanation, but encouraging elaboration of the experience. But there are also problems with the analytic paradigm for one who has taken the conceptual giant steps I propose.

One problem is the need to provide some kind of relief for both the child and her family as quickly as possible. The process of building the trusting relationship with the child takes too long. While this is happening, what is happening in the rest of the child's world? For example, Ryan Malone was a five-year-old boy who had been expelled from his private school kindergarten for fighting and swearing. The youngest of five children of a busy physician and an aspiring landscape architect, Ryan had been taken to various specialists throughout his short life to correct his feet, his teeth, and his speech. Now, his mother took him to a child psychiatrist, who recommended a course of psychoanalysis. But what was to be done about school or anything else while everyone waited for the relationship between Ryan and his analyst to be established?

A second problem concerns what happens when the relationship with the therapist is established; what kind of betrayal or breach of trust with one's family is encouraged? How does a child experience himself continuing to manifest symptoms in a context now where everyone is waiting for the therapy to start showing effects? My thoughts were that the child would experience himself as being untouchable, his parents as out of control, and the analyst as some kind of wizard, holding the bag of magic to be doled out at his discretion.

A third problem is a concern about the therapist's intrusion into the family's life. This is expected in therapy, but it can be dealt with through various degrees of directness and awareness. My own feeling is that the effects of the therapy on the whole family should be recognized and maximized rather than ignored. This means keeping in touch with other family members, knowing the child's siblings, seeing the child's home, and visiting with the child's teachers. Furthermore, if the therapist becomes so intimately involved with the child, what is happening to the child's relationships with her immediate family, and theirs with her?

Any therapist resides in one level of the child's ecosystem. In the concentric circle model of the ecosystem, the therapist system is in the first extrafamilial sphere, the exosystem. It is important to remember that two ecological realms are closer, more vital, and more influential to the child than that of the therapist: the nuclear family and the extended family influence. When a therapist crosses into the most immediate sphere of the child, as I believe happens in intensive individual therapy, the ecology is violated, and the relationships with natural contextual resources are disrupted in a fashion that is neither careful, thoughtful, nor facilitative of those natural resources. Rather, the therapist may try to substitute himself for these vital linkages in the child's daily world. It seems to me that a therapist who undertakes such a relationship should be prepared to make a formal adoption.

A fourth area of difficulty is an ethical concern about the expectation that the therapist knows what is best for other people's children. There is no doubt that a child therapist has expertise and a kind of experience that a child and her family do not have, but there is also no doubt that people in the child's everyday context have experiences with this particular child that make them especially qualified to make sensible decisions on the child's behalf.

A fifth concern is the application of a framework of interpretation of the child's experiences that is derived from an understanding not of the child in his particular situation but of issues and processes thought to be universal and developed and formulated between professionals. For child analysis, this framework would be psychodynamic. And there are other frameworks of explanation, such as constitutional, the disease model, or behavioral learning models, which can be equally unilateral in their application. The therapist needs to have a theoretical framework, and all of the frameworks just mentioned provide a useful vocabulary of explanation and understanding. However, it is essential to blend this framework with the metaphorical language of the child and family and, rather than offering interpretation or explanation, to develop the possibility for experiencing change.

The Malones Go to Work for Themselves

Ryan's mother sought a second opinion, and the family was invited in. When I involved the family in the assessment for problem finding and solution definition, the process of changing the context in which Ryan experienced conflict, as well as the conflicts, began to be addressed immediately, in a way that involved everyone in examining the problem and wondering about a solution. Ryan was seen first with his whole family. Ryan was the youngest. Ryan's siblings were "clean," and during the session they kept quiet, obviously avoiding any attention being focused on them. Ryan's father, who was pleasant about rearranging his schedule to come to the session, was also keeping a low profile. He clearly loved his family, and he clearly would do anything for them; they only had to ask. The main actors in the session were Mrs. Malone and Ryan. She fired questions at Ryan, and Ryan fired reckless, defiant answers back. As the exchange became more intense, the mother, in exasperation, said that he didn't even act like a member of the family. Ryan replied that he didn't want to be a member of this family anyway. He said that he preferred to be a foster child.

I asked the group, "Is this really a family?" Mrs. Malone sighed, signifying her response to this question. She had tried her best to make a family, provide a center of gravity that would draw her husband into family activities, and provide a perfect life for her children. And her five-year-old son was telling her that there was no family—that she had failed. Dr. Malone and the children just stared. I then asked Mrs. Malone, "What would happen if you resigned from your task of constructing the family?" Again, she responded, and the others were silent. I asked Ryan, "If your mother stopped talking, right now, and you stopped talking, who do you think would start talking, first?" Ryan was silent. His mother was silent. The other children were wide-eyed and silent. Dr. Malone began a monologue about how his wife was constantly dissatisfied with how they all spent time together. The older kids were doing fine, he said, and so was Ryan, but she was never satisfied. Ryan was the only one who stood up to her. There was one more question for the session, and it was addressed to eleven-year-old Tim, the oldest: "Do you suppose that Ryan or your Dad is better at getting your mother's goat?" The family came together in an explosion of giggling.

Treatment for the Malone family consisted of involving Dr. Malone with his wife in joint decisions about the family, encouraging Mrs. Malone to seek her husband's opinions about the children, and so forth. Ryan brought the family work to a crisis in one session when his defiance so exasperated his mother that she was brought to tears. Dr. Malone, who adored his wife, became enraged, grabbed his son, and shook him. Ryan began to cry hysterically, while his father continued to berate him for upsetting his mother. I whispered in Dr. Malone's ear, "I think he understands that you mean what you say, but now he's upset. Is there anything that might comfort him?" So the father, with some prompting, tenderly folded his little boy in his arms and rocked him, while the child sobbed quietly, and the mother looked on in amazement. Ryan returned to school within five sessions. Both parents set clear expectations of his behavior in school, and they promised to come to the school to pick him up if he repeated any of the behaviors that the school had found unacceptable. Dr. Malone made himself available at times, which allowed his wife to become absorbed in her schoolwork.

Principles of Systems Therapy

The aim of systems therapy is to change relationship systems, to alter the patterns of interaction at all levels of the biopsychosocial continuum. This was nicely illustrated by Minuchin's grand rounds presentation at Hahnemann University in 1982, when he presented work of three family systems therapists—himself, Virginia Satir, and Carl Whitaker. He had videotaped material to illustrate his points, and some of the pieces showed the different therapists working with the same family. The three therapists had different styles and operated according to different theoretical frameworks. At the end of the presentation, he turned to the audience and asked, "What do these three people who call themselves family therapists have in common?" The answer: "They all believe that effective therapeutic movement is brought about by changing the relationship system."

Systemic therapists have some common beliefs about the locus of change, the person of the therapist, the use of interpretation, and the use of play which further distinguish their practice from traditional child therapy. The systems therapist has a fluid relationship with his or her own context and the patient system. Often a student who is studying different psychotherapies is likely to try different techniques with her patients, and when the patients feel the effects of experimentation, it can be useful to discuss new ideas with them. According to psychoanalyst Edgar Levenson (1983), this is a principle of Sullivanian analysis; that is, the analyst is a genuine participant in the therapy, bringing his or her own experiences and associations to the therapeutic arena. It is not unique to systems therapists, but one cannot work in a systems framework without acknowledging the exchange between therapist system and client system.

The therapist's position in relation to the patient or patient system reflects the therapist's understanding of how change takes place in treatment and likewise affects the clients' understanding. The systems therapist believes that change occurs through shifts in relationships, in the way others are perceived and acted upon and in the way these actions are reciprocated. "Ahas" are the crucial experiences in change according to systems therapists. They are described as kaleidoscopic, referring to the stability of elements but the sudden irreversible shift in pattern that occurs when a kaleidoscope is turned (Hoffman 1981). The metaphor of the kaleidoscope emphasizes the systems therapist's focus on pattern and changing pattern rather than on the analysis of the elements themselves.

Play has been borrowed extensively in systems therapy. Systems therapists play in many ways. Systemic play is based more on psychologist

Robert White's (1959) ideas about a competence drive than on the notion that play is an expression of children's anxieties and problems. In systemic therapy, play becomes a way in which members of a system can actually experience themselves in the system. Structural family therapy grew out of work with relatively nonverbal, action-oriented families of delinquent boys (Minuchin et al. 1967). Employing enactments, marking boundaries, and making things happen are all activities of structural family therapy. Sculpting is a way of allowing family members to represent their perceptions of their relationships with other family members and to enact their wishes in terms of these same relationships. Playing and pretending are important activities of strategic therapist Chloe Madanes's (1985) approaches in working with families. Some therapists have families play with puppets, draw family portraits, put on plays, or, to develop order and turn taking, play games such as "whispering down the lane" or "pass the hat."

Principles of Systemic Child Therapy

The principles of child treatment from a systems perspective obviously employ the giant steps. The therapist's apprehension of different perceptions is reflected in appreciation of the shaping of meaning of the therapeutic context and of the different available levels of logic and experience. Patterns which have been identified can be disrupted so that new ones form. The system's competence is affirmed when the therapist recognizes that when systems find their own ways to change, or evolve into new patterns, this is usually a more satisfactory outcome than if the change is prescribed by the therapist.

The Relevance of Therapeutic Contexts

The first principle of systemic child therapy is that the context of the therapy is relevant, and it changes according to a number of variables. One contextual variable is the therapist's belief system. No therapist is atheoretical, and each therapist's prior experiences influence what he expects and how he enters a family system. A therapist's belief that poor families are disorganized because they fail to keep appointments regularly will definitely influence how the therapist greets such a family and will undoubtedly be played out in the family's response, probably showing their underorganization by further failure to keep appointments. Thus, an important lesson for systems therapists is to examine their own belief systems as relevant to the process of therapy.

A second factor is the system's expectation of the therapist. Our society is extremely "help" oriented, and many people look to the helping professionals to give them answers in the form of explanation—"Why does Johnny do these things?"—or in the form of prescriptions, either as medication or instructions—"Tell us what to do to get better." Some people, however, feel challenged by such a role for the therapist and, instead, take the position that they will give the therapist answers. One father, particularly sensitive to being told anything by a young resident, shouted, "You don't have to tell me about my daughter; I've heard of Odious Wrecks and all that stuff!" Many family systems enter therapy because it is a condition of their relationship with the court or child protective services or of a youth's probation. The families are often sullen, cooperating with the letter, but defensive about the spirit, of the therapy. One can approach these families only when including the referring system in the therapy in some way, such as having the clients require an explanation of the referral from the referring system.

A third factor is where the therapy takes place. If it is in a marriage counseling agency, then everyone's a priori focus will be on the marital relationship. If it is in a child guidance clinic, attention will be on relationships around the identified child. There will also be differences associated with the therapy site—whether a private office, a public clinic, the therapist's office, the family's home, the child's school, a courtroom, an attorney's office, the common room of the child welfare agency, or a meeting room at city hall.

A fourth factor is the source of initiation of the therapy: Whose idea was it, who referred the case, and what do they understand about their presence in therapy? On the therapist's side, How was she chosen, what is her relationship to the referring parties, and what is she being asked to do? These differences are particularly obvious when the therapist is involved in some kind of dispute, such as a custody battle. Who engaged the therapist and who is paying the bills will have a critical effect on the therapist's orientation, hypotheses, and activities with the system regardless of how neutral the therapist tries to be. It is for this reason that individuals doing custody evaluations take such pains to neutralize the referral process at the front end (see Gardner 1982). A fifth factor is the mood. Everyone's mood changes from day to day. Some days people will want to talk seriously, and on others they will feel more playful. This is true, of course, for both the therapist and the various members of the system. With all of these variations it is impossible to imagine how there could be a standard procedure for one therapist in all of his cases, let alone for all therapists. Thus, therapist responsiveness to the particular context of the system with which he is working is more important than following a procedure that can be replicated.

Levels of Observation and Experience

A second principle of systems therapy is the many levels of observation necessary for assessment, planning, and implementation of treatment. The systems therapist works with many different levels. If the therapist is working with a family in the office, the levels of operation will include having dyadic interactions with individual family members, working with subsystems or members of a particular generation, working with the whole family system, becoming a part of the system, or pulling out to look at the system from without. When the therapist includes a wider context in her work, other spheres of the child's ecosystem will be included: the parents' relationship systems, including family, friends, and work; the child's school contacts, including peers as well as teachers; and others significant in the family's experience of itself. How the therapist contacts these other systems elements varies from one system to another.

LEVELS WITHIN FAMILY THERAPY

The aim of the systems therapist is to change patterns that seem to occur around the symptom area. This can be done in a variety of ways and at a variety of levels. In order to change these patterns, the therapist can work with an individual, a subsystem, or the whole family and can change the composition of the sessions according to intervention plans. Bowen's (1978) system of treatment is primarily oriented toward individuals. The therapist coaches an individual to make forays into the family for the purpose of changing their patterns. In the Bowen model, the family system is mapped through the descriptions of the protagonist, who is the patient. The changes in the system are also reflected in the perceptions and reports of the protagonist; thus, in a sense, the family could be understood as a projection of the individual.

I prefer to use occasional sessions of coaching individuals within the context of working with the entire family system. Working this way, the map of the family is a shared experience of therapist and family members. For example, after observing a repetitive sequence between a divorced mother and father and their young adult son, I coached the father to resign his persistent efforts to offer support to his son, who constantly criticized, insulted, and demeaned him. This meant that the father would stop doing things such as finding jobs, buying cars, or sending extra money to his son. When the father resigned, the young man had to turn to his mother. It was then possible to work with the ways in which the mother–son dyad triangled in the father, as they attempted to seduce him back to his previous thankless role or derided his new position, labeling it as selfish or not living up to paternal obligations. With my considerable endorsement, the father was able to evaluate his position in relation to both his son and ex-wife and to make a more considered decision about how to respond to his son. In addition, the mother and son reflected on their activities and their outcomes. Thus, they were able to change a long-standing pattern through the coaching of one individual to behave differently.

It is also possible, having identified some patterns to be changed through seeing the whole family, to work with only the parents. This is particularly useful in systems where the parents have made their business the children's business. This sometimes occurs in democratic-style, or "open," families where decisions are made by consensus. It may also occur when parents' confidence in their own ability to lead, guide, and comfort their children is less strong than their admiration or respect for the children. These families are in danger of equalizing roles and functions among family members with the effect that parents cannot parent, and children have to parent to the detriment of being children.

One example was that of a ten-year-old boy whose worries about world problems such as hunger and the threat of nuclear catastrophe were so great that he had difficulty sleeping. When he was seen with his parents and siblings, it became apparent that his parents were so impressed with their son's ability to grasp the significance of these important world issues, that they had not known how to comfort him. The parents were seen alone, briefly, to differentiate them from the boy. They were encouraged to offer a bedtime ritual acceptable to a ten-year-old. This included their involvement in setting bedtime, talking with him after he had gotten into bed, and checking on him from time to time through the evening before they went to bed, to make sure that he was comfortable, or if he was awake and worrying, to sit with him to calm him down. After the institution of this plan, the boy slept soundly. It was necessary to work with the parents alone, because they needed to examine parenting behavior as differentiated from ten-year-old behavior.

Often parents seem to be asking the children's permission to set limits or discipline them. This is a common finding with "out-of-control" youngsters of all ages. With very young children, giving the parents the task of getting the child under control in the session is a very effective way of differentiating the parents and changing the pattern. With older children, such as adolescents, physical control is not appropriate, and it is often useful to send the adolescents out of the room for a time while one has a "secret" talk with the parents, which they are encouraged to keep as a "mystery" to their children. Then there will be something that the children don't know about their parents. Instead of objects of disdain, the parents will be objects of curiosity; instead of being predictable, they may do unexpected things. The family system can shift around these simple moves in therapy.

This was a necessary intervention to begin to reestablish parental dignity and authority in the case of Sarah and Maggie, who were sixteen and eighteen, respectively. Throughout these girls' lives their parents had been both burdened with the responsibilities of raising their children and delighted and amazed by their children's accomplishments. By adolescence, however, Sarah and Maggie were quite uncontrolled. Being of a quiet nature, Maggie was not an obvious problem, and at eighteen she went off to college. This left Sarah alone with their parents, who continued to be uncertain about what to do with her. Generally, they dealt with their uncertainty by asking her. With her parents she was rude, derisive, mocking, and obnoxiously intrusive and familiar. After about half an hour of listening to her insolence, I asked her to leave and wait for her parents in the waiting room. I spent the next half hour swearing her parents to secrecy about what we were talking about and then convincing them to arrange private meetings without Sarah several times a week. This enabled them to develop phrases like "we think . . . ," "we talked, and we decided . . . ," "that is none of your affair . . . ," and "what we talked about when we were alone was our business."

THE LEVEL OF THE THERAPIST'S EXPERIENCE

In psychodynamic thinking, the way a therapist experiences a particular family system reflects the way the therapist has experienced himself in his own family. For example, a young man whose father abandoned his family when he was young may think of fathers in client families as unreliable, but he will experience a subtle hostility toward mothers in these families. This theory suggests that what the therapist experiences with the family is information about the therapist.

The therapist does bring her own experiences to a family, and each client family also creates a special context when it includes the therapist. Thus, what the therapist experiences with a family is also information about the family, and it is critical to recognize this in order for the therapist to grasp family patterns and assess her own level of helpless involvement in the family system. Extremes of emotion such as anger, sadness, helplessness, or silliness experienced by the therapist are usually indications about the family, and are often indications of the therapist's helpless involvement in the family patterns. Indignation at a mother's ruthless punishment of a child (such as a beating in the session, or a year without television), for example, is more likely to reflect the therapist's having sided with the child than the therapist's own experience with unjust punishment. (And therapists do tend to side with children.) The problem with this, however, is that the child is going to go home and live with the mother, not with the therapist. So if the therapist sides with the child and embarrasses the mother, the mother will probably take it out on the child. Thus, it is better for the therapist to assess the source of the indignation and to ask herself, "How does this mother get people (like me) indignant at her, and how might this relate to the recalcitrance of the child?" Having narrowly escaped what undoubtedly would have become a stabilizing transaction— that is, criticizing the mother's punishment from the powerful position of expert, thus confirming her sense that she needs to sock it to the little one—the therapist can then turn to the child and say, with awe, "How is it that you get your mother so angry that she gives you such a terrible punishment?" This therapist has used her experience to observe the system and to act upon it rather than be sucked into it.

The system's effect on the therapist may not be as direct. The therapist may find himself worrying about what his supervisor would say if she knew what he said in that session. Viewed psychodynamically, this could reflect the male trainee's discomfort with women supervisors, a residue from his family experience. It could also be information about how the trainee gets along with the particular supervisor, as well as information about the family he is seeing when he has these worries. The family has cornered him so that he has acted in a fashion of which he thinks the supervisor might disapprove. Or perhaps the family is sneaky, and its sneakiness is translated into his feeling sneaky. Because many patterns are isomorphic at different levels of a system, it is worth exploring how the therapist's responses may be isomorphic with family agendas.

This same kind of influence of the family can be felt when the therapist presents a case to colleagues. In some way, the presentation picks up a flavor of the family; certain information is emphasized that makes the family seem dirty or crazy or scary or unorganized or pristine or untouchable. Information presented doesn't jibe, representing the confusion and double messages within the family. In short, the possible similarity between the therapist's experience is often isomorphic with important patterns in the family and is, therefore, information about the system.

LARGER SYSTEMS

The therapist's attitude is also informative when a therapist deals with other systems connected with the family, such as the school. For example, many therapists who are approached by a family of a child with a school problem find themselves indignant at the way a child has been treated in school. Apart from the possible justification for this indignation, the indignation itself is information about the way the family and school systems are getting along with each other. If the therapist wants to intervene effectively, he or she needs to recognize this and attempt to identify how the school personnel chose their particular form of action. Welfare workers are often seen by therapists as intrusive and judgmental. Have therapists ever thought about how they are seen by welfare workers? Nevertheless, the fact that the worker is seen in this particular way is information about how the family organizes "helpers" in their larger system. If the therapist and worker feel mutually critical, it may mean that the family system plays a fabulous game of "let's you and he fight," and if they do, the family goes unchanged. If, instead, the therapist and the worker could join forces with each other and with the family to think through solutions to the problems each has identified within the system of which they are now all a part, then change is more likely.

METALEVELS

More than any other approach to psychotherapy, the family systems approach has developed the role of the observer. Through live observation, use of videotape, live supervision, and use of the therapeutic team behind the one-way mirror, practitioners of family systems therapy concentrate on the observer's level of experience and influence. From the observer position, the therapist is operating from a metalevel. The metalevel is a conceptual plane from which the therapist tries to frame the experiences with the dysfunctional system.

The emphasis on the system viewed from different levels is so integral to the training experience of the systems therapist that even when there is no one-way mirror or video screen, the therapist should be constantly aware of herself both in the therapeutic system and as an observer of herself in the therapeutic system. An individual therapist can be seen to move in and out of the system. For example, at different times in the same session child psychiatrist Ronald Liebman (1973) joins in playful interaction with the children in a family or in "the doghouse" with the father in the family, and then draws himself out by giving a task for an enactment

127

and retreating behind a pad of paper on which he takes notes. Another therapist gets up, takes off his jacket, pulls his chair back, turns away from the parties having a discussion so that they do not draw him in, and, occasionally, leaves the room. Another therapist talks with a cotherapist about some family interaction, excluding the family from his conversation. All of these are therapeutic operations at a metalevel. The members of the system experience themselves reflected in a frame that is outside the frame of their activity—a frame in which they are not participants and from which they can choose which aspects to adopt and which to ignore.

The metalevel has been developed by some groups as a position from which to offer powerful interventions. The prescriptions developed by the team behind a one-way mirror in Milan, Italy (Selvini Palazzoli et al. 1978), and at the Ackerman Institute (Papp 1980) are examples. In front of the one-way mirror the family experiences the process of data gathering as they respond to questions posed by a disciplined team of therapists. They probably do not appreciate the ways that the data gathering is shaping their own perceptions of themselves. The data gathered include the answers to the questions and the observed responses between family members. The therapists and their colleagues behind the mirror meet to review the data, and the family is given some instructions based on the formulation that has taken place at the metalevel of the team. The family doesn't witness the therapists trying to reshape their experiences through interpretation or enactments.

From the metalevel the therapist can frame metaphors, and these, when effective, become a framework within which the patient system can work, allowing them to get out of the framework in which they are stuck. Master therapist Milton Erickson, for example, talks with a couple who is squeamish about sex, using the metaphor of a delicious dinner (Haley 1973). Madanes (1985) develops the metaphor to the level of an "as if" or pretend experience, where a family will actually enact a pretend version of the problem as the therapist understands it.

Different Frameworks

A third principle of systemic therapy is that the therapist always operates from a different frame than does the family. In an era where research generates information about children that is both more specific and more conflicting than that available before, a child therapist may not necessarily be better informed than the child's parents; that is, the child therapist doesn't know with more certainty. On the contrary, contemporary child therapists have to know more things with less certainty. They must have an extensive array of ideas and options from which to choose when approaching a particular situation. To me it is rather like the country doctor's bag, full of tools and medicine samples, a special combination of which will be tried in each new case. New information acquired by the professional will go into the bag to be tried out with something else already proven useful. The child and his family benefit more, I believe, from the therapist's experience and from the fact that the therapist's experience is different from their own, than from any particular system of knowledge the therapist may have. That is, the therapist operating from outside the system experiences it differently from the way those inside the system experience it and therefore has a different perspective to offer.

Since levels or expanding frames of experience and intervention are integral to the practice of family systems therapy, it is not surprising that one of the forefathers of family systems therapy was Milton Erickson, although he was not a family therapist. His therapeutic approach seemed to have developed out of work with hypnosis, which, in turn, developed out of the ordeal of paralysis, during which he was totally helpless except for his powers of observation. Anyone who had ever met Erickson personally would report about how familiar he seemed to be on the first meeting. He had the ability to pick up and integrate small details quickly, like Sherlock Holmes. He used this material at a metalevel to have the patient experience the familiar in a way that would be different. Several principles of systems therapy derive from Erickson's work, presented by Jay Haley (1973), among others. The first is that the therapist can be helpless, removed from the activity of change within the system, and can use only the powers of observation (from the metalevel) to act upon the system. The second follows from this, that the system changes on its own, often outside of the therapist's office, having found its own meaning. In fact, many systems therapists space therapy sessions far apart to give the family the chance to change. (How different this is from the perspective of the child analyst described at the beginning of this chapter.) The third, which also follows from this, is that the therapist's "helplessness" is actually a position of anonymity or neutrality, one from which the therapist's theories and values are minimally involved in the therapy experience. The fourth follows from the third, that if the therapist's personal viewpoint is of minimal importance, then properties of the system will be maximally important.

Triads and Systems Therapy

A fourth principle of systems therapy is that interpersonal systems are built on units of three or more, and one must therefore work conceptually with triadic units (triadic patterns are discussed in chapter 4). In the early 1970s Gerald Zuk (1971) identified this as a basic difference between family therapy and traditional therapies. Individual therapy and marital therapies were conceptualized dyadically: transference is a dyadic relationship, and the marital therapist usually excludes himself from consideration of the dyadic marital interaction. With the introduction of the concept of triadic relationships, many difficulties are encountered, because despite the fact that triads seem to be the smallest stable structures, it is habitual to think in terms of dyadic relationships at many levels of experience.

This habit of mind appears to be associated with the descriptive, nominal aspects of our Aristotelian language and epistemology. We are accustomed to describing the world as it is. To deal with ambiguities, we describe polarities such as good and evil, light and dark, yin and yang. We talk about symmetry, usually meaning bilateral symmetry, and complementarity, the fit between two parts. In therapy we talk of dialogue, and many family therapists, having been captivated by philosopher Martin Buber's fascination with the "between," have described the construction of the experiential dialectic "between" as an important therapeutic process (Boszormenyi-Nagy and Krasner 1986). The dialectic, however, is a process, not a thing. The "between" that is constructed in the dialectic makes dialogue a triadic experience. These triadic principles were described by philosopher Georg Hegel's description of the process of evolution of ideas through thesis, antithesis, and synthesis. In the process orientation of systems therapy, too, there are no dyadic interactions. What appears to be occurring between only two people always involves a conceptual third, whether it be an actual person, a governing principle, or an agency operating at another system level. It is extremely important that the systems therapist recognize and work with triads.

Marital counseling has been referred to by Carl Whitaker as social supervision (personal communication, 1982). Many have commented on the impossibility of changing a family system by working with a couple. In his 1983 keynote address to the American Association of Marital and Family Therapists, Jay Haley articulated several of the pitfalls of mistaking marital (dyadic) therapy for systems therapy. He pointed out that the dyadic unit is not stable, and it is difficult to think about. In working with a couple, he noted, there is a tendency either to break it down to the individuals and use the language descriptive of individual functioning or to shift to the larger unit of the triad. He pointed out, further, that there are only two terms that have been arrived at as descriptive terminology for dyads: *symmetry,* referring to the competitive dyadic interaction, and *com-*

plementarity, referring to a kind of fit. Finally, Haley noted that focus on a dyad tends to force the observer to ignore the structure in which the dyad functions. This structure is bound to include other relationships, such as, in instances where children are the focus of attention, the child's contribution to his or her parents' functioning.

Working with Families, Family Therapy, and Systems Therapy

Clearly, different therapists operate from different premises about how to change the family relationship system. In chapter 1 a difference between those who believe family therapy is a modality and those who see it as an organizing way to think about behavior change was noted. Some theorists have attempted to translate individual dynamics into family systems. These theories are not, in my opinion, truly systemic. They do enhance the theories of the individual by using direct observation rather than inference. They are limited, however, by the inductive process through which they are derived. Translating concepts and terminology from one logical, systemic level to another usually results in paradoxes and confusion. Applying analytic practice to family systems often requires breaking down the systems to deal with individuals. Or, as in the instance of object relations family therapy, where the theory addresses relational processes, the practice of interpretation keeps the therapist at a superior level of knowledge and understanding relative to the patients.

By focusing only on the level of the family or on the level of the marital system, mistaking it for "family," other family therapists have failed to include the child in the system within which they were working. When a child is the identified patient, a family therapist often understands the child's problems as representing or stemming from, or even serving to distract from, other problems in the family. There is a great deal of support for this idea, especially if the child's problems are of a purely emotional or behavioral, as opposed to organic, nature. Many see the child as simply acting out family distress, variously getting help for the family, saving the marriage, or covering for a troubled sibling. Family therapists who understand the child's problems as functioning for the system may move directly to the subsystem in which they think the trouble resides, bypassing the child and often the rest of the family. Usually, those who look at children's problems in this way are not comfortable working with children in the room. They tend to define the problem as having to do with parts of the system they can work with, such as the parents. They often end up doing parent effectiveness training or marital therapy. Parent effectiveness training has the irony that the therapist, who usually works with the parents because he is consciously or unconsciously uncomfortable working with the children, is now instructing the parents about how to help their children! One can see the likely futility of such work. If a child is symptomatic in the context of a dysfunctional marital relationship, the therapist probably will substitute for the child in the marital triangling process, thereby stabilizing the marital relationship in much the same way that the child did. The child, thus freed by the therapist, may actually improve. The family system, however, doesn't necessarily change through this process; thus, when the therapist withdraws, the children are once again called on to participate in the triangling.

There are also major differences among family systems therapists (i.e., those who believe that effective change occurs through changing the relationship system). One point of disagreement is over whether the therapy should be symptom oriented and corrective only or, instead, aimed at long-lasting and permanent change in the family. That is, should the therapist's efforts be directed just at resolving current dysfunction, or should the therapist guide the family to a deeper assessment of their relational experiences so that they can rearrange them? The extremes are represented by the strategic and systemic family therapists, who believe in symptom removal, and by contextual and object relations family therapists, who believe in the need to work through generations of emotional processes. The differences are substantial enough for these groups of family therapists to feel that they may be engaged in quite different practices.

The change-oriented schools, which include systemic, brief, and strategic therapy models, use a transformational approach to change. That is, the techniques of these approaches are directed at how people construct reality and how these constructions can be altered so that both the perceptions and, concomitantly, the ways of being are transformed kaleidoscopically. The therapists are deliberate in their analyses of the system and construction of the solutions, but they don't feel that it is necessary to include the family in discussing the philosophical aspects of the model. The depth models of family therapy are operationally much closer to the psychodynamic approach in the deliberate analysis of structures and relationships in the family and the careful carrying out of tasks to achieve deliberate changes in the relationships. This work is a project undertaken between participating family members and the therapist. A structural model is somewhere in between. Because relationships between family members are reorganized in sessions and in tasks given with rather explicit purposes, family members are often aware of what is being tried. At the same time, their experiences may be transformed by the actual rearrangements in authority, proximity, and turn taking. In practice, though, most family therapists take a less well defined, eclectic position that directs the therapy toward congruence with the style and beliefs of the system being addressed.

Systems Find Their Own Ways to Change

Whatever the underlying beliefs about the methodology, systems therapists all focus on activating resources within the system, largely by appealing to the system to find its own solutions. All systems approaches use framing and reframing, some more explicitly than others. When a different frame is presented, the members of a system are invited to a metaview of themselves, a position from which they can make some decisions about what to do. Child psychiatrist David Keith (1989) describes a family seeking help as like a cubist painting. All of the features are there somewhere, but it often takes the therapist to find them. As the therapist comments, "Did you know that your nose was over your left ear?" the family system's members can then evaluate themselves and decide on a preferred arrangement.

Therapists do not need to help systems by instructing them about how to change. Instead, systems therapists facilitate change by encouraging members of the system to experience themselves in different, more comfortable, and more competent relationships to one another. Reframing is an important part of this; activating resources is another. All systems have something going for them, and it is the therapist's duty to discover those strengths, however hidden they may seem to be. Indeed, one of the most important reframing jobs many therapists have to do on themselves is to convert from a deficit-seeking orientation to a resource-seeking one. Positive connotation is a technique to accomplish just this. In finding a positive connotation for symptoms and behaviors that the family members feel burdened or ashamed about, the therapist may assist them in feeling less ashamed and more able to deal with what they experience as a problem. Another approach involves reviewing solutions and resources for implementing them—focusing on the system's problem-solving energies rather than on defeats and failures.

Finally, it appears that individuals, families, and larger systems have many more repertoires than they actually use. One description of system dysfunction is when there are so many constraints on the varieties of repertoires employed that dysfunctional sequences are carried out over and over. As with resources, the systems therapist recognizes that there are other repertoires available to the system. Blocking the usual ones may induce the system to experiment with others, leading to alternatives and to greater system flexibility.

CHAPTER 7

Therapy Practice

When all four of the conceptual giant steps are taken, diagnosing and treatment are transformed according to systemic principles. The most important of these—apprehending multiple perceptions and definitions of problems—is easiest done when the observer/therapist can appreciate multiple levels of the ecosystem. From these multiple perspectives the therapist can also integrate different viewpoints and activate the resources of the system at all its levels. There are no sets of rules or methods that dictate how to think or act. Theoretical frameworks as well as treatment approaches are just skeletons upon which to build the distinctive shapes that will be the work between a particular theoretician or therapist and a particular puzzle or system. In this chapter I present further details of doing treatment. The extended case example began as the treatment of an individual child. This was deliberately chosen to illustrate that systemic treatment does not necessarily mean treatment of a whole multiperson system, such as a family, school, or agency. On the other hand, systemic treatment cannot proceed without consideration of the families, schools, and agencies that might contribute to the patterns experienced as problematic or to the changes that would be experienced as solutions.

Meeting the System

As discussed in chapter 6, the context of therapy is critical. The initial contact between therapist and the system provides important contextual cues and opportunities.

News of Difference

Even before a therapist comes face to face with members of the system, she should have some hypotheses about what is coming up. Usually there is information from a phone call, a referring professional, or an intake form. It is extremely important for the therapist to review these hypotheses prior to the actual session, for these thoughts shape the therapist's expectations and behavior, and there is some evidence that the therapist's expectations and behavior may also shape the system's initial responses.

A particularly striking example of this was in a role-play exercise of a first encounter. The therapist was presented with a single mother, aged twenty-four, and her four children, ages eight, six, five, and four, who attended the session with the maternal grandmother and uncle with whom the mother and her children were living. The six-year-old, only boy had the identified problem of fighting in the school yard. The therapist's hypothesis was that this family was overwhelmed and underorganized, and after meeting the various members of the family, he inquired, "What seems to be the problem?" The role-play mother heaved a great sigh and responded, "What isn't a problem?" She then rattled off a list of problems including abandonment by her husband, trouble with welfare, her inability to get a job, problems with child care, complaints by her mother, and so on, thus confirming the therapist's initial hypothesis.

If the therapist has identified his prenotions about the system, dissonances can also be picked up. For example, the therapist might expect that a particular presenting problem is likely to be in the context of a rigid authoritarian system and find, instead, a relaxed, underorganized one. Or the therapist may expect that a child's symptom functions in some way to protect other family members, only to find that the child has a specific disability. Bateson is often quoted on his statement that information is "news of difference" (1979, 76). Therapists who prepare themselves, as I have described, will get information by experiencing the differences.

The First Encounter

The first encounter between therapist and system is the one in which all sides size each other up. For some therapists this is a conscious part of the therapy, and it is called the "social" phase or the "joining" phase. Other therapists do not emphasize the process of forming a relationship system as much as data gathering. Most systems therapists, however, acknowledge that data gathering sets the tone for the therapy. The contextual therapist must be "multidirected" in order to hear fairly each system member's side. In taking this stance, the contextual therapist establishes an atmosphere of a fair hearing that sets a tone for the development of fair-mindedness, or multilaterality on the part of the family members. The data gathering by Mara Selvini Palazzoli and colleagues (1978) in Milan, Italy, includes circular questioning. Circular questions are asked of one member of a system about the interactions of others. The questions may be about hypothetical situations such as, "If your sister decided to quit school, who would be more disappointed, your mother or your father?" Or they may be about things that will happen in the future, such as, "When your sister leaves for college, who will miss her more, your mother or your father?" The answers to the questions generate data. The process of the questioning generates an experience, directing the family members' attention to the relational consequences of actions and decisions.

The deliberate stances of the contextual and Milan therapists about data gathering illustrate what is true of all data gathering, even if the therapist thinks that she is just getting the facts: the act of asking the questions shapes the experience of both the therapist and the system. Through preparing a genogram, enacting the scene around a particular event, or even telling the history of the presenting problem or the identified patient's early childhood, the system will experience itself in a particular way shaped by the way in which the therapist has asked the members to present themselves. Thus, the first encounters between therapist and system are occasions for sizing each other up and joining in a mutual project. Systems therapists vary in the way their theoretical orientation shapes their directing of this experience, and some are more conscious than others of this shaping as a deliberate activity.

The first encounter with the system, even over the telephone, begins a process of joining that continues throughout the therapy. In the first face-to-face encounters with members of the system, the therapist must carefully develop a framework for working with them, no matter how long the work has gone on and especially when new people enter the therapy system. For example, when a new baby is born, a grandmother comes to visit, Dad returns from the merchant marines, a sibling is home from college, or the family's minister comes in, each requires an orientation of therapist to the new person and to the system transformed by that person's presence. The first principle of my framework of operation is, then, to accommodate to the system. This can be done by actively socializing, asking questions of individuals to make personal contact with each one, and offering bits of information about the therapist to match some of theirs to establish common grounds. For example, when meeting a child's school counselor for the first time, I usually ask about his experience in the particular school, some of the procedures in the school, and the kinds of contacts he has had with teachers and the child's family. I may then offer some information about my experience with school systems, both to tell him that I have experience and also to tell him that it is different from his. Then I point out that I am inexperienced in this context and ask him to help me, thereby establishing an active process between the therapist/consultant and another member of the system.

After each member in a whole family has been contacted, nuances of family style, the family's definition of the problem, and the family's selection of spokesperson will provide a context for the therapist's response. For instance, in one family the father gave his version of the story to the therapist while his wife and daughters listened. He finished, then touched his wife and said, "I've done all the talking, now you talk." The therapist picked up the transfer and tracked it, saying, "Is it like a relay race; now you finish, now she goes?" The family responded with surprise and a little laugh at having their actions described thus, and the mother then told her version of the story. In supplying the relay race analogy, the therapist had proposed that their different versions would move the family toward the goal and be complementary rather than competitive. Thus, the therapist and the family enacted a kind of game in which the family moved, and the therapist observed and then touched them ever so slightly, influencing the direction in which they proceeded. Even after the first session there are continuing evaluations. The family system brings new information to each encounter with the therapist and leaves changed through the contact with the therapist. The therapist continues to evaluate and revise treatment plans and goals.

Assessment Is Embedded in Treatment

The kind of observation being described in this chapter is "therapy-observation," and it is inseparable from therapy itself. The sophisticated systems therapist does not expect the system to change in the office or as a result of carrying out some instructions. The activities between therapist and members of a system can be conceptualized as a series of experiments with constructions of reality and self-perceptions, all with the object of increasing the range of possibilities. All manner of techniques may be employed to do this, many of which occur to the therapist on the spur of the moment.

When Salvador Minuchin placed a tyrannical youngster on a chair to tower over the rest of his family, Minuchin illustrated what he experienced as a family incongruity. He could have simply told them, "Your boy is a tyrant," but they probably already knew that. Putting the boy on a chair tested his balance and changed his perspective, while family members literally had to look up to him. Minuchin did not expect the youngster to purchase a pair of stilts or to always stand on chairs. In fact, what the family does with such a perception is their own business. If they do nothing, the therapist will find another illustration. The assessment that "this youngster acts as if he is in charge of the whole family" occurred at the split second of observation, followed by the intervention, "You stand on this chair, so you can be taller than your father."

In an essay on technique in family therapy, Frank Pittman (1984) described several maneuvers undertaken in the therapist's desperate effort to activate the family system's new responses to their situation. One was placing a snowy wet cocker spaniel in the arms of a catatonic woman; another was having a father stand on his head for his child. Pittman explained that these are not techniques to be applied by therapists in similar situations, but examples of therapist resourcefulness in response to the demands of particular systems at particular times.

Mapping

In preparing for upcoming sessions the therapist should review all of her previous experience with the family. She can prepare a map that illustrates the system's structure, as she last observed it, and that demonstrates boundaries, coalitions, and alliances.

For example, in the family of an asthmatic boy, the mother and boy may appear to have a stable, cross-generational coalition, excluding the father and siblings. Another kind of map would illustrate the process of symptomatic cycles as currently understood by the therapist. In the same family it may be hypothesized that tension in the parent system is related to the child's asthma, which draws attention away from the parents. While the parents are taking care of the child, other arguments may come up specifically around decisions about caring for the child. These tensions are acceptable and understandable to the family in light of the precariousness of the child. This evolution of tensions involving the child's asthma can be diagrammed in a third sort of map.

Therapy maps should include the therapist, identifying where the therapist may have been placed by the family, where the therapist is likely to get stuck, and where he would like to act within the system. Further, the maps should include other systems levels. In the instance of the asthmatic boy, for example, the fact that the pediatric allergist dealt exclusively with the child's mother should be included in the map; the allergist can be added to the mother–child coalition. Or linked maps representing different levels of the system may be developed to illustrate the patterns that are isomorphic at different levels of the system (see chapter 4). I detailed these repeating patterns during an observation of a family therapy session of a child who was a psychiatric inpatient (Combrinck-Graham 1987). The individual, family, therapy, inpatient, and observational levels all had similar themes of being stuck or blocked, reflected in the identified teenager's constipation and encopresis. When an intervention was made, we could trace its cathartic effects through each level of the system. Such observations invited me to intervene at any or in several levels of the system.

The therapist uses the maps to think of how and where she may want to enter the system to change it. The therapist should also review the personal metaphors that are associated with the patient system. What worldviews do they present; how does she feel about the upcoming session; what descriptions is she using? She will then think of the directions she may want to take with the system. Does she want to simplify a too-complex process by focusing and repeating a certain theme, or does she want to encourage a too-rigid system to elaborate more complex actions by blocking the repetitive transactions? Finally, what are the goals of the therapeutic system? When the therapist actually meets the system after this preparation, she uses the map as a skeleton. The content the patients bring to the session can be used as the flesh.

In the family with the severely asthmatic boy the therapist's plan was to disrupt the coalition between the mother and the asthmatic child by involving the boy more either with his father or his siblings. The family came to the session with a story about another child's bad dreams. This led to a discussion of where people sleep and who sleeps with whom. It turned out that the asthmatic child usually had his attacks at night. He would awaken his mother, and she would then sleep on the couch where she could hear her son and not disturb her hardworking husband. The other child's bad dream took her into the parents' bedroom, where she ended up sleeping with her father. Some playful discussion of musical beds led to the idea that the mother and father could take turns tending to the boy's asthma and the girl's bad dreams. They would have to let the children know, before they went to bed, whose turn it was. It was agreed that the father would have the next turn with the boy and would be on call until the boy needed him one night; then it would be the mother's turn, and so on. The structural map had suggested a coalition between the mother and son in which asthma seemed to play a role. The family's presentation of the girl's nightmares offered the content in which the therapist could suggest changes in the map or restructure the family around the symptoms. After that, the boy had one asthma attack and awakened his mother, who gently reminded him that it was his father's turn. His father got up, took care of him, and then returned to his own bed with his wife. The child's nocturnal asthma improved dramatically. The sister had no more nightmares.

A marital problem was not discussed as an explanation for the fact that the parents often did not sleep together. Nor was the child's nocturnal interaction with his mother ascribed to the playing out of the Oedipal experience. Both of these are plausible descriptions of the events presented by the family, but in this case, the family's own explanation was taken at face value. The therapist recognized that family members were playing out repetitive patterns that appeared to have evolved to serve certain family needs—to take care of the child's illness and to allow the father enough rest so that he could continue to work. If the proposed solution had not been effective, it might have been necessary to pursue other levels of explanation for the sequence. The therapist's map could be wrong, and the system might behave in a way that suggests a different diagram of its structure or sequences. The therapist's map is always a hypothesis, and the therapist must always confirm or disconfirm it through the system's responses to the therapist's interventions.

Recognizing Triads

A systems therapist's work must always comprehend the triadic basis of interactions. This means that all assessments must recognize that even when there are only two principals, or the problems seem to occur primarily within the interaction between only two people, the therapist must ask, In what context do these two people have this interaction? Probes into the triadic aspects of a mother and child living alone together would include questions concerning where the child's father is, who helps the pair, where the child goes to school, and explorations of church, work, neighborhood, and economic status. If a child is presented because of intractable behavior despite the most extensive discipline and deprivation of privileges and pleasures, the therapist may see a determined parent consistently setting limits and punishments and ask how this child can continue to be so rebellious. Looking at the triadic system will inevitably yield an answer. The child may continue to rebel against the one parent in the context of encouragement by the other parent. Or the parents' coalition to discipline the child is in the context of the child's continuing to need discipline.

The therapist always needs to include himself in conceptualizing triadic interactions in systems therapy. Doing this both allows for strategic entry into the system and prevents the therapist from getting coopted by the system. The therapist may, in wanting to rearrange a particular set of alliances and coalitions, use himself as a "go-between" (Zuk 1971) by forming a coalition with two previously unconnected parties. In another triadic entry, a therapist may unbalance a triad by joining a powerful coalition and forcing the system to rebalance, with someone else taking the side of the scapegoat. For example, if a child's parents overdiscipline him, a therapist can attack the child in such a fashion that one of the parents comes to his aid, taking his side against the therapist and, perhaps, the other parent. An unwary therapist can be sucked into triadic family patterns. As noted in the previous chapter, the therapist who tries to release a child from playing a role in the parents' marital dysfunction usually becomes involved in a similar role to that of the child, thus stabilizing the system. On the other hand, if the therapist deliberately replaces a third in a triad, there is the possibility of changing the triad's patterns.

Ongoing Treatment

It is impossible to specify a point where assessment ends and treatment begins. The process of systems therapy seems to be an ongoing one of testing hypotheses with actual probes, which may be in the form of requesting enactments, giving tasks, or reframing so that the way the system experiences its functioning shifts. If the purpose of the therapy is to perturb the system, the therapist's activity will be directed, as indicated, to assessing patterns that need to be disrupted and then to disrupting them. Some forms of disruption are through the kinds of structural rearrangements proposed by Minuchin (1974) and Minuchin and Fishman (1981). These include actual rearrangements of family members or other members of the system that involve manipulating space and access in a variety of ways. Other therapists do these perturbations in more cognitive or experiential ways. Boszormenyi-Nagy and associates (1973, 1986) explore the family members' assumptions about each other, suggesting that an individual who has been seen as abusive or exploitative also has a side and may, in fact, have been abused and exploited at some point. The therapist thereby perturbs family myths and presses for relational rearrangements.

Similarly, Bowenians coach an individual to go home to challenge habitual patterns to stimulate new relational experiences.

Understood this way, therapy continues for as long as it takes for these rearrangements to happen. This may occur in a single session, but it takes longer if a system is particularly entrenched in its patterns. It is difficult for an entrenched system to change because of its embeddedness in other, unchanging contexts. Unfortunately, the therapist's own activities may be one of these unchanging contexts and may perpetuate dysfunctional patterns. This idea leads to the proposal that "resistance" includes the therapist in some way. The therapist may not have yet appreciated how the system changes or may change later. The therapist's aggressive interventions may actually activate and support sameness in the family.

One particular difficulty with finding how the system is functioning is limiting oneself to studying only a few layers of it. Looking only at the function of the parental subsystem as parents fail to manage their child, for example, overlooks the child's contribution to the failure. Although this is a common attitude among therapists who work with systems of children, a more common problem is the failure to assess the context of the family and the problem. The parents of a child who doesn't complete her homework are likely to be called by someone at the school and told that their child is failing to meet the school's standards. The parents will have the complicated feeling of being blamed, which may make them angry and embarrassed, and of needing to justify their child's behavior to the school. A mixed message is transmitted to the child, which does not help her complete her work. Working only with parents and child may ignore the maintaining influence of the school. Another example is that of the abusive family who continues to abuse, despite the therapist's efforts to change the system so the abuse stops. Usually this happens because the family is also in a system in which they are being "abused" by intrusions, surveillance, and threats from the welfare or criminal justice system. Therapists cannot successfully disturb family functions that are, in essence, being maintained by other systems. A third example is systems that are wedded to a variety of different beliefs about change. When a systems therapist works with a system in which members of the system are involved in other kinds of therapy, for example, it may be difficult to change the system because the reframing, tasks, and reenactments are being invalidated by the other therapists. These other therapists or their ideas must be incorporated in the assessment of the system and the plan for rearrangement in order for the systems therapist to be successful.

Ending Therapy

Systems therapy ends when the system has rearranged itself to solve its own problems. This may occur when the symptom has resolved or when the system has found constructive means for taking care of it. If the therapy has been successful and the therapist has not become too involved or credited herself for the changes made by the system, the family may later return to the therapist if problems arise again. In one sense, then, systems therapy never ends, for the useful therapist has become part of the family's resource system. In any event, the concept of a termination phase of treatment is not common in the systems therapies, because the relationship with the therapist has not been the basis of either treatment or the system's change. The therapist is, actually, incidental to the change. This does not mean to say that the therapist has no meaningful relationships with members of the system, but these relationships are not central to the process of change, as the transference is central to the process of psychoanalysis, because the enduring relationships within the system are those that are the focus of treatment. Thus, the therapist may continue to relate to members of the system after the therapy has ended. When the system is an individual or a family, the therapist may have a role as a family doctor, one whom members of the family may consult from time to time. When the system is a school or agency, the consultant may have continuing business about several different children.

Systems Therapy: An Example

The following example has been chosen for several reasons. First, it was a rather longer course of treatment than is typical for the kind of systems therapy I have proposed. Second, it prominently involved a child. Third, it illustrates the uses of several therapeutic modalities. Fourth, it illustrates how the process of reframing can be drawn out if other belief systems are actively encouraged at the same time.

Dr. Rosenbaum, who knew me by reputation, called me to refer a patient. She asked, "Do you ever see children individually?" "Of course," I cheerfully responded, intrigued with the question. Gina Peters, an eight-year-old, was the younger of two girls in her family, and she was experiencing more upper respiratory infections than other children in her class, thus needing to stay home more. Her mother also thought that Gina was unhappy. Gina's mother was in therapy with the colleague who had called me. Her father had just completed therapy with his own psychiatrist, and her older sister had had her own therapist for a while, too. So, although Gina did seem to be experiencing some difficulties, another impetus for therapy for her at this time appeared to be that it was her turn to have her own therapist. I inquired about any family therapy. Dr. Rosenbaum said she was sure that the parents would come in from time to time but that they wanted something for Gina. I was presented with a request for individual child therapy. To accommodate to the system, which, I appreciated included Dr. Rosenbaum as well as Gina's family, I accepted the terms of the referral. The presenting problems were Gina's frequent illnesses, school absences, and "unhappiness."

I agreed to see Gina, who was brought for her first session by her parents. Her mother had her own freelance interior design business; her father was successfully established in a small but lucrative business. Her mother also brought some reports of psychological tests done at a center where the older sister, Ashley, had also been tested. I was not clear why Gina had been tested, but perhaps since Ashley had had tests, her parents had thought it a good idea to have Gina tested, too. The tests showed some mild difficulties with visual–motor integration, information that was hard to reconcile with Gina's superior performance in all subjects in school. In her parents' presence Gina reported that school was a negative experience, claimed that she was not smart, and said that she had no friends. Furthermore, although she was a beautiful child, she claimed that she was ugly. Gina was carrying a Cabbage Patch Kid, one of six that she and Ashley shared. She also talked about other fantastic toys that she owned or had been promised. The parents complained that Gina could never accept a compliment and would burst into tears or run from the room if anyone crossed her. She was always fighting with her sister. Gina's parents felt helpless about how to make her happy and wanted to turn her over to me.

Although I was puzzled about what was going on in Gina's family, I acceded to the family's desire for me to see Gina individually, as it appeared to be the best way to join the family. My hypothesis at this time was that the parents were like cowbirds—those birds that lay their eggs in other birds' nests so that their offspring can be raised by someone else. I appreciated their sense of helplessness about whether they had the skills to provide a happy environment for Gina even though they clearly had financial resources.

In her first session alone with me, Gina proved to be a delightful, resourceful, and entertaining youngster. We worked together for four sessions, during which we played with the Cabbage Patch Kids and did a lot of drawing games. In her first session Gina told me that she was afraid of the dark. When pressed, she told me that there was a monster in her closet. I asked her to draw me a picture of it. She started out with a fuzzy, catlike creature, but with urging from me it grew more menacing, developing vampire features. In a careful rendering of her room as it was, she drew the monster in her closet. I then asked her to give it a name, and we talked about what she does when she gets scared. When she said that she goes into her parents' room, we each drew a picture of what might happen when Gina goes into her parents' room. Gina showed herself lying on the floor at the foot of their bed, whereas I had her between her parents right in the middle of the bed. Gina thought this was hilarious. She took her picture of the monster home to hang on her closet door, and she never again complained about being scared of the dark. My idea of using drawing came about, first, because Gina liked to draw and thought she was good at it. We used it as a way for Gina to represent her fears and her solutions. By insisting that she be specific about details like location and name of the monster, I forced Gina to take control of the monster and the fears. Moving on to her familial solutions, I suggested, by my own fantasy, a comforting inclusion in a manner that Gina could enjoy and did not need to argue with. This was an exercise in reframing and had the beneficial effect of dispelling the night fears.

Another drawing project came out of Gina's comment that she hated substitute teachers. I asked her why, and she indicated that she worried about whether they would do things right. I suggested that we draw a picture of a classroom in the total disarray that could happen when there was a substitute. Gina established the basic design of the classroom, then together we drew overturned desks and wastepaper baskets, with crumpled paper, gum wrappers, and apple cores strewn about the room. The children's seats were tipped, and many of the children were out of their seats. Books on the teacher's desk were open and pages were coming out. The blackboard was scribbled on, and there were many misspelled words and wrong answers to math problems (Gina's idea). The map on the wall was falling down, a filing cabinet was overflowing onto the floor, and the door was coming off its hinges. Gina had a moment's hesitation about letting the room get so messy; then she entered the project with gusto. After we finished the messy room, I proposed that we clean up the classroom for the regular teacher. So we drew another picture with everything back in order. In this second major exercise in reframing, Gina's concerns about adults losing control were tackled, using our playfulness and humor. First, she could be involved in messing up and then in cleaning up.

Gina's father brought her to her sessions because they were scheduled on his afternoon off. At one point he asked to see me alone, but he agreed to include Gina, at my request. He complained that Gina was just out of sorts all the time and that she blamed everyone else for everything. For example, if someone said that her room needed to be cleaned up, Gina would say that someone else messed it up. Gina did not like having her father in the office, refused to discuss anything with him there, and tried to change the subject. Finally he left, and I suggested that she draw a picture of her father messing up her room. Again she tackled the project with gusto, depicting her father with a devilish grin, throwing clothes around the room, a bubble coming out of his mouth saying, "I bet she won't know who did this." At this point I suggested that she draw herself discovering her father at work. And there she was, running into the room, hair flying, Cabbage Patch under her arm, a triumphant bubble over her head saying, "Gotcha!"

We tested the absurdity of some of her stances by using her humor in the drawings. While Gina was doing her drawing, I was drawing my picture of her family. It had the parents and Ashley standing over Gina's prostrate figure, pointing their fingers at her. A few tears were falling from Gina's eyes. When Gina saw the picture, she was delighted. "It's my family blaming me," she said. "Right," I said. "What's going to happen, next?" First Gina said that there needed to be a bucket to catch her tears, so she drew one. Then she pointed out that there would need to be a lot of buckets. A line of buckets appeared; those full of tears had blue corroded handles, and those in line for tears had shiny brass handles. "What will happen when they are all full?" I asked. "The room will fill up with water," said Gina. "Let's draw it." I drew her family members with water up to their noses. Gina drew herself in a rowboat, high and dry, and asking, "How's the water?" "Now what will happen?" I asked. "There's a drain in the floor," she said, putting it in under the water, "and we can pull the plug and let the water out." So we drew a third picture. I drew the family members, dripping wet and miserable. Gina drew herself, standing high and dry next to the overturned rowboat, happily saying to her family, "Want to try that again?"

Involving the Parents

In these first few sessions I had discovered that this was a delightful and resourceful child. She had enjoyed facing her fears and bringing her substantial imagination to the rescue. We had also begun to construct a view of how she saw herself in the family. Over her protests, we scheduled a meeting with her parents but did not at this point include Ashley. Gina was prepared to hate the session with her parents, and she spent much of her time complaining, sulking, being negative, and generally confirming, by her behavior, their complaints about her. Hoping to pull them together through Gina's skills, I asked them each to draw a picture of the family with everyone doing something. Gina drew herself and Ashley fighting. Gina's mother drew two pictures, one of Gina and Ashley fighting, the other of Gina and herself sewing. Gina's father drew everyone—mother cooking, father watching TV, Ashley with her earphones on, and Gina sulking. Together we remarked on the fact that no one was doing anything with anyone else, and Mr. Peters said that's the way it is in the family. Could he draw a solution? After much talk and consideration, he drew himself next to his wife, helping her cook. Mrs. Peters's reaction was to say, "Why do you always see me cooking?" She then went on to describe her current disaffection with her domestic role and her guilt about leaving the children while she went to work. Mr. Peters added that this same guilt was stifling the kids. He complained that she still walked Gina out to the school bus, which stopped at their own corner. Gina occupied herself in another part of the room while this conversation was going on.

Themes of separateness and helplessness about the separateness became apparent in this session. Thus, although each of the family members was successful in many endeavors, and although Gina was obviously a bright and resourceful child, these skills were not being recognized or applied in the relationship system. Mr. Peters depicted family separateness, and when he finally attempted to join his wife, in fantasy, she rejected his fantasy because it was not on her terms. This was conceptualized as a multilevel problem. His disappointment with her working was directed at her. She wanted to work, but, in effect, responded to his criticism by feeling guilty about the children. This led her to overprotect the children, especially Gina. Gina's frequent illnesses, clinginess, and expressed dissatisfaction with school could be understood in this sequence, both confirming her mother's sense that the children needed her more, and confirming her father's point that the mother should be more involved with the family.

Dr. Rosenbaum and I spoke about this, and she invited Mr. Peters into some of her sessions with Mrs. Peters. The theme there became enjoying themselves together. This was the beginning of bringing Mrs. Peters's beliefs about how therapy should go closer to a systems view, because she began to appreciate that some of her own problems involved her husband. But both parents continued to feel that Gina's problems needed to be addressed by someone other than themselves, so I continued to work with Gina, who remained enthusiastic about our sessions. She frequently brought dolls, who usually had something to say at the beginning of the session and then watched the two of us play. When we played it became more obvious that Gina was not a collaborator. We had taken turns in our joint efforts in the past. More and more Gina would tell me to wait while she drew something or carried out some plan, putting her back to me and her body between me and the project she was painstakingly executing. I would impatiently comment that I didn't like waiting and that I wanted to play with her. We began to do spelling tests where I would think up more difficult words and she would spell phonetically. She was very good at it and developed a scoring system. We did a "kinetic family tree." While putting all of her extended family members in their own generations, each person became a whole figure depicted doing something. This demonstrated that Gina felt more comfortable with her grandparents and her uncle's family than with her own parents.

Mr. Peters brought Gina to her sessions, and when I asked him how he was, he usually complained that he was overworked, that his new car was a cheap toy, or that Gina was impossible. I asked Gina why her father was so unhappy. She refused to discuss it, saying that she didn't know. I persisted, saying, "We're going to do something in this room that will tell us why you think your father is so unhappy." Gina rose to the challenge and began to draw a picture of a rainbow (a favorite exercise for school-aged children who can't think of anything else to draw). I said that this was about her father, but she insisted that rainbows had nothing to do with her father. We made up a progressive story about the rainbows, where we each told a part. It was a story about a drought and a farmer who noticed a rainbow and called his neighbor. The neighbor was very grumpy and didn't want to be disturbed. The farmer pointed to the rainbow, but the neighbor didn't see it. Trying to figure out how to get his grouchy neighbor to see, the farmer drew a picture of the rainbow. "Oh, a rainbow," said the neighbor. "Why didn't you say so in the first place?" That night there was a rainstorm, and the drought was over. I felt that the story had addressed Gina's experience of her father's cantankerousness—as the farmer tried to bring good news to the grumpy neighbor, so Gina felt frustrated in pleasing her father. But she, too, was like the grumpy neighbor. The exercise, however, did not spell out this interpretation. It dealt with Gina's resourcefulness in solving the problem with the grumpy neighbor even as she was feeling put out with me for pursuing it.

A Family Project

I had worked more with Gina's appreciation of her family and her own connectedness, but I was feeling more and more uncomfortable having such a good time with someone else's child, week after week. Gina's mother appreciated Gina's enthusiasm for her meetings with me, and she didn't want to intrude on her daughter's special relationship. Gina's father pointed out that he didn't see any changes at home. Gina was demonstrating her competitiveness and her unwillingness to collaborate in the sessions. She was still doing well socially, with many sleepovers and birthday parties, and she was doing well academically. She continued to experience a lot of academic pressure, but, after she began to see me, she was sick only once, with the chicken pox. We began to work on a fantasy collage involving torn tissue paper and cardboard shapes of various colors. We cut and pasted a scene with two girls, trees and flowers, a fence, a dog, and a sun with snakes coming out of it, resembling the hair of one of the girls. Gina said that the girl was going to marry the sun. Working on this was a new experience. We collaborated. Gina would ask me to cut or paste something for her. If I cut something that she liked, we would plan where to put it. We covered one large sheet of easel paper, and it seemed that we could spread to another, using this collaborative process.

Finally Gina's mother came in. She admired the fantasy but was not sure where she could fit in. I waited. She and Gina decided to build a house on the next sheet. It was made of a manila folder that flipped up to show the inside of the house. Gina got to work making shutters and a door while her mother mostly watched and helped her. The next session, Mr. Peters joined us. He laid out the rooms and put in the plumbing and electricity (gray paper strips for piping, telephone wires for the electric wiring), while Gina and her mother made decorated wallpaper walls that pasted over the wiring and flipped up to show it. Gina worked on decorating her bedroom with color-coordinated bedspread and curtains, plus dolls and toys. It was agreed that Ashley needed to be a part of this project, and Gina generously allotted a space for Ashley's bedroom. Ashley joined and decorated her bedroom. The family moved to contemplation of the common rooms, so Mr. Peters put in kitchen fixtures. Ashley decided that the family needed Chinese take-out food to go on the kitchen table, so she made tiny containers decorated with Chinese figures and pasted them on the table.

At this point the family worked like this: Gina worked on her own room or a small fantasy piece, often unconnected with the joint project. Ashley clearly enjoyed the challenge of working with these materials, and she, too, worked by herself, but with a sense of the whole project. Mr. Peters furnished the house with utilitarian pieces, then went to work on the master bedroom. He worked swiftly and without consulting his wife about the layout of "their" bedroom, so that when he had put a few things in, she protested. I suggested that they design the master bedroom together.

Mr. Peters would then say, "What do you want me to do?" Mrs. Peters would demure, he would begin a project, I would ask if that was something they had decided together, she would say, "No," and he would ask, "What do you want me to do?" Mrs. Peters tended to sit back and watch her family work. She finally undertook to decorate a bedspread for the master bed, and at a later session, she asked her husband to make a study for her. He asked Gina to help him, but she refused. But he did consult his wife for every piece, and when it was done, she was very pleased with it.

Now the whole family was coming to the sessions. They were working industriously on a project that they were enjoying, although they were not working together. A characteristic sequence involved everyone, except Mom, being immersed in some productive activity. Mom's role was to appreciate everyone. Dad never got appreciated enough. Ashley's work was exceptional, and she got a lot of praise. Gina, whose work was also exceptional, but different from Ashley's, appeared to decide not to compete, so she chose to work on something other than the family project. The tension centered on the relationship between the sisters. Ashley took an older-sister critical position about Gina; Gina reacted wildly upset, and the flames were fanned by Mom supporting the reasonableness of Ashley's position and Dad losing his temper at Gina. Gina then either stormed out of the room, slamming doors and refusing to return, or she sat under the table, refusing to come out. The parents then looked at me with, "You see? This is what we have been talking about." I responded, "What do you want to have happen here?"

The first time this happened, Dad sat back and said, "Let her do something about it. She always protects Gina. You get her to come out from under the table." Mom said, "Okay, I will." Dad said, "She won't, you know, she never does." Mrs. Peters sat down on the floor and asked Gina to come out. Gina refused. Mrs. Peters then told Gina to come out. Gina still refused. Mrs. Peters then pulled Gina out and put her on a chair. This was quite a struggle. Mr. Peters watched with arms folded, apparently expecting his wife to give up. She probably would have given up, but I kept asking her if she was satisfied with Gina's behavior, so she kept insisting that Gina sit in the chair. Finally, Gina sat in the chair but maintained her stance that she wouldn't work with the family. Mrs. Peters was congratulated by both her husband and me, and Gina was congratulated by me, and the session was over.

The family enjoyed coming together and working on the project, which clearly utilized a lot of their talents but did not, at first, challenge their ways of being together. Gina's withdrawal from the family project was like her withdrawals at home, over which the parents felt helpless. Their helplessness was accentuated by mutual blaming for Gina's problem in which neither of them brought Gina into the family activity. The enactment in the session had a different outcome, but since no one seemed convinced that it would make a difference, I congratulated Gina, because she was obviously not going to make a change until she was convinced that there were other changes in the family.

Forming New Ways of Relating

On other occasions the parents were asked to decide, together, where they wanted Gina to be in the session. Thus, if Gina was rude or withdrew in an obtrusive fashion, they would decide whether to exclude her or to expect that she stay with the family, accepting that they could not force her to work on the project. In one session they had Gina sit facing the wall until she decided to join. Gina's staying power was much stronger than her parents'. They kept wanting the "punishment" to be over, but Gina maintained her stance that she didn't want to be a part of this work. The parents usually insisted that Gina remain in the room, even though she wasn't with the family, and they occasionally had to collaborate on physically keeping her in the room. Ashley became very uncomfortable with this; and when getting more absorbed in her work didn't distract her from what was going on, she tried to leave the room.

The parents' helplessness about dealing with Gina's negative and self-excluding behavior was related to blaming: Father blamed Mother that she gave in too easily and never followed through, and Mother blamed Father that he was too quick-tempered. They expected me to transform Gina; I expected them to do something about it. Mrs. Peters followed through, and they had to transcend their differences as a parent team in order to decide on their expectations of Gina and to implement the plan. Ashley's discomfort and eventual departure from the room seemed to maintain the old family style of not completing, giving up, and defining the whole exercise as futile. When Ashley left, however, the parents were asked to make a decision about what they expected from her and to implement that, as well. This led to a battle between the parents and Ashley, with Gina becoming upset at their treatment of her sister.

The collage house became a background activity to keep hands busy while we talked about the family. Ashley's complaints shifted from Gina to her parents—that they didn't appreciate her enough, that they didn't give her enough independence, and that they always wanted to do things together as a family that she didn't necessarily want to do. Her complaint could be summarized: You don't listen to me. The family was asked to plan their activities for the weekend. Dad said he wanted to take a drive to the mountains, where they were looking for a vacation spot. Mom said she'd like to do that, too, and Gina said she would go along. Ashley said she didn't want to go, but that she would be happy to stay home alone for a few hours. They negotiated this. The parents wanted assurance that Ashley would be happy and safe; Ashley needed to convince them that she had something to do. They listened.

In contrast to Ashley's quest for more independence, Gina continued to demand close involvement from her parents. She continued to be moody and contrary both in the sessions and outside. For example, she would complain that she had no shirts to wear; her mother would come up to her closet and show her the shirts, and Gina would insist that they hadn't been there. It was so nonsensical that one could only conclude that she wanted more contact, on any terms. I raised the question about what the family would do when they no longer had a baby. "We don't have a baby," they said. I suggested that Gina was sustaining her role as baby and that it was probably important for the family. Therefore, I suggested, they should think about having another baby ("Oh, no, not that") or of figuring out what kind of family they would be without a baby.

It was helpful for the parents to think of some of Gina's problem behaviors as inducing them to treat her like a baby. Gina protested that she was not a baby, and everyone agreed but pointed out that she sometimes acted like one. I added that she did it probably for her parents when she saw that they needed a baby. She was not comforted by this observation. The parents, though, found that every time Gina acted up, they had to consider whether they needed a baby or not. This refocused their critical inquiry from, "Why is she doing this?" to, "Do we need a baby now?" Gina's behaviors were now understood not as her trying to get out of the family but as her trying to be herself and find her way into the family.

The family completed the house, a greenhouse, and a "magic carpet" picnic. They mounted the collage on a piece of plywood and set aside a place for it in their own house. They had completed their project, and they could think of nothing else they wanted to do with it. I asked them how they would rather spend their Saturday mornings. Dad said that he liked coming to the sessions because this was the only time the family got together. What other ways would he like to spend time with his family? They all thought they'd rather be playing tennis. Four weeks later they returned for a final session. We sat around the table where houses and fantasies had been built and where struggles for recognition and individual identity had been carried out. Ashley started to tease her father, and I asked her, "What is your father good at?" "I know," said Gina, "let me say." She then listed five special qualities about her father, who glowed. They all agreed that tennis was a much better way to spend time together than fighting in a therapist's office.

Systems Therapy and the Giant Steps

Members of the Peters family were seen for twenty-five sessions over fifteen months. Contact with the system began with the mother's therapist and involved entering the system on their terms before slowly transforming it to terms in which members of the system could manage with each other. The child's problems with seeing herself as attractive and competent came to be understood as relating to a family in which everyone was clamoring for individualized recognition and acknowledgement. These shifts in perception, reflective of the first giant step, were essential to the family members seeing each other in a more positive way and becoming engaged with each other. Step 2 involved identifying and confronting patterns of mutual blaming and helplessness, while also taking step 3 employing the family's own creative resources and activating their own good judgment about what they wanted and how to go about solving sticky problems.

Finally, for step 4, working together productively on a project that was ultimately frivolous allowed for the enactment of family systems problems and solutions. Challenged to change their views of each other—Gina to trust her parents, the parents to feel confident containing and comforting Gina, Ashley to differentiate herself as an older sister and as a more independent family member—the family system shifted in many ways that allowed the members both to enjoy being together and to appreciate each other's differences.

PART III

Larger Systems

CHAPTER 8

The Mental Health System: Dichotomies and Exclusive Categories

We have yet to write the history of that other form of madness, by which men, in an act of sovereign reason, confine their neighbors, and communicate and recognize each other through the merciless language of non-madness; to define the moment of this conspiracy before it was permanently established in the realm of truth, before it was revived by the lyricism of protest. We must try to return, in history, to that zero point in the course of madness at which madness is an undifferentiated experience, a not yet divided experience of division itself. We must describe, from the start of its trajectory, that "other form" which relegates Reason and Madness to one side or the other of its action as things henceforth external, deaf to all exchange, and as though dead to one another.
—MICHEL FOUCAULT, *Madness and Civilization,* 1965

Mental health systems have developed to take care of those who suffer from mental disturbances. Like childhood, as discussed in chapter 2, mental illness has been a shifting set of categories. History has recorded many changes in the way mental illness has been framed and the way people have responded to it. The term *mental illness* implies that there is a disease process disturbing the emotional or psychological functioning of "afflicted" individuals, and this reflects the dominant framework for identifying and responding to individuals whose behavior, mood, and thinking are sufficiently deviant from the norm to set them aside in a special category.

Whether or not mental illness reflects a true disease process is still debatable in epistemological and philosophical circles. I referred to a process called the medicalization of social deviance in chapter 1, a process by which certain socially aberrant behavior is designated as illness. Thomas Szasz (1961) has accused doctors of constructing mental illness in a form they think they can treat. Hafner (1987) speculated that whatever is meant by *illness* must be distinguished from health as a norm, deviations from the norm that have cultural or legal implications, and distress related to untoward life events. He opined that none of the so-called mental illnesses has been sufficiently delineated, none meets the criteria to be called a disease in the sense that the pioneering German psychiatrist Emil Kraepelin had hoped, and few meet the criteria of syndromes composed of characteristic symptom clusters. Nevertheless, mental disturbances are treated as if they are diseases, and using the disease framework allows fruitful scientific inquiry into their biological bases.

The definition of mental illness in children and adolescents is even more elusive than in adults, because children rarely show the intractable forms of psychosis and disturbances of affect called mental illness in adults and because children's serious mental disturbances, such as autism and pervasive developmental disorders, are so clearly associated with disabilities that are not classified as mental disturbances but as neurological or organic impairments. In fact, the children's mental health system evolved from concern about a very different population than did the adult mental health system. Child mental health grew out of concern about "wayward youth" (Aichorn [1925] 1935)—youth gone astray, those gone against society, and delinquents—whereas, up to the present, adult mental health has attempted to make a clear distinction between the antisocial and the mentally ill. The first child mental health clinic was founded in 1909 out of the juvenile court system in Chicago. It was started by a psychiatrist, psychologist, and social worker who elaborated the multidisciplinary approach to the study and treatment of a child through their work with children referred by the courts. The psychological approaches, however, were derived from what was evolving for adults, primarily psychoanalytic understanding of the mental processes, and the use of asylums and the emerging psychotherapies as corrective processes.

Although problems of classification continue to plague the mental health field, mental health systems operate as if classification is well established. They operate as if there is a clear basis for deciding who should—and should not—be treated in the mental health system and as if there are clear criteria for establishing what treatments are most suitable to what types of disturbances. The result is a confusing set of dichotomies and categories. For example, a child might be deflected from a mental health setting because he is bad, not mad. Categorization of people with problems can become a serious fragmenting problem.

The mental health system operates with an imposing array of dichotomies—such as madness versus reason, badness, stupidity, or malice; outpatient versus inpatient treatment; family versus individual psychotherapy;

public versus private care; and standards of care versus malpractice—and categories—like psychosis, neurosis, or character disorder; and psychodynamic, cognitive-behavioral, or psychoeducational treatment. This chapter examines these categories in existing mental health systems, and it should become apparent how the giant steps I propose can break down some of these compartments to more workable situations.

Public and Private Systems

Over the more than eighty years of child mental health, two systems have evolved—a public system and a private system. The private system functions to help parents manage troubling and difficult children. It is based largely on private enterprise, a powerful motivator for progress in managing problem children. In the private system there is no clear distinction between problems that can be managed among a family's natural counselors and resources, such as relatives, neighbors, a clergyman, or a pediatrician, and those that need expert assistance from a mental health professional. The much-criticized advertisements for psychiatric hospitals are good examples. These ads cite many common adolescent behaviors, such as moodiness and irritability, and encourage families to bring these youngsters for hospitalization. Another illustration, however, is one provided by a colleague of mine when he was justifying public relations for child mental health professionals in mental health awareness week. He described a standoff between a mother and her eight-year-old daughter about selecting her clothing each day. Obviously, if the mother and daughter are entangled in such a daily routine of arguing and irritation, they could use intervention from third parties. But when should this third party be a mental health professional? Only, it seems, after the other nuclear family members, extended family members, and other natural resources have been consulted. To suggest that this is a situation requiring mental health intervention poses that the child's behavior is disturbed (although in the consultation, at least six out of ten professionals would say it was the mother's problem) and would bypass the competent resources within the family. This kind of definition of the function of child mental health professionals in the private sector violates the ecology of children and families by bringing mental health professionals into a pseudo-intimate relationship and by setting up the professionals as experts without whom families dare not function.

The public and private systems have different motivations. The public system has been focused less on assisting parents and more on providing alternative environments (asylums) for children whose parents are seen as incapable or destructive. It has been both developed and limited by cost containment. The public system suffers from a sense of inferiority to the private system. It is also driven by developments in the latter, for the attitude of entitlement to mental health intervention cultivated in the private sector is brought to the public sector, both by parents whose resources have been exhausted and by professionals who believe that standards are set in the private sector. Nevertheless, important effective means of addressing disturbed children that could ultimately transform the mental health service delivery system have emerged out of public necessity.

In the private sector services tend to be offered over longer periods and usually are more intense. During the 1980s there was a nearly tenfold increase in the use of psychiatric hospitalization for evaluations, protection, and definitive treatment of children from the private sector (Weithorn 1988). In contrast, during the same period the number of beds for children and adolescents in state hospitals tended to stay the same or decrease. Public sector treatments focused on symptom relief and function maintenance are briefer. Long stays in public institutions usually occur because of difficulty in finding a placement. Public systems are trying to expand services to manage children in their homes and communities. Psychiatrists tend to be more involved with private sector types of treatment, social workers with the public sector, and psychologists with both. These differences have an economic impact that makes it very difficult to do objective evaluations of treatment efficacy, but it is abundantly clear that the rich and insured get a different sort of treatment from the poor and uninsured. It is also likely that both extremes suffer—the former from too much treatment, which takes over, creates dependence on therapists, and provides explanations rather than activating solutions to problematic behaviors and feelings, and the latter from insufficient attention and inadequate services; both suffer from lack of continuity of care.

As a part of this lack of adequate data or consensus about efficacy there is considerable competition between child-serving agencies about who should be serving which children. In the public sector this takes the form of shunting youngsters back and forth between child-serving agencies, such as corrections, welfare, and mental health. In most cases children's education is considered secondary in importance after their emotional needs. Again, there seems to be a difference between the public sector and the private sector. In the private sector, if the child or adolescent has financial resources, some form of mental health services probably will be deemed appropriate for him in lieu of what might actually be a more appropriate response from other quarters, such as corrections.

I encountered Kurt, a young man in a private psychiatric hospital, who had been arrested twice—once for dealing drugs. Kurt's father was reputed to be "as rich as H. Ross Perot." Kurt had been in the hospital for four months, something less than the amount of time he might have served for a jail sentence. He had received a diagnosis of "combined partial seizure disorder" and was being treated with anticonvulsants. No electroencephalogram had confirmed this diagnosis, but the treating physician reported that these impulsive youngsters responded well to the anticonvulsant treatment. In another private clinic I found that many youngsters who were in trouble with the law and were dropping out of school were being given the diagnosis of attention deficit hyperactivity disorder (ADHD) and being treated with stimulants. Here, as with Kurt, the youngsters were admitted to a hospital unit at the time of serious crisis with the law, to be started on the medication and then gradually be moved to less restrictive treatment environments. Did this approach work? The physician in charge of the program said it did. He claimed that the youngsters were much more able to control their impulses and were, therefore, able to pay more attention in school and do better there. As they did better in school, they seemed to feel better and more hopeful about themselves. He reported that the schools and the parents were ecstatic about the changes in these kids. And the kids themselves bore testimony to their appreciation for this treatment.

Public facilities are often overcrowded and beleaguered by demands to admit children they don't feel are appropriate for hospitalization. Furthermore, public institutional care reflects the multiple viewpoints of a heterogeneous staff in public service, and these multiple viewpoints often lead to a messy treatment approach. One state hospital adolescent unit leader, apparently ignoring the roots of child mental health, refuses to admit youngsters he deems to be "antisocial." He claims that such youth are untreatable. Yet public facilities are full of kids whose primary problems are disturbances of behavior (at least 60 percent). One public mental health system was sued because of mixing children with "conduct disorders" with "mentally ill" children, a suit that suggested that someone thought they could make the distinction, just as the unit leader thought he could. In chapter 2 I described the case of Robert, whose lawbreaking behavior brought his family and community into crises. The judge remanded him to mental health and required the department to contain him in their state facility. But the pressure comes, too, from child welfare, where the desperate behaviors of youngsters that might be interpreted as means of survival are seen as dangerous (which they probably are) and signs of emotional disturbance. The public mental health facilities then become providers of intensive supervision for youngsters whose dangerous behaviors require supervision but who frequently do not respond to the treatment available in a mental health setting.

Remedial Processes in Mental Health

Mental health systems for both children and adults operate with four fundamental remedial processes: diagnosis (or designation), containment, psychotherapy, and medication. They are listed in order of historical evolution, although medication in some form has always been a part of treatment.

Designation

The first principle of mental health handling is classification of a person as requiring such treatment. The process of classification in medicine, as I discussed in chapter 5 on diagnosing, requires inclusionary and exclusionary criteria with the effect, often, of sustaining mutually exclusive dichotomies. A first step is to clarify which illnesses are physical and which are mental, psychological, or emotional. This differentiation supports the psyche versus soma dichotomy. Two overlapping classes of illnesses are psychophysiological, those in which the psychological state influences the physiological condition, such as peptic ulcer or hypertension; and psychosomatic, in which the state of mind may create the symptoms. These two become less distinct when the reciprocal influences of mind and body are appreciated. Prolonged states of stress and anxiety may alter brain and body chemistry, and physical illness usually has significant psychological effects. But the distinction between medical and psychiatric illness is still overdrawn. Psychiatric consultants in medical or pediatric facilities may encounter consultation requests coming out of this kind of exclusionary thinking, such as, "We find no physical causes of this patient's symptoms; please evaluate for psychiatric problems."

History has shown that how the mentally unfit are designated has significant implications for how they are treated. People designated as mad during the Renaissance were put on "ships of fools" that travelled the waterways of Europe, ridding their own societies of the burdens of managing crazed individuals and producing a bizarre show for those villages and cities the ships passed. In the seventeenth and eighteenth centuries there was little distinction between mentally disturbed individuals and the indigents and criminals with whom they were imprisoned (Foucault 1965). Little distinction was made between the chronically mentally ill and the mentally deficient, until the emergence of the "talking cure," or verbalization in psychotherapy. Mentally deficient people did not benefit from the talking cure, nor did the undereducated or intellectually unsophisticated. Separate categories were made for the retarded and the emotionally disturbed, and until very recently mentally retarded people were not thought to have mental illnesses. All of their disturbances in behavior, mood, and thought were considered to be part of their retardation.

Now a new designation permits retarded people to be both retarded and mentally ill. Dual diagnosis has become an important new category in mental health. Lawsuits in many states have required that special programs be developed in mental hospitals directed at the "dually diagnosed." This is partly due to a clarification of mental illness symptoms, such as psychosis, mania, and depression, and the inclusion among symptoms of mental illness, destructive aggression, apparently unprovoked violence, and withdrawal from involvement in activities or social contact. Dual diagnosis was originally developed to address the psychological problems of the retarded, but it is now also applied to those who have substance abuse and mental illness, and a new set of programs for this dual diagnosis population is being developed.

I have already referred to the distinction between mad and bad and how this distinction becomes blurred, or the bad are seen as mad under circumstances not strictly related to psychological functioning. On the one hand there is the class of people who have committed crimes and who are designated as "not guilty by reason of insanity." On the other hand there is increasing evidence that among those who have committed and been convicted of crimes, at least among children, there is a significant history of deprivation and damage, which would explain the badness as madness, or at least as resulting from emotional disturbance. But demographic examination of the denizens of juvenile correctional facilities and of public state hospitals demonstrates definitively that classification is largely based on factors having nothing to do with mental disturbance in the youths. These factors are race, socioeconomic status, and gender. Specifically, black males go to corrections for their antisocial acts; white females go to mental hospitals. The range between depends on socioeconomic status and previous history.

When the first giant step is applied to these categorical differences, the validity of each side is recognized and accepted, and the task is to integrate rather than separate. Mentally retarded people may be psychotic, sad,

manic, aggressive, and withdrawn because of the psychological circumstances of being mentally retarded. This is more easily understood when
the context of their disturbed behavior is examined, looking for patterns
in which the behavior is a part (giant step 2). For someone with cognitive
limitations to misunderstand or misinterpret, with the resulting psychotic
distortions, is logical. It makes sense for such a person to experience sadness, hopelessness, or low self-esteem; anxiety and panic in confronting
social situations in which one's deviance is apparent; aggression at those
who are perceived to limit and control; or withdrawal and self-stimulation
in a context where external stimulation is overwhelming or confusing.
Mental disturbance in disabled people usually represents an effort to cope
and may, in many instances, effectively communicate the sender's message
when other forms of communication are not available to the patient (step
3). Furthermore, understanding the emotional disturbance contextually
and relating it to the type of disability the patient has widens the options
for treatment. Medications that have been found to be useful for alleviat-
ing psychosis, anxiety, depression, or aggression can then be supplemented
with sensitive planning for activities and the milieu.

Similarly, there is ordinarily a relationship between substance abuse and
mental illness. Indeed, substance abuse is classified as a mental illness. The
use of substances by depressed individuals or psychotic individuals is a
time-honored form of self-medication. The problem here seems to have
been the elaboration of the disease model of substance dependence, an
even more problematic model than that of mental disturbance. The U.S.
Supreme Court upheld the Veterans Administration's refusal to pay for
alcoholism treatment, labeling alcoholism as "willful misconduct." Here is
another dichotomy to argue about—illness versus misconduct. There is
clearly a voluntary, weakness-of-the-will component of substance dependence, but to take the puritanical position that it is merely willful misconduct absolutely overlooks the significant emotional and adjustment problems that underlie the use, and the physiological changes that accompany
addiction. The best programs for individuals with substance dependence—
or any kind of addiction or compulsive behavior (such as gambling or sex
abuse)—provide reeducation and resocialization in which the individuals
can examine themselves, both their assets and liabilities, and make a new
plan.

Finally, there is no doubt that most antisocial individuals come from
disturbed environments and have distorted ways of thinking. As with the
exclusion of so many from the talking cure, antisocial individuals have not
been seen as good candidates for psychotherapy. Furthermore, as I have
noted, many antisocial or delinquent youths come from other groups that

have been excluded from the mental illness class on the grounds that they are not candidates for psychotherapy. It is clear that two issues must be addressed with the disturbed individual who commits antisocial acts: accountability and habilitation. The dichotomous classification of bad versus mad leaves accountability to the correctional system and treatment to the mental health system, when both should be components of a service plan for such individuals.

DEFINING THE POPULATION TO BE SERVED

Despite the absoluteness of categories, professionals have not actually agreed on which children need mental health services. According to various epidemiological studies, between 12 percent and 22 percent of all U.S. children are mentally ill (see, for example, Kazdin 1989). Despite the criteria clearly presented in diagnostic and statistical manuals, diagnostic and assessment packages vary by state, profession, and group using the package. Some studies clearly underestimate the needs of children, but others probably overestimate their emotional distress or at least the possibility that the mental health system, as it now is, could provide some relief for them. One variation that confuses the picture is which group of children is sampled—a clinical or nonclinical population. When state mental health departments do needs assessments, they find that 5 percent of all children and adolescents are severely emotionally disturbed, and about half of these need attention from the public system. These surveys are usually based on complaints or requests for service, either from the consumers or service providers. Another type of study was conducted of a primary care pediatric population in a health maintenance organization, or HMO (Costello and colleagues 1988). The researchers found a weighted prevalence of one or more *DSM-III* disorders of 22 percent, whereas a little under 4 percent had been referred for mental health services. Here the dismaying number of previously unidentified problems found in the children raises the question, What is the significance of meeting diagnostic criteria without complaint? Another study, with similar aims to estimate the prevalence of childhood maladjustment, was performed in Puerto Rico (Bird and colleagues 1988). Prevalence of moderate to severe maladjustment was identified among 15.8 percent of randomly selected children from a sample of Puerto Rican households. These investigators distinguished between the significance of scoring in a significant level on the Child Behavior Checklist (CBCL), where they observed a generally high score in Puerto Rican children (thus suggesting some cultural variation); actually meeting criteria for *DSM-III* diagnosis; and displaying a condition of sufficient severity to warrant clinical attention.

Still another approach to defining the population to be served by mental health is an examination of those youngsters who have been designated as needing mental health services and are actually receiving those. As described briefly in chapter 1, a large-scale project of this sort was conducted by the Florida Research and Training Center, looking at 800 youngsters ages seven to seventeen in residential and day treatment settings who had been designated as severely emotionally disturbed (Friedman et al. 1989). Who are these children? they asked. The investigators used an extensive evaluation protocol including diagnostic schedules, a review of school performance, psychological and educational testing, and interviews of parents and teachers. They found a heterogeneous group of children whom they referred to as "mad, bad, sad, and can't add." The "mad" children were those who were psychotic and comprised less than 10 percent of the total group. The "bad" children were those who had disturbances of conduct characterized by impulsivity and failure to conform to social expectations and limits. About 60 percent of the children exhibited these characteristics. About 40 percent of the children were "sad," reflecting a sense of hopelessness and helplessness about their current situations and futures, and there was significant overlap between "sad" and "bad." And 90 percent of the children were at least three grades below age level. Much of this failure can be explained on the basis of the disturbances suffered by the children, but it is also true that educational failures contribute to hopelessness and helplessness and their associated behaviors.

OTHER FACTORS IN DETERMINING APPROPRIATE CARE

Among conditions designated as mental there are also some strict categories, including neurosis, psychosis, character disorders, substance abuse, and eating disorders. The coincidence of substance abuse and eating disorders is common. Is there a process common to both, or are such individuals suffering from dual diagnosis? Studies of the sequelae of child abuse, particularly child sex abuse, have led anew to the interest in dissociative processes, originally thought to be neurotic. Now we are finding that an impressive number of women in psychiatric hospitals have histories of sexual molestation (Craine et al. 1988). Many of these women have complex symptoms variously called schizophrenia, bipolar variant, and borderline personality disorder. It is certainly possible that a clear traumatic experience, such as child abuse, may be linked with a syndrome of mental disorders, forming a new diagnostic category. The current classification system is, in fact, a hodgepodge of descriptive syndromes named for the characteristic behaviors (such as conduct disorder) and syndromes named for presumed etiology (such as attention deficit hyperactivity disorder).

One final important implication of diagnosis, or designation, is the implied standard of care. This is particularly significant to a profession increasingly practiced in a litigious environment. A mental health professional may not always be correct in anticipating what a patient can do, but she must be careful. Some have attributed to this the skyrocketing rate of adolescent hospitalization, which has become a standard of care. But what sort of care? In the hospital the adolescent is presumably protected from himself and from other destructive impulses, the family and the society are protected from the adolescent, and the professional is protected from a lawsuit. Standards of care are also becoming increasingly specified and exclusive, not necessarily to the overall benefit of the patient.

An example is Edward, a sixteen-year-old boy living with his single father after the two were abandoned by his mother. Edward has been an indifferent student and is in a vocational track in his junior year in high school. He developed a crush on his science teacher, and he was distressed when he observed her leaving school one day with one of the male teachers. He chose for a special project in science a study of poisons—how they work, how they can be administered, and how they might be detected. Edward's science teacher was aware of his feelings and connected the interest in poison with his sense of rejection and resentment. She kindly tried to direct him to another project, but he persisted. When she brought her concerns to the principal, Edward's work was reviewed, and he was suspended until a psychiatrist could verify that he was not a danger to the science teacher or anyone else. The psychiatrist met Edward and his father. They were rather disconnected from each other, and the psychiatrist learned that Edward had a fascination with horror films, murders, and science fiction. Edward denied malevolent intent toward the science teacher, even though he admitted to liking her and feeling that she did not think enough of him. He showed no sign of thought disorder and none of the vegetative signs of depression, though much of his preoccupation and isolation appeared to have a depressed quality to it.

The doctor didn't think Edward was a serious danger to the science teacher; she was prepared to take his word that he was not. Furthermore, she felt that through an extended evaluation with Edward and his father and some psychotherapy, he might modify his withdrawn and eccentric stances and become more integrated into his peer group. But she could not guarantee that he was not a danger, and she recognized that the standard of care required that he be hospitalized for everyone's protection until such a guarantee could be established. She had a further dilemma, however. She recognized that hospitalization would mean a declaration of mental illness to Edward. This would be one more strike against him, and rather than helping him become less eccentric, this could confirm that he was truly deviant and authenticate his chosen life-style. On the other hand, if Edward were not hospitalized and he did hurt someone, she would be held responsible and liable because she had not followed the standard of care for a potentially dangerous adolescent. This should be familiar as a dilemma of clinical experience (discussed in chapter 3), and it is the kind of dilemma fostered by the compartmentalized framework of the mental health system.

Containment

Until the development of the talking cure, all mental health treatment was done in institutions. The most direct implication of designating individuals as mentally ill is to contain them and to separate them from "normal" society. Containment is one motivation for institutionalization; asylum is another. Asylum implies safety and refuge; containment implies control. Mentally disturbed people are separated because they are disturbing. Much of what they do is harmless, but nevertheless distressing because it is so deviant. However, much of what they do is harmful, either because it is irresponsible (like smoking in bed) or actively dangerous (like threatening or harming oneself or others). Containment is just that, and only within the last century has there been some form of active treatment available in some hospitals or asylums that adds to what nature might do to heal the individual. Emotionally disturbed children are also separated when it is thought that they are symptomatic because of an unhealthy environment. Thus, in addition to containment and asylum, mental health institutions have served as corrective emotional environments for children.

DARREL'S EVALUATION: AN EXAMPLE

Imagine this scene. A master's level psychologist, a woman in her late twenties, is evaluating an individual child, Darrel. He becomes loud and threatens to beat her with an electric cord, then talks about undressing her. For the young woman, who represents nothing more than a step in an elaborate system of evaluation and triage, these would be frightening threats from a male, if he were bigger and stronger and in any way able to carry out these threats. But imagine that Darrel is six years old. Does that change the response? It should. It should also change the meaning to be attributed to the threats, the meaning to be attributed to the emotional state of the individual making the threats, and the response. In the situation involving Darrel, he had been brought to the local hospital to be evaluated for signs of physical abuse, presumably by one of his parents.

168

Signs affirming the likelihood of abuse had been found, and Darrel had been taken into custody by the welfare department. His parents then disappeared. Once in custody, he had to be placed somewhere, and the young psychologist was evaluating him for this. She concluded from these utterances, as well as his generally frantic behavior, that Darrel was emotionally disturbed—possibly psychotic—and he was sent at once to the state hospital and was admitted.

This example reveals several elements common to the induction of many children into the mental health system. First is a failure to differentiate the importance of behaviors on the basis of development. Second is the practice of cataloguing observed data without either speculating about the meaning of the data in the context in which it is being observed or experimenting with how the data change according to the responses of the observer (who is, after all, also a stimulus). The third element is a different level of systemic understanding: that of the systems now available to handle children who, for whatever reason, cannot remain in the care of their own families. Within this element are several key points. The first is the drastic reduction in the quantity of beds in well-organized and well-structured residential homes for dependent and neglected children. The second, less well documented, but often commented upon, is the reduction in the availability of foster homes willing to handle an aggressive youngster. Third is the common practice of having professionals without child and adolescent training performing intakes for state hospitals, especially during evenings and weekends. Fourth is the practice of admitting a child because of his symptomatic behavior rather than through any consideration of whether the hospital might have an appropriate remedy for his problems. Increasingly, then, psychiatric hospitals have been used as the sanctuary for the more difficult to manage of the youngsters who have been ejected from their families.

Let's examine each of these elements of the vignette and imagine what other possibilities there might have been for Darrel. First, if the evaluator had taken development into account, or if she had simply taken the child's size into account, she would have had to realize that, unless she permitted it, there is no way the child could have beaten her with an electric cord or taken off her clothes. Thus, there are three reasons a six-year-old would say something like that. Either he is distorting his own personal power, he is imitating something he has heard as a way of coping with a strange and probably unpleasant situation (e.g., threatening to hurt), or he has somehow appreciated that this form of behavior gives him a greater sense of control than another form of behavior (this is not inconsistent with either of the other two). For any one of these reasons, however, the developmentally aware evaluator must realize that attempting to intimidate is a desperate move; succeeding in intimidation will put the child in more frightening control than a youngster of that age can generally tolerate. These developmental considerations would naturally modify the meaning of the data.

The developmental considerations should also modify the way the observer responds. The kindest thing to do, given the child's desperation, is to reassure him that nothing of the sort will happen. Given in the form of reassurance, this reminder that he is small and helpless and that the examiner is bigger and capable of making decisions and offering comfort will not put the child down. There is a variety of responses to the threat to beat her with a cord. She could take the interpretive approach and say, "You really feel angry that you're in this situation with me, and you would like to hurt someone. I guess you have had others hurt you when they were angry?" She could take the warm, but firm approach, "Don't be silly, I'm not going to let you do a thing like that." Or she could take the corrective instructional approach, "You are just a little boy, and I'm a grown woman. You look pretty strong; but I'm much stronger than you. I won't allow you to hurt me, and if you want to tell me how you feel, you had better find a better way to express it than threatening me." Any one of the three of these would evoke a response from the child, which could range from relief expressed by relaxing to crying to crawling into her lap to more desperate efforts to exhibit his power and control. In the latter case, she would need to fulfill her boast of being stronger than he, both by physically restraining him and by recruiting more assistance if necessary.

If the child is relieved by the assurance of adult strength and caring, placement in a setting where this can be followed up on is most appropriate. In most cases this should not be a mental health facility. If the child becomes more active and aggressive, then it is clear that he needs more supervision and firm management. It is not clear why a mental health facility would be the best place to provide this. In fact, if he went to a mental health facility, such a child probably would be placed on medication to control his aggressive behavior and placed in time-out or seclusion or even restraints when these behaviors escalate.

THE APPROACH TO NED

Darrel did get admitted to a mental health facility, and we lost track of him. His fate might have been similar to that of Ned, an eight-year-old I met in a private hospital, who was working on his second hospital year. Ned had been discharged after one year in the hospital, even though no one felt very confident about having a handle on his behavior. They had tried a variety of medications and behavioral programs, offering both rewards and restrictions for his persistently aggressive behavior to both adults and peers; his disruption of groups, including the community, his classroom, and his family; and his destruction of property, with smashing, tearing, and fire setting. After only a few weeks at home, Ned was back in the hospital after he had run away several times, had stolen candy and a lighter from the local general store, and was described by his family as scary and out of control. Here is another example of how the mental health system seemed to provide relief in a form that did nothing to prepare the child, his family, or the community for working out life together.

Prior to his first hospitalization, Ned's family had struggled with their difficult child, but they had struggled with conviction. When he came home after a year, they no longer struggled, because they thought he was emotionally disturbed and needed professional help. In a meeting with the hospital staff, Ned's mother reported that, thanks to them, she had been able to pursue her philanthropic community work, uninterrupted by the need to rush home or to school because of some trouble Ned had gotten into. Ned's father, a busy, well-traveled executive, said, "Keep him till he's better." Ned was, in fact, a difficult child who had not been successfully managed by any adults for a large portion of his eight years. He had virtually no education. The police would come when called, but seeing the youth of the child, would leave. Once in the hospital, Ned was still uncontrolled and uneducated. The hospital staff were thoroughly frustrated and angry with him, and his parents' confession of their relief only made the staff more outraged.

THE ROLE OF PSYCHIATRIC HOSPITALS

Psychiatric hospitals are usually handled in a manner unlike medical or surgical hospitals both in the reasons for admission and for the treatment given therein. Medical and surgical patients are admitted to the hospital because there is a specific treatment in mind that can be done only in the hospital. Psychiatric patients are admitted for the variety of reasons already discussed. This fact—that psychiatric patients, especially if they are children, are admitted for the various reasons of containment, protection, asylum, treatment, and removal—makes psychiatric hospitalization a very confusing process. Generally, professionals avoid the lack of specificity about hospital treatment by emphasizing the distinction between inpatient and outpatient care. But there are varieties of inpatient or out-of-home care that ought to be specified and clarified so children could be admitted to the level of care most suited to their needs.

My own preference would be to have the psychiatric hospital assume a similar place in mental health care to that of the general hospital for medical and surgical care; that is, patients are admitted to a hospital for a treatment that can be delivered only there. Severity of disturbance would be a criterion for admission only if there were an articulated therapeutic response. Danger to oneself or others would require the same planning to justify hospitalization, because it has been demonstrated repeatedly that these kinds of behaviors can be managed effectively outside of hospitals. Asylum and respite can be provided in a hospital, although models developed in medicine and surgery would suggest that some form of hospice could serve better, and there are now many successful examples of community-based respite, especially for individuals with developmental disabilities and their families. The psychiatric hospital should not be substituted for other institutional needs. If the purpose of removal of a disturbed child from a home is to provide a more salubrious environment, hospitals should not be the place to do this. Rather, a long-term residential center where treatment is available would be more suitable. Here, the emphasis should be placed on residence, a place where a child can live, rather than on residential treatment, a type of treatment.

Psychotherapy

Psychotherapy was developed primarily in the treatment of nonhospitalized patients. In the 1940s and 1950s psychotherapy done in hospitals was prolonged, and many patients remained there for years. This approximated the corrective environment, but it required a stability of relationships not often experienced in today's fast-moving world. It also required public confidence in the effectiveness of such expensive treatment, underwritten by insurance and approved by utilization review committees. Once again, there is no evidence that a hospital environment is most suitable to this long-term rehabilitation, even if one believes that the rehabilitation is the most appropriate treatment. There is now considerable controversy about the effectiveness of psychotherapy with severely disturbed, hospitalized individuals. One lawsuit against a venerable psychiatric hospital pits the current "standard of care" for depression (antidepressant medication) against time-honored psychotherapy. In the evolving family treatment of severely and chronically mentally ill individuals, the patients are excluded from psychoeducational sessions because they are demanding, disruptive, and disturbed, and because the family needs a rest from them. Once again, there is a dichotomy. Why can't severely disturbed patients have psychotherapy and other treatments? Isn't this the humane form of treatment? What might go through the head of a hospitalized patient who knows that her family is coming for sessions from which she is excluded? Don't tell me she is too disturbed to care!

In the mental health system for children and adolescents, psychotherapy is a mishmash of insight-oriented psychodynamic approaches, cognitive behavior approaches, parent education, and family therapy. These often are dealt with as mutually exclusive categories: You can't do behavior therapy focusing on insight (yet the father of behavior therapy, Joseph Wolpe, is an analyst). You shouldn't see the child alone if he has a family, yet, why not, if the family understands what transpires and approves? Children are really innocent, and their problems are caused by parental mismanagement. To see a child alone places an unnecessary burden on him. Or working exclusively with the family ignores the child's personal feelings. In the end, every program for children and adolescents has a mixture of psychotherapies. The respectful thing to do is to let mental health professionals practice the way they know best. This may work well enough in outpatient clinics where patients and their therapists are relatively compartmentalized. But it does not work well in any setting requiring a team approach, such as inpatient care, day treatment, or home visiting. Tolerance for differences of approach to psychotherapy leads to confusion and contradictions, usually experienced by the patient and her parents. Besides the often mutually exclusive categories of the psychotherapies, psychotherapy is usually separate from other therapeutic experiences. Also, although a treatment plan may skillfully address therapeutic issues in the school milieu and peer group activities, institutional requirements and quality assurance plans may require a clearly delineated personal psychotherapy as the patient's right.

ALTERNATIVES IN TREATING NED

In Ned's case the hospital staff felt out of control of his treatment program because they felt out of control of him. The components of the program were behavior control and medication, neither of which had worked well. The behavior program that had been developed in abstraction was based on isolating Ned from the group to the point that he spent virtually no time with other children and was on constant one-to-one supervision by the staff. Ned persisted in being an exceptional child and having a completely different schedule and set of expectations from the rest of the patients. The program for him had been conceived by the clinical staff but had to be carried out by the patient care staff who had been subjected to his physical assaults, biting, kicking, and spitting. When he arrived in a meeting with his therapist, a psychologist, he affectionately climbed into his lap. In our conference the patient care staff revealed (to the horror of the clinical staff) that to pass time and especially to reward Ned when things had gone well, they took him for ice cream and candy.

One further aspect of Ned's treatment had included a variety of stimulant medications (for his possible attention deficit) and neuroleptics (for his impulsivity and aggression). The staff did not feel that the medication made a difference, but they persisted in giving it as the only workable option. This impasse in Ned's treatment reflects an increasingly common problem for mental health treatment teams—the failure of mental health technology (which is, after all, psychotherapy and psychopharmacology) to manage the exploding population of children with behavior problems who come into their programs. The children's problems are formulated in terms of their psychopathology or neurobiological instability, whereas the social aspects of their maladjustment are not as effectively assessed or understood.

In my consultation with the hospital staff it seemed most important to provide the range of experiences necessary for a young child. I also felt that Ned was dangerously out of control, and this was frightening to him as well as self-perpetuating. When I first met Ned, he was demonstrating his prowess at boxing with a dummy. He then led a merry chase through the hospital and ended up sharing the floor under a bed with me. It had apparently been a while since he had seen an adult under a bed! He was coy about coming to a meeting with the staff and his family and seemed prepared to dodge and play with the staff to avoid this. Ned's parents agreed that he should be at the meeting and were willing to bring him into the room. Ned protested and was dragged up the hall by one foot, the other aiming deadly kicks at his determined mother while the father walked along shouting commands to his wife and the boy. As Ned arrived in the room, I immobilized him on my lap and continued the conference. He barely protested, struggled hardly at all, and within ten minutes was able to sit in his own chair and participate in some family storytelling.

It would have been impossible to assess Ned's academic skills directly, but after the stories were told, there was time to draw illustrations of the stories. It was thus possible to see that Ned had very poor paper-and-pencil skills and could hardly spell or read. He was physically coordinated and almost nonverbal, although when he did talk, he was adequately articulate. It appeared that he found it much simpler to act out than to negotiate verbally. I recommended that the focus of Ned's treatment be on keeping Ned within the situations he needed to be a part of to develop more appropriate social behavior and to improve his academic skills. This would mean establishing the primacy of adult decisions for him and maintaining adult control, as I had done in immobilizing him in the meeting.

My physical actions with him had said, "You need to be in this meeting. It is about you. Your mother and father want you to be here. Thus, I am prepared to take whatever action is necessary to make sure you remain in this meeting." I proposed that this be a paradigm for community meetings and classroom experiences.

This approach would probably have led to progress within the hospital, but improving his behavior in the hospital would have done very little about the patterns established at home and in the neighborhood. It was essential to involve Ned's parents in the hospital plan. They lived at some distance from the hospital and complained that they couldn't be there much because of the distance and because they were so busy. The staff were very discouraged about their involvement and clearly frustrated with the entire situation, facing another long spate of abuse from Ned. The task, then, was to assist the staff in involving Ned's parents as essential allies and assistants. This required setting limits on the family's abandonment of Ned's problems to the hospital. To begin with, Ned's parents had to be given information about the problem and suggested solutions. First, they had to be disabused of any notions that the child had a mental illness. Instead, they needed to appreciate that he was seriously out of his own and adults' control. Furthermore, all of the adults could recognize that Ned was not an easy child to manage—definitely more difficult than most. And no one would be under the illusion that it would be easy to convince Ned that adults could and would take charge in order to guide his growing up.

Ned's story, like those of so many other children and adolescents described in this book, illustrates the confusion of the mental health system and some of the essentials of the solution. The confusion in the system results from discontinuity, lack of clarity about who should be served in which system, disagreements about what is effective treatment, and a technology derived from a combination of psychodynamic and biomedical principles that does little to address the social and educational needs of the children, not to mention hold them accountable for the consequences of their acts.

Medication

Medication in some form has always had a role in the care of the mentally ill. For years medication consisted of sedatives, tonics, and some herbal remedies, with specific properties not well documented but invested by tradition and lore. The renaissance in psychotropic medications began with the discovery of the calming and antipsychotic effects of chlorpromazine in the late 1950s. The discovery of antidepressants and of lithium's effectiveness in mania and the development of new and more specific psychotropic agents have been enthusiastically promoted, especially by psychiatrists, whose medical background has been vindicated by the effectiveness of these drugs. Furthermore, the effectiveness of drugs supports the medical hypotheses about mental disturbances. So widespread is the enthusiasm about medication for mental disturbances that caution is often thrown to the winds, as psychotropics are tried for a variety of disturbing conditions for which they are not specifically indicated—in case they might work. Most psychotropic medications have a broad spectrum of effects. For example, stimulants slow people down and increase intensity. This is true whether the people are hyperactive, have attention deficit, or neither. Most neuroleptics have sedative properties; they tend to slow down aggressive, violent, and impulsive people. Few believe that neuroleptics have any specific effects on areas of the brain that control aggression and impulsivity, but their use for aggressive children and adults is widespread. As mentioned earlier, antidepressant medication has become the standard of care for depression (although recent findings have emphasized that mild depressions may do best with reassurance, intermediate depressions may respond equally well to psychotherapy or medication, and psychotic depressions may respond only to more complex medical treatment). Medication is also rapidly becoming a part of the standard compendium of care for mentally disturbed children and adolescents, even though little is actually known about the long-term effects of such substances on developing brains. And often medication is used instead of psychotherapy. It is another dichotomy in the mental health system—medication versus psychotherapy.

Medication is not the panacea that one wishes it were, and some have argued cogently that neuroleptics can facilitate and maintain the chronicity of schizophrenias through interference with purposeful function; that tricyclics can increase the number of relapsing psychological episodes in patients with affective disorders; that use of a variety of medications for various forms of ennui enhances the narcissistic underlying character; and that use of a variety of sedatives and anxiolytics diminishes the ability to cope with problems of everyday life (Mandell 1986). The last two instances address what I would call "medicalization of normal problems of life," although it is obviously necessary to distinguish illness, which should be treated with whatever means available, from life stresses and strains.

Chapter 1 began with the presentation of Daniel, who had been designated as mentally disturbed, had been medicated with up to four different medications simultaneously, and had, upon his reaction to the withdrawal of these drugs, been given the diagnosis of a psychotic process. The use of medications with Daniel illustrates a role they have played in the mental health system for children. The assumption is that because the child has a mental disturbance, or because one is suspected, some medication must surely be appropriate. The medication rapidly becomes a substitute for other management and substitutes for accountabilities of all systems—the child, who is so ill that he must be medicated; the parents and school, who must wait for the medication to work before they can expect progress in the child; and the mental health system, which has become so compartmentalized that it has nothing else to offer!

Mental Health as a Service System

Aside from the problems with coordination and provision of adequate services, a major problem with mental health systems is that in many ways they exist as alternatives to services provided by other child-serving agencies. In contemplating what to do with a particular child (such as Tyrone, the hyperactive child described in chapter 11, or Karen, a child separated from her family because of the denied accusations of sexual abuse, as described in chapter 9), professionals act as if there is a real choice and there are criteria for deciding when a child should remain in a foster home or go to a hospital, whether a youngster should remain in a correctional facility or go to a residential treatment center, or when a child should be in a residential school rather than a program sponsored by mental health. The problem with these decisions when a child ends up in the mental health system is that this system is not prepared to supply the necessary education, residential security, and legal accountability. On the other hand, it is quite possible to supply mental health services in settings where children are receiving these fundamental services as long as treatment is integrated into the child's daily life, instead of taking over. Furthermore, once a child enters the mental health system, other systems seem to become less able and willing to cope with the child. In reviewing a series of children under twelve presenting for admission to a state hospital, my colleagues and I found that one of the most important factors in their admission was at least one previous admission! In many ways, when children are taken into mental health, it is like a narcotic. Service providers and families seem to keep coming back for more. It is very difficult to reestablish a sense of competence and potential success in the community after this. The stories of Ned, in this chapter, and of Johnny, in chapter 10, are excellent examples. Becoming involved with mental health is a self-perpetuating process.

Most who are familiar with the mental health systems for children and adolescents would agree that current service systems are disastrously uneven, disconnected, and largely inadequate in either availability or appropriateness for the populations most needing service. The most comprehensive explanation for this is that children, as a group, are not adequately and systematically planned for in this society, despite its alleged child-centeredness. As I noted in chapter 1, children cannot advocate for themselves. It is an irony, then, that much attention to the needs of children and adolescents has been stimulated by two areas of child and adolescent behavior that rivet attention. One is suicide, and between the mid-1960s and mid-1980s, the rate of completed suicides in adolescents has increased 300 percent. In many states, teen suicides have focused public attention and alarm so that legislators have recognized the problem in a variety of ways. The second is aggressive behavior, which also seems to be increasing. Statistics are not available to document this, because there are differences of opinion about whether such behavior is antisocial or emotionally disturbed and which are instances of which. In several states there have been class-action suits on behalf of emotionally disturbed aggressive youngsters that have resulted in the need to develop integrated systems to provide treatment for them. In North Carolina, for example, one such response to a lawsuit is called the "Willie M. Program." It has served as a model for an entire child and adolescent mental health system in the public sector.

A tragic twist in the public recognition of aggression as an expression of emotional disturbance in children is a lawsuit brought by parents of an adopted child against the adoption agency. At eleven this child was reportedly aggressive and out of control and therefore had been designated mentally ill. The adoption agency was sued because they failed to give the parents information about the mental health of the child's natural parents.

Making Decisions about Mental Health Care: A Proposal

Decisions about mental health care ostensibly have been made on the basis of the condition of the individual being presented for treatment. I have indicated that there are other factors, many of which usually go unacknowledged. It would be more effective to base decision making on factors about a variety of domains. One method involves assessment at three levels.

1. The condition of the child: This includes the current state of distress and interference with expected functioning, as well as the history of efforts to treat it.
2. The condition of the child's family and community. Are they able to care for the child? If the family is exhausted or depleted, what support group or other resources might they have that could assist them?
3. The suitability of the available treatment for the child and the family. Particularly with psychiatric hospitalization, this is rarely considered. Yet the indications for and uses of hospital treatment for children and adolescents might be greatly expanded if the type of treatment were a part of the admission criteria.

An example is Ruth, who refused to speak in school. This state of affairs had been tolerated through her first three years of elementary school, but when she reached fourth grade, the teacher said that it was just no longer possible for Ruth to make the progress she was expected to. Ruth, singly and with her family, had been in outpatient treatment off and on since she was in kindergarten. Still, she refused to speak outside the family. Ruth's condition was not life-threatening—she was not severely ill. But her condition did seriously threaten her development, and all outpatient efforts had failed. An assessment of the family led to the understanding that the family was a very closed unit, mistrusting and warding off outsiders. Yet the family did want Ruth to speak if this was required for her to succeed in school. Hospitalization of Ruth was proposed as a way of involving the family actively in a larger system (the hospital), in order to lower the boundaries of mistrust and suspicion. Ruth's mother was accorded collaborator status, and she was asked to come each day to assist with other children in Ruth's hospital school-room. As Ruth's mother talked with the other children and with the staff, the desired effect of her increased trust and affiliation with school authorities and mental health professionals was achieved. Gradually Ruth began to talk—first to her mother, in class, then to other children, and finally to her teacher.

One must conclude that the mental health system is still operating with serious limitations. These limits are posed by adherence to the appearance of distinct categories, the expansion of the range of problems for which the mental health system has responsibility, and the narrow range of available responses, a range that is progressively restricted by standard setting, accreditation, peer review, and utilization review, as well as legal actions. (The transformation of the mental health system when giant step 4 is taken is elaborated in chapter 13.) Clearly, the current system, both through its institutions and its methods of practice, does not operate as a system of systems coordinated for their mutual benefit.

The mental health system is evolving, both in response to developments in diagnosis, etiology, and treatments, and in response to pressures from other overburdened systems, but in its movement there is no overall vision or goal. What should a mental health system be? What, in fact, is mental health? I have offered a definition in presenting the fourth giant step: mental health is a state of systems. The mental health system cannot be effective without the corresponding effectiveness of other systems serving children, including their families, in the innermost domains, and the other child-serving agencies in those domains shared by the mental health system.

CHAPTER 9

Child Welfare: A Conundrum

While many families may communicate with mixed messages, the mixed message in large human service systems is unique; it centers on the opposing and dualistic mandates of such systems, involving care giving on the one hand and social control on the other. These mandates, which frequently confuse the clients of such systems, also often confuse the workers in their daily interactions with each other and with clients. In addition, what may be seen as care giving by the larger system may, in fact, be experienced as social control by the clients.

—EVAN IMBER-BLACK, *Families and Larger Systems,* 1988

Child welfare systems exist to provide shelter and protection for dependent and neglected children. Child welfare reflects a society's general attitude toward its children, and this attitude pervades all of the systems of care for children, even those children who are not dependent and neglected. Since the formation of organizations to protect children in the latter part of the nineteenth century, child welfare philosophies have been dominated by the belief that families were responsible for children's difficulties, so that if a child was not thriving, it was best to remove him from the family and raise him in another, healthier environment. The background of this attitude was undoubtedly rooted in at least two developments. The first was the emergence in the eighteenth century of the moral attitude toward children that regarded children as innocent and adults as corrupt (Ariès 1962). Children are always in danger of being corrupted by adults, according to these notions. A second, which may have grown out of the first, was the moral attitude that underlay the development of child labor laws and that directly challenged the then-prevailing practice of treating children as chattels to be used for whatever purposes the father wished. Both of these developments supported the notion that children should be removed. The practice of removing children was pursued with increasing zeal with the formation of the Society for Prevention of Cruelty to Children, the Children's Aid Society, and other agencies with similar objectives throughout the country.

Evolving Views on Children's Placement

A more recent conflicting point of view, however, is that the best environment for children is in their own families. This idea evolved from several different sources. First, placement of children out of the home has not effectively improved their condition. There is substantial evidence that even with placements intended to be temporary, children frequently don't return to their families; and when children remain out of their families, they usually reside in more than one foster home. Furthermore, many of the most severely emotionally disturbed children are those who have experienced multiple placements. Second, as the demand for foster care has increased recently, so have the problems. Good foster families are harder to come by, because there are fewer families who can afford to do foster care rather than have both parents work, and because there are more frequent accusations by children of abuse by foster parents which, when unfounded, diminish the rewards of fostering children. Third, there is now a substantial experience demonstrating that families can be helped to be effective supportive environments for their own children, and there is an increasingly sophisticated technology developing to assist families in doing this.

All of these factors may be secondary to a significant economic factor: it is cheaper to maintain children in their own families. It is important to consider the influence of economic motivation, especially when one recognizes that the child welfare system has been cutting back on residential beds (deinstitutionalizing) since the 1930s. Whether the philosophical attachment to family support, preservation, and permanency planning conveniently justifies the economic incentive or has evolved pari passu can't be determined, but it is ironic that the political embrace of the family comes at a time when many families appear to be less prepared to look after their children than, perhaps, in any other era in modern history (including the Depression). Specifically, there are more teenaged parents whose offspring are often produced after inadequate prenatal care; there are more families decimated by street drugs, particularly cocaine and crack; and there are more families in which children are born with serious vulnerabilities, including fetal alcohol syndrome, cocaine and crack addiction, and AIDS. It is also ironic that this embrace of the family is during an era of virtual panic about child sexual abuse and its inevitable damage.

Nevertheless, now, after a history of rescuing children from their families, child welfare systems received a federal mandate in the Adoption Assistance and Child Welfare Act of 1980, to turn to families as children's best hope for lasting relationships and a sense of identity and belonging in one's relationship system. This change has not been undertaken without ambivalence. In fact, child welfare systems all over the country represent the conflict and confusion about switching the paradigm or attitude from one that said, "Families are bad for children, and children should be removed from bad families," to one that says, "Families are the best chance children have." The latter view does not deny that some—even many—children suffer exploitation, abuse, and neglect from their families. It simply observes that most parents love their children, there is more to family violence than individual psychopathology, prosecution and punishment for abuse are solutions that perpetuate the problem, the alternatives are usually not more satisfactory, and there are layers of systems that must be evaluated and changed in order to ameliorate conditions in which children can be protected.

Thus, the child welfare climate since 1980 has been characterized by contradictory missions: one based on the notion that children should be saved from their families and another based on the experience that children do better with their families. This contradiction represents the crux of the revolution in child mental health. The conversion to the point of view that children belong in their families and that families can be assisted to maintain themselves is the change involved when the giant steps are taken by those called on to deal with children and families troubled by poverty, mental illness, substance abuse, illness, and death—families whose lives are so distracted that caring for children must come last rather than first. It is a shift that is advocated in the 1980 Child Welfare Act, which emphasizes efforts to keep children and families together, to restore children to their own families, and to have thoughtful and timely permanency planning based on the outcome of these efforts. It is a shift that is echoed in states that have passed family preservation legislation, requiring that aggressive services to support families be developed and made available to all eligible children. But it must be recognized that this is not just switching from one pole (families are bad) to another (families are now good). For the family advocacy movement in child welfare to successfully accomplish what the child removal movement did not, one cannot simply shift gears and "correct" the families. It is essential to assess the historical and current contexts of family abuse and neglect, perhaps to "correct" the contexts so that the family members have more energy to devote to the care of each other.

Mental Health Professionals' Role

For mental health professionals who work with children in the welfare system, the metaposition of consultant makes it possible to take the giant steps to review the interaction of the child welfare system with the complicated life of a child ward, his family, the workers, the staff at group homes or shelters, and foster families. The first giant step—recognizing that reality is how it is framed—must be taken at the outset to assess the troubled families of children who come into contact with the welfare system in a way that will enhance these families' chances of capably caring for their own children. This means moving beyond the conviction that there is a linear relationship between family hardship and childhood disorders to an appreciation of the many factors that contribute both to dysfunction and resilience. When the mental health professional becomes involved at later stages of the welfare process, more facets of experience have to be apprehended. For example, children in foster care are often referred because of problems of adjustment in the foster home. Frequently these problems are exacerbated around visits with their birth, or biological, parents. Foster parents and welfare workers may present the natural parents as inappropriate, inconsistent, and emotionally harmful to the child. They may ask that the professional recommend that parental rights be terminated and the child be placed permanently in the foster home, in the best interests of the child. It is particularly crucial in such cases to remember that the parents have a side and an investment in their child. They should be part of any evaluation of ultimate custody, and this evaluation is best done by the same professional who has evaluated the child and the foster family and who approaches the evaluation with multilateral partiality.

The second step—apprehending patterns relevant to the issues of concern—is necessary to comprehend the roles of all the systems in several involved domains of the children's experience. Most particularly, it is crucial to appreciate how these patterns involving abuse and neglect may be perpetuated by those who actually wish to help. In chapter 4 a pattern associated with domestic violence was outlined. A variation of this pattern of escalating attempts to gain control and establish status is frequently operating in the interactions of the welfare system. Thus, attempts to protect by removing a child also humiliate the child's parents. One response to the perceived intrusion is to attempt to control the child further with more harsh discipline. An extended consequence of such patterns, however, goes into the adulthood of children who have been wards of the welfare system. They carry with them patterns of abuse and violence, and a legacy of disrupted loyalties that probably will be perpetuated with their own children and in their adult interactions, as parents, with the welfare system.

The third step—assessing resources and building on competence—is the basis for successful intervention with both families and children in the welfare system. Thus, with such families one must acknowledge that the families not only harm their children sometimes but also contribute to the children's welfare, health, and resilience. By the same token, one must recognize that the welfare system both perpetuates dysfunction and ensures proper protection for children. Even given areas of competence, however, families sometimes may not be able to care for their own children, and they may make a competent decision to place a child, for her own welfare. But the competence of parents whose children are in placement needs to be highlighted so that positive aspects of their relationships with their children can be fostered and sustained. Salvador Minuchin and associates conduct family meetings with foster families and birth families to sustain the competent involvement of parents and to develop a collaborative working relationship between adults who are concerned for the children's welfare.

The fourth step, of course, is the goal—to help the system achieve a level of organization in which each individual's integrity and health are protected and enhanced by the system. Critical to families who encounter the child welfare system, the parents' integrity and health have to be as much a goal for the final system organization as the children's. But also critical to the welfare system are the workers' well-being and satisfaction and a structuring of the organizations that permits genuine welfare work rather than social intrusion.

In this chapter I present several families involved with the welfare system to illustrate how the child focus of the system often places both child and family in jeopardy. I describe ways of evaluating the situation that involve the helpers, as well as the child and family, and that lead to a different (and, ideally, more beneficial) course of action. Finally, I discuss family preservation, both as an alternative to removing children from their families and as a reflection of a systemic response to the welfare conundrum.

The Robertsons: An Example of Fragmenting Escalation

The Robertsons are a middle-class black family who had moved into a blue-collar white neighborhood. Mr. Robertson works as a stevedore; Mrs. Robertson is a teacher. They have two children, a girl, Karen, and a boy, Keith, three years younger. Karen was born with a benign tumor on her bottom. This was removed in the neonatal period, but careful follow-up required semiannual visits to the medical center, where she was extensively examined, including a digital probe into the vagina and rectum to determine that there was no tumor impinging. Karen's parents reported that they were reluctant to spank her for fear that they would cause recurrence of the tumor, so Karen developed with little discipline. When she was five an incident happened that her mother interpreted, first, as possible sexual abuse by the father. The mother reported the incident to the police. Instantly the mother and children were whisked away to a shelter, and when the mother recanted her accusation, the children were taken away from her and placed in a foster home.

The father persistently denied that he had touched his daughter, and the mother, after her first accusation (based on a suggestion from Karen that she and Daddy had a secret), also staunchly denied that this could have happened. Both parents then worked to get their children back. The child protective system in this area had acted swiftly and with great moral outrage, however. There had been extensive questioning of both mother and daughter immediately after the report, with no clear statement by the child. The mother had not actually witnessed the incident. The father was not questioned at this point. This early interview was followed by an interview by a policewoman, using anatomically correct dolls. Some months later came an interview with a child sex abuse expert, also using the dolls. In none of these instances did the child unequivocally indicate that her father had sexually abused her. She did, however, show an unusual attention to her own perineal area and to that of the dolls, and despite her medical history focusing on this area, this was taken as evidence of her sexual abuse.

What ensued was a preoccupation with proving that Karen had been sexually abused and basing any future family reunification on the father's admission of guilt. To be on the safe side, two-year-old Keith was also placed out of the home, although no accusations of any abuse whatsoever had been made about him. Mr. and Mrs. Robertson sought legal counsel, but because of their lack of sophistication and financial resources, they did not initially get good representation. In their defense of themselves they were also regarded as confusing (as Mrs. Robertson seemed to change her story) and uncooperative (as they refused to admit that the father had abused Karen). Nevertheless, during the first three years after the children were placed, the parents faithfully made their visits and telephone calls and tried to keep up with the needs of their children. They also attended required therapy, which included marital counseling, individual treatment for Mrs. Robertson, and an offenders' group for Mr. Robertson. According to one marital counselor, the couple worked effectively on issues that probably led to the accusations in the first place—Mr. Robertson's slipping out to drink a beer when their religious commitments forbade it and their difficulties managing conflict, which led him to become physically threatening and her to become passive-aggressive. The couple reported more marital satisfaction, and they discontinued treatment on the grounds that they did not need it. Mr. Robertson became disgusted by the offenders' group, where the pressure to confess his crime was as strong as the pressure on an alcoholic in Alcoholics Anonymous. He reported that he clearly didn't belong there, and finally quit. These terminations were regarded as evidence of lack of cooperation by the state's attorney and the child welfare service.

During this period, life was extremely difficult for Karen. She had been an undisciplined child at home. Her behavior in a foster home was regarded as the outcome of her sexual traumatization, and she was sent to a residential treatment center. Karen's therapy had her focus on anger at her father "for what he did to her," and she was encouraged to dictate letters to him expressing her feelings. Since Karen's trauma was regarded as the primary factor in her behavior, it was considered most urgent to deal with this. The parents were blamed, further, for not acknowledging the abuse, making the child out to be a liar, and suspending the resolution of the situation. Karen's educational development was relatively neglected, so that at eight years old, she was just entering second grade with very early primer skills.

Keith remained with the initial foster family, but he lost Karen when she was sent to residential treatment and subsequently placed with a different foster family. He was much beloved by the family, who expressed their interest in adopting him. But he, too, was constantly scrutinized. Was he showing effects of early abuse? Or were the signs of hyperactivity due to anxiety about the lack of resolution about where he belonged and who was his real family? Or did Keith have an attention deficit disorder? Before he was five, he was taken to be evaluated for a trial of Ritalin.

Intervention with the Deadlocked System

At the end of three years very little had been accomplished despite hours of treatment, drawers full of court records, several different attorneys representing the parents, and Karen's three different placements. Karen's story was still ambiguous, although her vocabulary had improved; the parents still maintained their innocence. The welfare department proposed to break the deadlock by petitioning for termination of parental rights. Their rationale was that these children's best chance for the future was permanent placement in families that they could call their own. They needed a resolution to the question of where they belonged. Karen needed a consistent response to her situation, not a disqualification by her parents, countered by unconditional acceptance by her therapists and workers. The parents were outraged by the suggestion that they should terminate parental rights: "These are our children." They engaged yet another attorney, this time from a large firm. This attorney contacted another expert to evaluate the situation to assist with the next step.

I was the expert, and after hearing the story, I hypothesized that the problems currently plaguing the systems involved many more people and issues than a troubled little girl and an adamant father. I proposed that I could offer nothing to the parents' case without the opportunity to work with and for the entire deadlocked system. This meant that my role should be supported by all the parties. The state's attorney and welfare workers expressed little optimism that anything could change, but they could think of no other way to proceed and reluctantly agreed. A meeting was set up to include as many of the involved parties as could attend. In attendance were workers for both children, the children's lawyer, the parents' lawyer, the parents' lay advocate, both parents, both children, and myself. Others, including the state's attorney and the foster parents, as well as some of the Robertsons' associates from the church, had been invited but did not attend.

The Search for Solutions

The evaluation lasted three hours. The first hour was spent with the entire group in a large conference room at the district child welfare office. The family and I sat around a large table, and the family was asked to draw a picture together. The rest of the attendees, free to interact and ask questions, sat nearby and watched. There was no question that even after nearly four years of separation the Robertsons were a family. The children were glad to see their parents and were excited by the new situation. Keith set to the assigned task of drawing the picture, planting himself in his father's lap and working with him. Karen was more reserved and stood, somewhat hesitantly, near her mother (which also placed her between her mother and her welfare worker). She tentatively began to draw in the upper left-hand corner of the piece of paper. She drew a girl in trouble, who was then saved by the mother. Mrs. Robertson had the most difficulty joining in the task. She appeared most aware of being evaluated and was least spontaneous in her interactions with the children. But once Karen handed her this bit of relationship material, she began to draw parts of the picture, connecting to her daughter.

The picture was of the family's house. The father and Keith had put in the backyard swing set, sandbox, and patio equipped with barbecue and furniture. Karen and her mother were drawing the house. The question came up about whether Karen wanted to be there, what she liked to do there, and whether she had any friends there. Karen was mute but wrote yes or no in response to the questions. It was at this point that I noticed Karen was getting different signals from her mother and her welfare worker, sitting on different sides of her. When asked a question about wanting to be with her family, Karen would spontaneously respond positively, then she would look at her worker and write the reverse. Her net response was zero, which is all I could conclude from the testimony about her alleged sexual abuse, as well.

I spent forty minutes of the second hour with Karen alone. In this period she continued her balancing, or canceling, behavior, drawing a picture of the Robertson home with the mother standing in the window watching Keith play ball and "the girl" crying "because her dog is dead, and her cat is on the roof, and it will die, too, if someone doesn't do something." As she explained this, she drew a cat precariously balanced on a sharply peaked roof. Karen's picture of her foster family represented no conflict but also no nurturance, no generation. It was just three girls together— herself, her teenaged foster sister, and her foster mother. During the conversation in this session, she alluded to "what he did with his hands," but she professed not to know what that was and indicated that I should fill in the blanks of her story.

I spent another forty minutes with the whole family, without attorneys and workers. Their task was to plan what they wanted to do next. I observed that they had not lived together for nearly four years and there were many things that would have to be worked out between them before they would feel comfortable together as a family. So the question was what would they propose to do to move securely in that direction. Mr. Robertson proposed that they should have more frequent and longer visits together. He complained that they never had a real opportunity to deal with "the bad" as well as "the good," and he expressed the concern that he could not handle his children. Mrs. Robertson added that she thought the children should visit at home and overnight. Keith was enthusiastic about this. Karen, however, was at first enthusiastic but became very doubtful when the attorneys and workers were invited back in during the last forty minutes, and she caught the eye of her worker. In this last forty minutes the family haltingly presented their proposal. This was difficult both because they were not very articulate and because they were so mistrustful. This latter problem became more pronounced when the children's attorney and the welfare workers said they would have to think about the proposal and had doubts because it was prolonging a situation where the children were kept in limbo about their ultimate futures. The meeting ended with the agreement to have a conference call between the parties after all had had a chance to review my report and recommendations.

I don't know how anyone will ever know for sure whether Mr. Robertson sexually abused Karen. I doubt if Karen actually knows, now that she has had so many interviews and so many assumptions have been made. It was also apparent that Karen had two distinct realities, with little logical connection between. As experienced in the session, this dissociation had a systemic influence—the inputs of mother and worker—but it was internalized enough to be maintained during Karen's private interview with me. Somehow, establishing whether or not Karen was fondled by her father and requiring confessions or admissions had to be transcended so that these parents and children could get on with the business of being a family. The parents were unequivocally in favor of that agenda; Keith was pretty enthusiastic, although he did express concern about leaving his foster mother; and Karen was interested, but ambivalent. My recommendation was that the family's proposal of more frequent, longer, and finally closer-to-home visits be adopted along with a whole family "therapy" designed to assist with identifying the rough spots and helping them all to evaluate how and even if they should work on smoothing things to the point that they could function as a family. The struggle between the parties shifted to an obvious power struggle about who would be acceptable as a family therapist, and only after a year was a family therapist appointed so the work could begin.

This is an unfortunate example where the child welfare agency's zealous intervention to protect children had its own dire consequences. Not only was the family sundered for more than five years, but a little girl underwent a process as close to brainwashing as might happen in a well-intentioned set of circumstances. In this situation there were no innocent parties and everyone was a victim. Specifically, the parents were to blame for involving their children in their conflicts in such a way that the complaint was initiated; later they were to blame for their secrecy and oppositional attitude toward the child welfare agency. The child welfare staff and their attorneys were to blame for making conclusions on minimal evidence gained in questionable circumstances. Specifically, they never interviewed the family together. In preparing their case, they did not interview or evaluate the father; they did not get his side of the story at all. Finally, the person who may have been most damaged by this series of events, Karen, must also bear some responsibility, for she allowed the ambiguity to persist. She never has made a clear statement.

As it is possible to describe responsibility, it is also possible to justify the actions of the various parties. One is particularly prone to do this for the child. But I believe that unless the role of the child in the perpetuation of this nightmare is not acknowledged, she will not be able to be accepted back into her family as a child, and her history in foster care suggests that she cannot be readily managed, much less nurtured, by others. Acknowledging the participants' responsibility for the situation also raises the question of trust. It appeared to me that the greatest calamity had been the destruction of trust in this family relationship. I proposed that this issue be addressed head on by pointing out that they had no basis for trusting one another. This was the work to be done in reconstructing the family.

The Bakers: Early Intervention

In contrast to the Robertsons, the Bakers were evaluated as a whole family before there was a lengthy separation, so that the repair to the family could focus primarily on the internal family issues. The Baker family consists of two parents and four children, all girls. They came to the attention of the welfare system shortly after the two youngest girls (twins) were born when their older sisters were three and eighteen months. The pediatrician reported that the children were unkempt, poorly nourished, and dirty; that the three-year-old still wore diapers; and that the mother appeared oblivious to their needs. The father, who was black, was a community organizer in a nearby city. He was busy with his work and, according to his wife, who was white, he seemed to limit his family life to his critical comments about her care of the home and the children.

Two services were provided to the family. The first was to arrange for marital counseling for the parents; the second was to provide homemakers to assist the mother. Marital counseling uncovered the mother's frustrated need for relief from domestic drudgery and addressed it by having the couple arrange for the father to stay home with his children two nights a week while his wife went out "to socialize." The mother saw the home-maker service as patronizing and intrusive. She felt that they came to instruct, not to relieve, so she developed all kinds of means to avoid them, including taking the children out when they were expected or absolutely ignoring them when they were there. Eventually Mrs. Baker convinced the homemakers that she was managing the situation, and they stopped the service. Actually, Mrs. Baker was not a sociable person, and this natural tendency to keep to herself was reinforced by the family's peripheral position in the community. She preferred reading to almost any other activity, including interacting with her children. On her nights out, she took courses, planning to matriculate for a bachelor's degree.

When the twins were four, Mrs. Baker intimated to her counselor that she thought her husband was fondling them. The system moved swiftly. Within hours the twins were removed from the home; a day later the two older girls were taken, too. Physical exam of each twin revealed a dilated vaginal introitus, suggesting frequent and regular sexual fondling. Physical exam of the two older girls revealed nothing, and they remained silent about whether their father had fondled them. Criminal charges originally made against Mr. Baker were dropped because of the stress on young children needing to testify in court. Mrs. Baker was advised to leave her husband lest she be charged as an accessory, thus jeopardizing her chances for keeping her children. She did all of this, but the children remained in custody for more than two months. At first all four girls were placed in the same foster home, but the twins' behavior was so "disturbed" that they were moved to a special foster home. The parents were allowed to visit with their children separately every two weeks. Visits took place at the local office of the child welfare agency, and it was reported that each parent brought many presents for the children in what was interpreted as an attempt to woo the children and prevent them from revealing any family secrets.

Up to this point the welfare department had acted appropriately for an agency designed to protect children. Early the agency had provided ser-vices to help the family reorganize itself to provide more adult satisfaction so that they would have more resources to care for their children. The combination of marital counseling and homemaker services was well con-ceived, from this point of view. But these interventions did not take into consideration the social isolation of this racially mixed family living in predominantly white suburbs. In this family social isolation was associated with an intense sense of privacy and the invasion of the homemakers. Mrs. Baker did not need a companion and felt the visits as intrusive. Furthermore, the marital counseling offering a standard intervention of involving the husband more to relieve the wife did not address the particular dynamics of this couple: the unavailable wife in a family whose social setting isolated all of the family members from their peers. The plan also did not take into consideration the parents' own family histories. Mrs. Baker's mother had had multiple men in her life who had abused her and possibly the children. She had not experienced family life as warm and nurturing or men as intellectual companions and problem-solving partners. Mr. Baker's history was more vaguely remembered. He was the son of a fundamentalist preacher who raised his children with extreme discipline, commanding strict loyalty verging on servitude within the family. In retrospect, the father's sexual involvement with his daughters might have been predicted.

The Evaluative Process

The Bakers were evaluated after the children had been in placement for a month. This evaluation was delayed for a variety of legal reasons. The evaluation took place at the child welfare office where the parent visits had been. All four children and both parents attended, and the six were seen together for about an hour before the therapist broke the group down to three subsystems: the sibling group and each parent. As a whole group they were impressively noisy and enthusiastic about being together after a hiatus. Both parents had brought lavish toys, and the little girls were quite breathless with their prizes. The two older girls were sober and somewhat parental toward the twins. The twins climbed all over their father, who clearly appeared to be the warmer and more nurturing parent. Even in the short time of the visit, the mother was excluded and excluded herself from the high-affect interaction, offering a more detached, intellectualized point of view, and, finally, being ignored by her children.

During the interview with the sibling group the twins drew pictures; their sisters preferred not to. The twins chatted about Daddy touching them in "bad places" and about the foster homes. One twin drew a picture of a dragon having a baby through the abdomen, clearly demonstrating her failure to connect sexual fondling with reproduction. The other drew a girl and told a story about how the girl was attacked by a stranger, because she was a stranger. The attacker killed the girl, but she got up and killed the attacker, and was okay after that. This story appeared to illustrate the dangers experienced by this child at the hands of strangers (the foster families and workers as well as the evaluator).

Further psychological evaluation of the parents revealed an amorphous identity and sense of maturity on the father's part. He also showed signs of dissociation and amnesia, which corresponded to his own bewilderment about the sexual abuse. He stated, "I must have done it, but I don't remember having done it." He wondered, too, about the possibility that he had been molested by his own father. The mother showed the already observed intellectual defenses and interpersonal isolation. Family drawings by each of the parents illustrated what had been observed by the evaluator—the affective warmth of the father and the removal of the mother.

There was little doubt about how poorly structured the family was to care for four little girls. The father was loving and involved with his children, but he had stepped over a generational boundary in his sexualization of their relationship. And, in his claim of no memory for the interactions, he offered little reassurance that he would or could stop this kind of behavior of his own accord. The mother was distant, intellectual, and uninvolved. She loved her children but had little idea how to interact with them and was quickly turned off by the twins' excitement and physical warmth. The two older girls were sober and parental, thus putting aside their own childhoods. The twins were the focal point, scrutinized by experts for signs of trauma and by their sisters and parents for signs of betrayal.

What should be done with this family? Nothing at all could be done until some assessment was made of the family's strengths. Many of these have been described in the assessment, but they have been presented as deficits. The father's warmth and nurturing had succeeded in sustaining strong attachments and positive feelings among his children, who were staunchly loyal. The mother's intelligence had ultimately led to the revelation of incest and could be utilized in developing solutions for the future of the family. The older girls' sense of proportion and their substituting for parents for the twins when they were in foster care perpetuated coherence in the relationship system. Finally, the twins' basic positive affect and joyous affection for their family offered much hope for the future of the family.

The evaluator felt that the family should be viewed as the primary resource for the children. They were referred to a distinguished family therapist, whom they saw weekly over a period spanning more than a year. Sometimes the parents were seen alone; at other times the children were included. The children moved in with the mother to a residential home for battered women and children (the only kind of residence available for them at that time). In the home, work with other women and their children provided a beginning access for Mrs. Baker to a peer group as well as a support group in developing some of the interactional skills she so desperately needed with her own children. Visits with the father were confined to the therapist's office at first. It seemed likely that he would always need supervision and monitoring, although the family group did want to be reunited. One day, more than a year after the initial reports and separation, the evaluator happened to be walking by the therapist's office when the twins came tumbling out. "Oh, hi! Remember me? I met you and your family down at the child welfare office?" "Oh, yes!" replied the irrepressible duo. "Guess what? We might be able to go home as a family, if Daddy promises to stop touching us in bad places!"

It is likely that the Baker family will be able to live together once again as a family. In this family, as with the Robertsons, trust cannot be assumed and the family members will have to establish a new basis and new limits for trusting each other. Most important, Mrs. Baker will need to observe her daughters more closely and supervise her husband's contacts with them. She will have to learn a more protective attitude toward them. To prepare Mrs. Baker for this role, she will have to review and reevaluate the relational experiences that led her to withdraw, as she also experiences, in the present, the rewards of involvement with her children. It is certain, though, that the healthiest outcome for this family will be the triumph over their own intrafamilial disaster to resume control over themselves using social agents as assistants, not as police.

Assessing Troubled Families' Competence: The Family Life Interview

My experience with the Bakers encouraged me to advocate that at the first contact with child welfare a full family resource interview be conducted. Called a "family life interview," this protocol is a semistructured interview designed to involve the family system in its own decision-making process. The success of the interview depends on three factors: who is assembled for the interview; the focus of the interview to elicit the family's perception of itself and its options; and the inclusion of key family members in the decisions that must be made. A careful inventory of family contacts must be made in order to ascertain who might be helpful in such an interview. When there are parents or adult caretakers involved, they should be asked who should be included in the interview and assisted in their thinking by running through a list of potential relationships. Also, suggestive inquiries should be made about including extended family, siblings, "foster" parents, helpful neighbors, workers from involved agencies, members of the church, and so on. These individuals come not just to be advocates for the family but to represent their resource system and assist them in evaluating their current needs.

The meeting should be held at a time and place that can include as many of these individuals as possible within the time frame demanded by the situation. The content of the interview includes several key areas.

1. A review of the situation that is demanding this attention (e.g., baby Jane's failure to thrive; Susie's complaints that her mother beats her; the school's discovery of bruises all over Albert's arms and legs; the irritation and discharge in Margie's vagina, which are probably signs of sexual abuse) and the goal of the meeting, which is to agree on a course of action that will protect the children at this moment.

2. A review of the family situation—how they view themselves (e.g., who they are, who is in the family, what their strengths and weaknesses are), what vision they have for themselves (what kind of family they want to be, how they see things being better for them in the future), and what steps and assistance they feel they may need to move in that direction.

3. A spelling out of the steps, with the agency offering its resources (e.g., family preservation services, group home or foster placement) and the family reviewing theirs (e.g., Does the child need to be placed outside of the family? Can someone come in to supervise? Can the child go with a relative and still have access to the parents?). Immediate steps to protect the children must be taken, with a clear articulation of the participation and obligations of the various parties. What ongoing involvement will each parent have with his or her child in a foster home? What relationship would be developed between the foster parents and the natural parents and with what purpose in mind? What responsibilities would the welfare agency have to facilitate these contacts? Furthermore, what needs of the children should be addressed by the agency and foster home; and what do the parents need to do to make their home a safer and more nurturing environment for their children (e.g., entering a substance abuse program, entering treatment, getting finances and housing straightened out)?

4. A schedule for accomplishment of various goals needs to be set as well for review of progress and making of necessary adjustments.

This systematizes the approaches improvised in the assessments of the Robertsons, Bakers, and others who have been involved in the complex interaction with an agency dedicated to protecting children when they, as a family, have faltered in this function.

Family Preservation

Family preservation is the name given to a variety of programs designed to help families of children who are at risk of being removed from the family stay together in such a way that the children are adequately protected and cared for. These services are primarily offered out of the welfare system, but they have also been tested with families of children who are in danger of hospitalization. The earliest clearly articulated model of family preservation was that of the Homebuilders group in Washington (Kinney and Haapala 1978). This model involved one worker with a caseload of two families, available to these families over a twenty-four-hour, seven-day-a-week period lasting no more than six weeks. Early in the work with a particular family, visits would typically be long and intensive and would involve practical things like working out housing, sleeping arrangements, food supplies, heat, housecleaning, and so on. Emotional problems were approached using an individual cognitive-behavioral model, a modification of parent education. Outcome reports of family preservation programs have demonstrated that 68 percent to 80 percent of families evaluated to be at high risk for having children removed were able to stay together safely even up to a year after these services had been rendered (Knitzer and Cole 1989a, 1989b). Furthermore, they claimed that disturbing psychological processes had been effectively dealt with within the six-week period, so that follow-up counseling as a part of a continuing treatment plan was not necessary. It can be argued that such a recommendation might be counterproductive, because it would encourage dependency in a family who had just been helped to take charge. Other models have variations of the number of workers, the number of families in a caseload, and the length of time (ranging from six weeks to three months). Several models have employed a family systems theoretical base rather than the cognitive-behavioral one for coping with interpersonal and emotional problems within the family.

This exciting movement is designed for family support, but there are a number of impediments to its successful implementation. The most important impediment is the attitude about families discussed at the beginning of this chapter, which has prevailed in child welfare and which most of the critical public still holds—the view that families can be harmful and exploitative of their children; that this behavior is criminal; that children should be removed from such parents to a more appropriate relational environment; and that the parents should be punished. Illinois was the first state to pass family preservation legislation that requires such services to be available for all eligible families by the end of 1990. What this means is an enormous amount of work, for in addition to retraining agencies and workers to provide different kinds of services, workers also need to make a major shift in their attitude about children and families. This latter effort does not come easily, as the next example illustrates, because the way in which an agency is involved may exacerbate the family's difficulties.

Intervention with the Murphy Family

Ronnie, a ten-year-old middle child and only boy of his young mother (aged twenty-five), was referred to a child psychiatry clinic by his children-and-family service worker because he was depressed and angry. Basically, Ronnie was contrary and irritable, refusing to work on academic tasks and constantly getting into fights with his classmates. The worker presented the family situation as barely tolerable. Because Ronnie's mother wanted to keep her children, even after she had been reported for neglect (leaving them at home unattended for several hours at a time), the agency had instituted a form of family preservation that involved intensive supervision of Ms. Murphy. The worker reported that Ms. Murphy often did leave the children unattended, seemed to be irritable with them, had poor parenting skills, and probably wanted to keep them only because of the increased size of her welfare check. Ronnie's school problems were seen as the direct consequence of Ms. Murphy's indifferent parenting; he was a neglected, unloved child.

The therapist was surprised to find that Ronnie (whose mother brought him for his appointments) was a shy, but polite and responsive, child. Far from the usual shoulder-shrugging, monosyllabic ten-year-old boy, he gave full answers to the therapist's questions, even though he volunteered very little spontaneously. The therapist wondered, If Ronnie's mother is such a poor parent, how has he learned to be so polite and responsive? The therapist began to take the first giant step, playing with the question, If you were ten, how would you feel if someone (such as the social worker) thought so badly of your mother and subjected her and you to constant supervision accompanied by disparaging remarks and questions? Could this situation, alone, explain Ronnie's preoccupation, sadness, and inability to attend to academic and social issues? The therapist and supervisor believed that it could and embarked on a course that began with the observation of Ronnie's reserved responsiveness. We spoke to Ms. Murphy and the worker together, including Ronnie in the meeting, as well. We complimented Ms. Murphy on her fine boy, noting how polite he was and how loyal he seemed to be to her. We went on to observe that he seemed to be very concerned about her and the family, suggesting that Ronnie needed to feel that she and the family were okay so that he could concentrate on the tasks of a ten-year-old.

This was the entree for Ms. Murphy to talk about her difficulties getting a job, caring for three children, and trying to have some kind of social life of her own. Having had her first child at fifteen, she had not been able to finish high school. Her mother was an alcoholic; she hadn't seen her father since she was six years old. Ms. Murphy had left the children alone, both when she was working during the day and when she was dating. She maintained that they were good children; she had left strict instructions about what they were to do. They were not to go out of the apartment or let anyone in, and they had not disobeyed her. Ms. Murphy showed far greater strength and resourcefulness than had been reported. Indeed, many of the specific allegations of neglect appeared to be different when Ms. Murphy was viewed as a concerned mother struggling in isolation and poverty to make something for herself and her children. Furthermore, Ronnie's depression and acting out, rather than seeming to be an expression of neglect, were far more understandable as an outcome of his loyalty to a struggling mother, who was now under criticism from an agency in which there were adults visiting all the time, one of whom was assigned to help him.

We in the mental health profession saw our task at this point as having several facets. The first took form when we began to hear Ms. Murphy's side of the story (the beginning of multilateral partiality). This initiated both the Murphy family's feeling of competence and a change in the social service worker's view. Out of this initial step we had to work with the system so that the family continued to take steps in its own behalf but was able to use the services offered by welfare for assistance rather than see them as a critical imposition. Could child welfare assist Ms. Murphy in finding safe and reliable child care while she looked for a job? Yes, indeed they could. Could the agency assist Ms. Murphy in getting transportation to Ronnie's school to meet with his teachers and coordinate academic work assignments with home expectations? Could the agency help find some resources to aid Ronnie when his mother's own meager education left her feeling she could not help? In these ways the agency began to assist the Murphy family. The worker was gratified weekly at the strides made both by Ronnie (who, it turned out, had some special learning problems) and Ms. Murphy (who chose to work for her general equivalency diploma before seeking a job again).

In this case the efforts to "preserve" the Murphys had aggravated the beleaguered family, and Ronnie was the one whose signals got others' attention. The mental health professionals did not limit themselves simply to an evaluation of Ronnie or to an uncritical acceptance of Ms. Murphy's inadequacy as a parent. Instead, through taking the giant steps, they evaluated the integration of several elements of the system, which led to a more complimentary view of each element's efforts to manage. The welfare worker was not to blame for the critical position she took toward Ms. Murphy. She was acting according to a time-honored view. Family preservation had been turned into a form of holding the family hostage, as the welfare workers and supervisors still believed that this mother, if not carefully watched, was dangerous to her children. It also appeared likely that she would fail at whatever measures of her competence were to be used by the welfare system, because they did not recognize her preexisting competent efforts to hold her family together and improve their life-styles.

* * *

A pitfall of the family preservation movement is similar to one attached to the reunification movement: so much stock is put in families' natural benefits for their children that children are, indeed, inadequately protected. This happens either out of zealous embrace of the family as savior for all children or out of a hidden desire to prove that the family preservation movement is actually ineffective or bad for children.

I have proposed in this chapter that the solution to the conundrum of the welfare system is to save the children from their faltering families by helping families pull themselves together. But this does not mean simply switching from a position that families harm children to a position that families are ultimately good for their children. It means carefully and deliberately taking the giant steps that require an ear for both points of view, assessing patterns in which difficulties seem to occur (and in this case, these patterns must include the roles of welfare workers and agency policies), recognizing competence in all aspects of the system, and, of course, integrating a program in which all are coordinated in a mutually beneficial fashion.

CHAPTER 10

Mental Health and Legal Systems: A Clash of Paradigms

There are today certain countries who pride themselves on the enactment of special laws concerning juvenile delinquents. Their legislation makes due allowance for the immaturity of childhood and youth and also takes into account the common experience that penalties do not always achieve the hoped-for results, and that other means of training are required to complement the function of punishment. . . . We would be happy if legislation concerning juvenile delinquency freed itself from the exclusive wish to protect society against the youthful lawbreaker. If the laws would take into account the hard fact that both waywardness and criminality originate in psychic illness, that it is in our power today to heal the illness, further therapeutic methods could and should be found. In other words: we should not "reform," but bring remedy.

— AUGUST AICHORN, "The Juvenile Court," [1934] 1964

While the art of interpreting the law is what distinguishes judges, and the art of presenting a case is the work of attorneys, the legal system is built on a fundamental binary process of right and wrong: if it is not one, then it is the other. This necessary outcome of legal processes is in contrast to the approach of seeking solutions in patterns and relationships, and pursuing courses of action that are a part of the process, not a part of the outcome. Thus, when the systems of childhood involve the courts, there is a clash of paradigms that raises a number of problems. The first problem is the ambivalence with which the justice system applies its process to juveniles. In recognizing that the legal system should somehow be taking emotional circumstances into account, the system often fails in its basic function—to bring individuals to account to the laws of the civilization in which we live. This is particularly likely to happen with children and adolescents, and it is the ambiguous state out of which child mental health began in the early 1900s. The second problem relates to the way families are involved in court proceedings involving their children. Child psychiatrist Paul Mansheim (1989) has termed it "the family turned against itself." In the peculiar domain of overlap of family system and legal system, the family is often put on the defensive in such a way that they appear to be sacrificing certain members in order to save the family. This is true in cases of custody conflicts between parents, lawsuits on behalf of children, and situations when children are accused of illegal acts. Finally, special instances of the second problem are when there are accusations of child abuse or incest, when some family members are accused of harming others, and where the process of resolution is to dismantle the family or to pit subsystem against subsystem in an effort to do justice on behalf of one side versus the other. In this last instance, as discussed in chapter 9, establishing who is right will always be a compromise of family relationships. Either the charges are dropped because there are insufficient grounds (the parents are deemed right); the children change their stories, refusing to testify (the parents are deemed right); or it is found that abuse has taken place (the parents are deemed wrong, and the family is dismantled, its affectional bonds ignored and attenuated in the pursuit of justice—society's protection of its members).

Yet it is important for the legal system to function with the binary system of outcome. This discussion is not to level an attack on this basic process. In fact, in considering the problem of accountability, my argument is that the process is often diverted from the establishment of guilt or innocence by the exploration of excuses for a youngster, based either on his youth or his mental distress. It does seem, though, in consideration of the family as the child's primary relationship system, that many relationship issues do not belong in a system that has such cut-and-dried goals. The question in a custody case, for example, of Who is the best parent? does not contribute to a child's secure sense of attachment and identity. A better question would be, Given that these parents have irreconcilable differences and cannot live together, what is the best arrangement for them to jointly parent this child? Although the courts are raising these questions more often, when they do, they must refer out of the court system into the system of mediation. Many of these family issues just do not belong in court.

A basic recognition on the part of the judiciary that children, while parts of families, also have independent accountabilities will increase the likelihood of partnerships between arms of the court, such as probation officers and therapists with families, because blaming the family becomes part of a pattern in which problems persist. A family who is blamed tends to be ashamed and then may either take it out on the child or, quite the opposite, condone the child's behavior, closing ranks with the child against the shaming legal system. Next to the family, the legal system is the essential system of accountabilities for one's behavior in a given society. But people too often forget that the family does come first in socialization, or the establishment and maintenance of relational accountability. Thus, it is always important, first, to assist the family in this function rather than to undermine it. If there is no relational accountability, there will be no basis for social accountability, which is, after all, what legal accountability is all about.

This chapter examines three kinds of circumstances in which children and their families usually come in contact with the legal system: juvenile delinquency, abuse and family violence, and child custody. To apply the giant steps that must be taken so that the legal system is more constructively involved with children and their families, the relationship aspects in each instance of these types of circumstance are examined. First, it is necessary to recognize and work with different definitions of reality in order to accomplish a fair balance of the involved parties' needs. This means not endorsing the legal judgment that there is a correct solution to be found about relationships. But the legal sanctions that should be taken to uphold the law and civilized behavior under the law should be endorsed. Second, how involved systems and events form meaningful patterns, such as the pattern of perpetuating parent–child conflict through shame and blame, must be examined. Third, essential to every circumstance of children involved with the legal system is the assessment of competence. This is particularly important with youngsters who have delinquent and antisocial behavior, because the emphasis on these areas of their incompetence tends to magnify them so that the child identifies herself with her delinquency, and not with her kindness or loyalty, or with specific skills she may have or could develop. Finally, the integral belief in mental health as a condition of the involved systems working for the mutual benefit of their members must be maintained.

Juvenile Delinquency and Antisocial Behavior

The crisis with mental health in the juvenile justice system does not date simply from the closing of training schools in some states during the 1970s. Nor does it relate simply to the elimination of status offenses from the list of behaviors that can be found delinquent and that youngsters must be held accountable for under the law. Historically, the crisis goes back to the beginnings of the child mental health movement, when it was first carved out of juvenile justice. Prior to the designation of a separate discipline for examining and treating the emotional problems of children who committed antisocial acts, their treatment was an integral part of the legal response. Youths were sent to training schools, instead of prison, where the cultures varied according to the prevailing philosophy—from reform in the form of discipline, to education, in the form of involving the youngster in a productive activity in which he could feel competent and envision himself as a productive member of society. This latter was the vision of educator August Aichorn ([1923] 1964, [1925] 1935). As Aichorn became more familiar with psychoanalysis, he employed a psychodynamic method in uncovering conflicts that presumably lay behind the youthful errors, and then he helped them resolve the conflicts. Thus, he offered the youths in his training schools three levels of assistance. First, there was the placement in the training school as a legal consequence, a sentence. Second, there was the benefit of education, which developed the youth's competence. Third, there was attention to the youth's mental health and to assistance with the resolution of conflicts. In the late twenties and thirties, Aichorn (1934) became more involved with diverting youngsters from the legal system into treatment.

In the United States, the first children referred to be systematically examined for emotional difficulties were those who were repeatedly in trouble with the law. As discussed in chapter 8, the child mental health movement grew out of the dichotomy of bad or mad. Children and the mentally ill have in common that society does not hold them accountable for their antisocial acts. The juvenile justice system is structured this way; child murderers, unless tried as adults, must serve sentences that last only until the end of childhood. The juvenile system is different from the adult system and is designed to give kids a chance to go straight. This differentiation of the systems for children and adults represents a thoughtful recognition that children are more plastic than adults and have more possibilities of changing. It acknowledges the youthful peccadillo and the possibility that the wayward youth may grow up to be a responsible adult.

In recognizing the plasticity of youth, juvenile authorities have become very aware of the difficult conditions under which many youngsters live. A simple solution is often applied: the youth would be all right if he were not in the deleterious environment; let us send him to live somewhere else, where he can have healthier relationships. There are several problems with this solution. First, the deleterious environment is often with the youngster's family, who may act in a particularly outrageous fashion in the face of the courts' negatively critical attitude. Second, the proposed healthier relationships are to be with other youths in similar trouble and with staff who are relative strangers to the youth, work on shifts, and change their work positions frequently. However, there is no evidence that youngsters actually do better under such a plan, and some evidence exists that youngsters do better with a carefully devised plan that allows them to remain in their own community and in school. Furthermore, the plans for relocation usually are initiated without explicit standards for accountability built in, so the youngster, even while sentenced to residential placement, is de facto excused. As noted in chapter 8, there is also a dichotomy between those youths designated as needing mental health corrective settings and those retained in the correctional system. Although these decisions may be argued skillfully before a judge, as I have noted, they are made primarily on the basis of race, gender, and socioeconomic circumstances. But the distinction between correctional facilities and mental health settings can be dramatic, with the former emphasizing discipline and corrections, the latter emphasizing therapy, and neither doing more than what is legally required for education.

Youths between Mental Health and Juvenile Justice

Johnny is the third of four children and the only adopted child of a working-class urban family. His parents separated when he was twelve after a turbulent marriage. Having been removed from his biological mother in his first year of life, due to abuse and neglect, Johnny was placed with the family who subsequently adopted him. He had a series of adjustment difficulties, which became particularly acute when he began school. Two factors seemed to underlie these difficulties: one was his sensitivity to belonging and separation; the other was his difficulty in grasping academic material (he tested in the range of mild to moderate mentally handicapped). The difficulties were interpreted as emotional disturbances, and Johnny was hospitalized when he was seven. He was given a diagnosis of pervasive developmental disorder. The school system provided special education for him; and Johnny's foster family adopted him when he was eight. By fifteen he had been involved with the juvenile authorities for shoplifting; and at sixteen he was involved in a fistfight, which led to his being placed in detention for assault and battery.

Three pieces of information are important. Johnny's school situation had been rather successfully resolved by placement in a special school with a high degree of structure and built-in successes. Johnny's mental problems had been addressed in years of individual therapy, but the therapists had experienced enormous frustration with Johnny and with his parents because he failed to progress according to the therapist's goals of increasing insight about his behavior, which presumably would lead to his exhibiting better judgment. Third, each of his antisocial acts had been committed while he was with a group of friends, which meant that Johnny was a group delinquent and was strongly influenced by others. On the basis of Johnny's now ten-year-old mental diagnosis, his parents' dissolved marriage and continued conflict with each other, his frustrating therapy experiences, and his several brushes with the law, the juvenile authorities recommended that he be placed in a long-term residential treatment setting. To affirm that this was a good decision, they requested a psychiatric inpatient evaluation, the results of which confirmed their conclusions.

The juvenile authorities cared about this boy, and their recommendation was based on their best judgment about what would work for him. They had been frustrated with Johnny's mother for years. Their main objection was that she was preoccupied with herself, did not seem to care about Johnny, and was often not willing to attend court hearings or therapy sessions. Furthermore, she was not available to give him the supervision he so clearly needed. They dismissed her as a negative influence, and her response to this was to be irritable and insulting to them, often refusing to make herself available because of what she experienced as their patronizing attitude. They dismissed the father as not responsible; thus, he was not even invited to court hearings (he showed up only sporadically for meetings to which he was invited). They assumed that since the parents did not consistently attend the many court or therapy sessions set up for them, they did not want this child. And, indeed, Johnny's mother had at times told the probation officer that since he and the judge knew so well what was best for her child, they should raise him. In short, there was competition between the juvenile authorities (particularly Johnny's probation officer, his attorney, and the judge) and Johnny's mother. This was dramatically illustrated when a large number of concerned professionals gathered with Johnny's mother in the judge's chambers. Everyone had an opinion. No one asked Johnny's mother hers, and as the session progressed, she shook with frustrated anger and then quietly began to cry.

When a mental health team became involved with Johnny's family, we found that they had not been asked a number of basic questions, such as, Did they want their son at home? How might they assist in providing the supervision he needed? What did they think his problems were? Did they think he was mentally ill? When finally asked these questions, they said they did, in fact, want him home. They were willing to arrange for friends and relatives from their vast network to move into the home to be there for regular meals and supervision or to cover times when no one was home.

They felt that his problems were primarily ones of supervision and of being put down on the grounds of his alleged mental illness, and they did not feel that he was mentally ill. They did not want to have him placed in a residential treatment center.

Our evaluation of Johnny found him to be intellectually slow but not mentally ill or even seriously emotionally disturbed. He reflected a confident sense of attachment to his family. He was also so obliging that he would say contradictory things, apparently in order to please the person to whom he was talking. For example, if one worker told him he should have someone to talk to about his feelings, he would say that he needed that. If another person expressed the opinion that he would do better with some activity, he would affirm that that was what he needed. This quality fit well with the observation that he became involved in antisocial behavior with his peers. And it militated against the conclusion that he had a basically antisocial bent. His success in the special school experience affirmed that he used supervision, structure, and personal successes well, and his lack of success in talking psychotherapy suggested not that he and his family were resistant or untreatable but that this form of intervention was not appropriate for him. It is clear that we did not believe that residential treatment was appropriate for Johnny.

OPTIMAL APPROACHES

I do not believe that youth should necessarily be incarcerated for their crimes. I do believe that they should be held accountable. They need to be adjudicated delinquent and they need to be sentenced. If they are dangerous, they probably do need to be incarcerated. If they are repeat offenders, they probably need more than adjudication and probation. But they do not necessarily need to be viewed as mentally ill and given psychiatric treatment instead of a program reflecting accountability under the law. On the other hand, programs in prisons and community juvenile justice programs have to go beyond holding the youth accountable and punishing her for her crimes. They must also direct the youth into more productive activity, address the common educational deficits that these youngsters suffer, and assist the youngsters in finding a way to become contributing members of society.

Johnny's success if he were not to be sent to residential treatment depended on a well-coordinated community plan that combined these elements. He was returned to his special school, where he had been successful prior to his detention. His mother arranged for one of her grown nieces to be in the home, to provide a regular dinner on a schedule, to set expectations for Johnny's whereabouts, and to be there for him to talk to when he needed advice. Beyond this, the challenge was to develop a plan in the community that would involve Johnny in productive and pleasant social activities that utilized his areas of competence and also made him accountable to others. A program in a recreation center was developed in which he could assist younger children on sports teams, and he was involved in a youth group for vocational planning.

Such programs have to be invented through a collaboration between agencies involved in the care of a particular youngster, because they don't ordinarily exist as a part of any single child-caring system. But it is hard to set these kinds of things up when a habit of sending the youngsters away is so ingrained. This habit comes, as noted, from the eighty-year-old conviction that youthful antisocial behavior somehow stems from emotional disturbance, bred in the family. But it also comes from a money shortage and a shortage of resources to attend to these children through the court system itself. There is a strong incentive to get these youngsters involved with the mental health system so that services they need will be paid for through that system. In many cases, it is only through the mental health system that youngsters can be housed and get appropriate attention. Indeed, the previously cited estimate (Friedman et al 1989) that as many as 60 percent of youths in mental hospitals have a diagnosis of disordered conduct indicates that they have come to the attention of the system through behaviors that might also be called delinquent or antisocial.

Money is a problem, but the categorical separation of functions between the mental health system and the juvenile justice and correctional systems is a greater problem. Most juvenile systems do have a mental health section where youngsters are evaluated and even given treatment. But when the youngster is evaluated as seriously disturbed or distressed, he is transferred to a psychiatric hospital. This is because many think that the mental health system does "real" mental health, and that therapeutic programs required by the youth, but unavailable in corrections, will be in place there. Such categorical thinking also leads people to conclude that a seriously disturbed youth does not belong in the juvenile correction system—the mental health system should be responsible for caring for that youth. This is a parallel to some of the arguments that occur between child welfare and the mental health systems. Why shouldn't a disturbed youth serve a sentence and be treated at the same time? In the instance of Walter, whose case follows, there was some treatment available in the correctional facility where he served his sentence. But the discomfort of the correctional staff was supported by their belief that the boy belonged somewhere else, so that they did not take the steps to manage his disturbed behavior effectively. Furthermore, it became clear that much of his disturbance was related to the context of the facility.

THE CASE OF WALTER

Walter, a seventeen-year-old, was serving time in a correctional facility for the murder of his two-year-old brother. There was considerable evidence that Walter was psychotic when he killed him, but even more evidence showed that he was acting out resentment and a sense that the toddler boy had higher status than he, Walter; that his mother used him as a baby-sitter, sacrificing him for the baby. In the correctional facility Walter was isolated, strange, unpredictably violent, and actively paranoid. After several episodes when he viciously attacked staff members, he was transferred to state hospital units, where he remained a few weeks before being sent back, because, they reported, he was fine. The prison system and the mental health system represented two different places that passed Walter back and forth like a hot potato. Expert mental health consultation in the prison found numerous factors within the unit where Walter was incarcerated that contributed to all of the symptoms he displayed there. For example, he was treated differently from all of the other youths because of his known dangerousness. This different treatment, however, appeared to underlie his paranoid suspicions. If they weren't singling him out, then why did they treat him differently? Furthermore, there was disagreement between the staff members on different shifts and in different programs about how he should be treated. Thus, he experienced the staff members' diverse responses toward him, and he was in the middle of their arguments about him. And, finally, they did not hold him accountable for his menacing mien, his refusal to participate in required activities, or his actual physical harm of staff and other patients. They defined these as crazy. They gave up on him. All of these actions reinforced Walter's isolation and paranoia, and the disconnected state from which he would lash out at the staff. His brief sojourns in the state hospital were different, not because they knew better how to treat Walter but because the environment was new; he had no history, good or bad, with them; and as his behavior continued to be acceptable, they gave him uniform warmth and approval. He did well, and was returned to the prison time and time again.

It is possible to understand that there were certain sensitive interpersonal patterns in which Walter's assaultive and murderous behavior played an important role. Recognition of these patterns was useful in understanding and predicting Walter's behavior and in developing strategies to help him progress and become more productive. The patterns we discerned included both the situation in which he had murdered his brother and those situations in which he had assaulted the prison staff. A more conventional diagnostic approach would have identified the psychopathology within him, which included periodic psychoses and paranoia. But we recognized that because the behaviors were inconsistent and appeared to be context related, identifying sequences related to the assaultive behavior or episodes of increasing isolation and paranoia were meaningful. We also appreciated that this was a very disturbed youngster. His relationship skills were extremely poor, undoubtedly reflecting difficulties throughout his life, with a father who had been serving a life sentence for murder and a mother who was an alcoholic and had frequently depended on him to stay home to care for his infant brother. Themes of powerlessness and problems with status pervaded his early family life, as we understood it.

At the same time, there was little opportunity for Walter to be nurtured or to attend to his own development as a person by going to school regularly or by socializing with peers. Killing his brother repeated the family pattern of asserting status and calling attention to oneself by violence (the same behavior used by his father). This pattern was played out repeatedly in the correctional facility, where the boy's lack of social experience tended to place him outside the peer group, and he, in turn, isolated himself. Thus, deviance was amplified in a cybernetic fashion. It was further amplified by the differential treatment he received from the staff, who, on the one hand, experienced him as crazy and deviant and, on the other hand, were fearful and wary of what harm he might do to them. To the staff's escalation of isolation and differential treatment Walter responded with menace and increasing paranoia. This escalation usually culminated in an explosion of violence, thus bearing out the staff's view of the boy and precipitating a change in his status—sometimes a major adjustment in his activity program; at other times, a transfer to the state hospital. After this, the cycle would begin again.

We urged, and the prison superintendent concurred, that the staff should confront Walter with their fears (thus directly according him respect for his strength, which he required), and that they also expect him to participate in the unit activities and to be subject to the same system of rewards and penalties that the other boys received. In order to do this, they might have to place him in restraints for their own protection while administering a penalty he had earned for refusing to participate in a required activity. It was clearly agreed by the consultants and the superintendent that this action would change the pattern by involving the staff more directly with Walter, reducing his isolation and reducing the well-based paranoia that he was being treated differently from others. Yet the staff found it difficult to do this, and the pattern recycled once again. Instead, they chose to pursue their claim that mental health should be responsible for the boy, thus perpetuating at another systems level the same pattern of noninvolvement and nonaccountability that seems to have been a pattern of Walter's whole life.

An additional problem resulting from the disconnection between mental health and juvenile justice was that when he reached nineteen, Walter would be released from prison, because he had been held as a juvenile. He would have no further legal obligation to serve time or to be in treatment, yet he would be released from prison with no social skills, little education, no family with whom to live, and no vocation. It seems unlikely that Walter has much of an opportunity to make a difference in his life. Both systems have failed him, and he probably will commit another violent crime, not because he is a sick or bad person, but because these are the patterns of his life, and nothing has been done to change them.

Abuse and Family Violence

The issue of domestic violence and abuse further reveals how the legal system becomes involved in patterns where the family is turned against itself. Some of the consequences of child sexual abuse were discussed in chapter 9; similar consequences occur with children who are physically abused and neglected. It has been observed, however, that the attention to abused children is in inverse proportion to the real danger of the abuse (Miller 1989); the response to sexual abuse is much swifter than that to physical abuse, even though the latter may maim or kill a child. Also, in situations of ongoing spousal battles and wife beating where the children are the terrorized witnesses, abuse to the children is not even an issue. Usually, the children are not even involved in treatment, nor is their safety considered apart from that of their mother. Such facts raise several important issues. The first is the integrity of the family. When social and legal systems act in cases of domestic abuse, they move to rescue the victims. In doing so, they usually escalate the relationship issues that the abuse is about and turn the family against itself. The family is not held responsible for protecting and caring for itself, and social agencies take over, violating the family in the process.

This may seem like an easy thing to say, and it is not even a very controversial idea. But it is not an easy issue to incorporate into a more appropriate practice. Welfare agencies do get blamed for harm done to children; legal systems do get blamed for harm done to women for whom protection failed. Often this protection was in the form of incarcerating the abusive husband, who was released because there was no justification to infringe further on his civil rights. The step of removing the victims to a shelter, where they are temporarily protected, or removing the perpetrators to prison, where they are temporarily forced to contrition, is a necessary one that is sound only if it is recognized that separating the family is a temporary, or temporizing, solution. After this step has been taken, the victims usually receive counseling aimed at helping them examine how they get involved with abusive men and helping them establish a different level of independence. The perpetrators also receive treatment, which is aimed at helping them understand and master their violent tendencies. The perpetrators are often given a diagnosis, while some sex offenders are given medication to control sexual urges, and some physically violent are medicated to reduce impulsivity and violent reactions.

The rate at which women offered such treatment end up returning to the abusive mate is surprising, and the rate at which the abuse recurs is discouraging. One can only conclude that the treatment plan doesn't work! This is because there are patterns of relationship involving all members of the family that are not addressed by this response—patterns centered around loyalty, attachment, and dependency, as well as status and pride. A temporizing move to protect and hold accountable can be shared and collaborated with by family members who do not want to be hurt or to hurt. But the control by others of these moves and their duration becomes an issue of shame and humiliation for the family. A woman who returns to her husband after all the help and support she has received has to deal with her abandonment of the helping efforts, with turning against those . who had supported her. A man, humiliated and further enraged by seeing his wife joined by an outraged system, may be further stimulated to vindicate himself and to take it out on the most available parts of the system—not the whole faceless system that has escalated his shame, but his wife and possibly his children. In such cases, the attempted solution to the problem becomes the problem.

In presenting the case of the Bakers, I illustrated an approach that combines the safety precautions of separation with the opportunity for whole family work to address the issues, within the family, of how they will protect themselves. There are some developments in work with couples involved in spouse abuse that does address the loyalty, commitment, and dependency issues between them, but very little work has been done addressing the roles and needs of children in families where there is spouse abuse. There are at least two aspects of the children's participation that must be dealt with. The first is the terror experienced by children who witness these parental battles. Data gathered from many sources indicate that chronic conflict between parents is associated with adjustment problems in the children. Little work has been done to explore how children's helplessness as they watch or hear their mother being hurt plays a role in their ultimate maladjustment. The second aspect of the children's participation is more subtle: What active place do they have in the patterns of violence and the response to it? This point can be illustrated by a vignette from the Peterson family.

THE PETERSON FAMILY'S EXPERIENCE

The Peterson family consists of a father, mother, and two small children, Andy, aged four, and Nancy, aged two. Both parents, in their late twenties, are very attractive, and both have jobs that promise some career development and the opportunity for the family to attain a goal of a solid middle-class life-style. Mr. Peterson works as a manager of a local supermarket, and Mrs. Peterson is a paralegal in a large law firm. He earns a slightly larger salary than she, and he supervises all of the workers in the store during his shift; but both of them regard her job as being of higher status. He often worries about her relationship with the many male lawyers in the firm and frequently finds himself worrying that she is having an affair with one of them. She, not wanting to lord her status over him, does not talk much about work, a reticence that he interprets as evidence of her infidelities. Arguments ensue in which her initial efforts to convince him of her fidelity give way to fury at him, and she becomes silent. He then becomes so enraged that he strikes her. At this point, she takes the children and leaves, going to her mother's house. His anger is aggravated by his fear of abandonment, and he is beside himself with rage and desperate sadness. At those moments following his wife's departure with Andy and Nancy, he feels he has lost everything.

The Petersons sought treatment for themselves, and they brought the children because they were asked to. The children appeared to be comfortable and affectionate with both parents, and both parents seemed equally attentive to their needs as they talked with the therapist about their situation. As they were discussing Mrs. Peterson's departure from the house, the therapist asked about the children and how the decision was made about where the children should go. If she left and the children stayed in their own house (these fights usually occurred after the children had gone to sleep), would the children be all right with the father? If the father were to leave and go to his mother's, could he take the children? Where, indeed, did the children fit into this problem? Did he feel, when she took the children, that everyone was against him? Of course, he did. Her move, to go to her mother with the children, made him feel as if he were the problem and humiliated him. If she were to go and leave the children with him, it would be more clearly a shared problem, and a temporary solution, to cool off the situation.

Exploring these questions about the children, given that the children did not express a preference for one parent over the other, allowed the parents to view options differently. They had a range of choices about what to do when the violent pattern heated up. They also had a perspective on the pattern itself. In the first phase of treatment they agreed to rotate who left, who stayed, and who was responsible for the children. This established their responsibility for protecting themselves from the violence while they worked on the issues of status, jealousy, possessiveness, attachment, and communication styles that were involved in the violent patterns. It is easy to see how not addressing children in this situation could have led to the disturbed loyalties so commonly found in children with chronically battling or separating parents.

Child Custody

Child custody as a legal issue takes on several forms. The first is what has already been looked at in terms of parental competence and the welfare system. The second is the rare and complex issue of custodial rights in situations such as the case of Baby M, the child of a surrogate mother who ultimately decided she could not give up her baby. The third, and by far the most common, is the instance of divorcing parents and their continuing responsibilities in raising their children.

Why is the legal system involved in decisions about child welfare? Who is a judge to make a decision about where a child should live and how much contact that child should have with each of his parents and other concerned relatives? What are the bases in law upon which these decisions are made? In the Baby M case, there was a straightforward answer: there was a question about the validity of a contract between Baby M's natural father and mother for the mother to bear the child and give her up to the father and his wife. Was there another legal issue to come before the courts? Did the judge have the training and background to decide who should raise the baby and who should be in her relationship system? I think not. Even wise King Solomon could not make such a decision. Solomon's response to the two women fighting for custody of the baby was to initiate a process by which they would settle the dispute themselves.

The legal process might seem to have just this sort of goal—to determine who cares best for the children. The problem is that it operates on a quantitative basis—the preponderance of evidence, the amount of time spent with the children, the comparative willingness of each parent to involve the other in the children's lives. These are standards by which custody determinations are made in court. These standards beg several important questions. The first is respect for the value of the children's relationship system. The second is the parents' responsibility in planning for and caring for their children. A third is the necessity of developing a means by which the family system functions for the benefit of the children in the different circumstances determined by the fact of the parents' separation.

The value of the children's relationship system does not need further persuasive discussion here. What is distinctive about divorce and separation is the notion that this need not necessarily rupture the relationship system of the children. It does, however, alter it. It changes the access the children have to both of their parents. Individuals who may have had peripheral roles with the children, such as grandparents, may be brought closer. And new individuals, such as new friends, mates, and, eventually, spouses, will be introduced into the system. There are shifts in the relative amount of time a child will spend with one person or another, the role of the children in each parent's life, and so on. Many parents, on the advice of their attorneys, try to discredit the other parent. Many parents genuinely believe that the children will be emotionally harmed by the other parent. Often people feel that if it can be demonstrated that one parent has a meretricious relationship, has committed crimes, or shows evidence of other moral weakness or mental illness, then that parent should not have contact with the children. But the point I am making is that there it *is* a relationship system regardless of the undesirability of one parent to the other. Furthermore, if this system, in response to the way of making custody decisions prescribed by the legal system, develops patterns that discredit some who have different life-styles, moral positions, and so forth, then those patterns are communicated to the children.

CUSTODY IN THE VISOTSKY FAMILY

Let us take as an extreme example the Visotsky family. In this family, both parents had been indulged offspring of financially successful first-generation immigrants—the mother was the daughter of an Italian contractor; the father was the son of a Polish furrier. Mrs. Visotsky's siblings had gone into their father's business; Mr. Visotsky's had become doctors and lawyers. Mr. Visotsky's family therefore had more status than Mrs. Visotsky's. Nevertheless, it was the mother who initiated the separation;

both agreed to this fact. And when they initially separated, she had undisputed custody of the two little boys, Jason, aged five, and Mikey, aged three. Stories from each family conflicted about what happened next. Her family said that Mr. Visotsky's overcontrolling mother got on his case to go for custody. His mother wanted the kids, and she would make sure that her son did not lose custody over them. Someone in the father's brother's law firm was engaged to represent him. Mrs. Visotsky and her family also stated that Mr. Visotsky had a girlfriend, and he had been cheating on his wife for at least a year prior to the separation. The father's family said that the mother was a complete slut; that she entertained a string of men in her house, neglecting the children in her affairs. They also alleged that she used drugs and that she was always an unstable character. They cited incidents and produced hospital records to demonstrate this.

It is possible to see, already, how the polarizing of these views of one another for the purpose of increasing one's own chances of getting custody was seriously undermining to the children's views of their parents. Given that this is not an unusual kind of atmosphere, it is always astonishing to witness how the children define the value of their relationship with each parent on their own terms. As the battle waged on between the parents, between their families, and between their lawyers, the children began to imitate the vocabulary of their parents. In the presence of his father, Jason would refer to his mother as a bitch and a whore, and he indicated that he did not want to see her. Mikey would echo his brother in a babyish version of the words and actions that was horrifyingly cute. This conversation by the children convinced their father that he must fight for them. With their mother the boys were snuggling and affectionate. They did not call her names. They did, however, repeat the story about the time Daddy pushed her around and they were afraid that he was going to hurt her.

In conducting a court ordered evaluation, I noted that the parents each had weaknesses attributed to them. The mother had an unstable educational and career history, she had been in psychotherapy but had not stayed, she had a bad temper and was impulsive, and she had been a wild teenager. The father was dominated by his mother, was not settled in a career but was generously supported by his father, and was petulant and bullying. Neither, by the standards created in their battle, was a fit parent. Yet each had a meaningful relationship with the children. The attorneys were bent on resolving the conflict by giving one parent custody and allowing the other only limited access (having convinced themselves, on each side, of the latter's danger to the children). It was clear that mediation could not take place and this case would go to court. In court, frightful dirt would be raked up about each parent, and the judge would be forced to make a decision of the sort prescribed by the attorneys. The father's greater financial resources, as well as his family's social status, could not fail to have influence. If the judge believed that young children should be with their mother, that would be in Mrs. Visotsky's favor, unless Mr. Visotsky indicated that he was planning to marry his girlfriend and provide a stable two-adult family for the boys. In the end the decision was made to give custody to the father and to allow limited, alternate-weekend visitations with the mother. The lesson to the boys was that their mother was a bad person who had to be watched and that interpersonal problems get solved by power and influence.

CUSTODY IN THE MANCINI FAMILY

In another instance, Mr. Mancini, the father of five-year-old Lenny, had had several psychotic breaks following his return from Vietnam. Lenny's mother wanted an evaluation of her former husband, because she wanted to be certain that he was mentally capable of handling the child, alone. Lenny, in response to his mother's apprehensiveness, had begun to object to visiting with his father, and his mother wondered whether scary things were happening when they were together. Several things were apparent on evaluation. First, Mr. Mancini loved his son and wanted to spend time with him. Second, being the youngest child in his own family, he was unfamiliar with children, and he didn't always know how to handle Lenny. Third, Lenny was curious about his father, if a little apprehensive. A visiting arrangement was made in which Mr. Mancini sat down with Lenny and his mother before and after the visits to talk about the plans and recount how the visit had gone. As this process involved him with his son, he became more confident and was able to be more forthright about his illness and the times when he felt it might interfere with their time together. Mrs. Mancini began to trust him more, and Lenny had a relationship with his father.

Mr. Mancini's sensitivity flared up when, at age seven, Lenny was not so happy to give up weekends with his friends to be with his dad. Further difficulties were experienced around Mrs. Mancini's serious relationship and upcoming marriage to Mr. Costello. This required a renegotiation of expectations in a session including Lenny and both parents and Mr. Costello, again reassuring Mr. Mancini that neither Lenny nor his mother nor Mr. Costello was trying to cut him out of Lenny's life. They were able to come to some understanding about Mr. Costello's role with Lenny, and to deal with what was apparent—that Lenny's development necessitated more time with his own peers. Mr. Mancini was not excluded from Lenny's relationship system because of his illness. Arrangements were made that enabled him to have an active role in Lenny's life in such a way that everyone felt secure. Lenny was able to love his father, and he was also able to have a relationship with his father that developed on their own terms.

Giant Steps in Custody Conflicts

These examples illustrate that giant steps must be taken in the instances of conflicts over child custody. The first giant step—recognizing that reality is contextually dependent—is particularly important in examining these situations. Each side in the battle has a skewed version of reality, which becomes more skewed as the battle wages on. The nature of the court system accentuates these differences and tends to passionately entrap parties to the case. Mental health experts engaged by one side or another are particularly vulnerable to this, because despite their efforts to be objective and neutral, they are in danger of being coopted by whoever is paying their bill.

The second giant step—recognizing the patterns—helps us understand the accusations and counteraccusations in a different perspective. For example, a common accusation is that the father never interacted with the children, worked all the time, and left the child care to the mother. On observation, after separation, the father is charmingly engaged with his children; responsible about basic aspects of child care, such as feeding and bedtime, as well as entertainment; and feeling quite capable of caring for them full-time. Patterns during the marriage dictated that he work and she care for the children. Things can change. Furthermore, it is important to view the accusations themselves as forming new patterns that can be detrimental to the integrity of the children's relationship system.

The third step—building on competence and using the family's own resources—is illustrated in the Mancini case, where the tendency to discount Mr. Mancini because of his illness was countered by having Lenny and his mother participate in involving Mr. Mancini with his son. The question becomes not Can this parent be involved with his child at all? but How can this parent be safely involved with his child?

Finally, the outcome of solutions to custody conflict that preserve relationship systems through developing respect for the validity of different sides and the competence of individuals in the system (including the children) is the development of patterns within the system that attend to the parents' and the children's needs, thus maximizing the possibility of mental health. For some families coping with custody conflicts, a solution can be developed that incorporates ongoing interaction and renegotiation as circumstances change. Others seek outside assistance from counselors or mediators whenever such a change in one party's situation requires a change in the arrangements. This was the case in the Mancini family, and they became accustomed to returning to see me whenever they had a question of this sort, so that I became a part of their pattern and a part of their relationship system.

Binary Systems versus Mediated Systems

The legal system has important functions in the lives of children. Most important is the establishment and application of standards of account-ability to one's society. But particularly in relation to children, the legal system must also be accountable to the systems that are most vital to the children's continued development and survival. If the family, as the closest and most important domain of survival, security, self-definition, and ac-countability, is turned against itself when the legal system becomes in-volved, problems escalate. One final example illustrates this.

Donald was eleven when he and his seven-year-old brother set fire to a homeless man who had inhabited their neighborhood for several years. The man survived but was severely burned. He had thrived in this neigh-borhood because the inhabitants had more than tolerated his presence, often offering him hot coffee and blankets during the coldest periods. The crime perpetrated by Donald and his brother was a violation of the neigh-borhood ecology as well as an act of cruelty. When the police came to the Parker house to arrest Donald, his parents were embarrassed and speech-less. (Donald's brother was not held accountable at all because of his age.) They protested weakly that their son could not have done such a thing. Shortly afterward, they hired an attorney. Donald was not held in juvenile detention but was sent immediately for evaluation to a local child psychi-atric inpatient unit with the question Is this boy bad or mad? At this point, there were several levels of conflict, all of which militated against anyone holding Donald accountable or properly socializing him.

The first level of conflict was within the family. Because the police charged Donald and removed him from the home without preparation or discussion with the parents, the parents were bound to feel defensive of their son and angry with the police. They then had to take the position that Donald was innocent, and if it were proven that he had set the fire, that he was not in his right mind. The second level was in the community, where the Parker family would henceforth be known as the family of "that boy." The Parkers were then on the defensive from another front. A third level was the legal system, with the prosecution taking the position that the boy had to be brought to accountability *unless he was emotionally disturbed.* The parents' attorney (technically an advocate for the child) also chose to defend him on the grounds of his youth and his "innocence" about what he was doing.

I believe that in order for this incident to be properly handled, the parents needed to be approached first, presented with the evidence, and consulted about the consequences for their children. In order to form a working relationship with them, it would have been necessary to anticipate the community's reaction to the family, when it was learned which boys had caused the injury. It might have been necessary to convene a neighborhood meeting to discuss the episode and to remind everyone that such a community needed to assist and protect its members and their children, as well as the unfortunate street people with whom they shared their territory.

In this way, the family and the legal system could have worked together to evaluate what should be done with both boys. This would include not just an evaluation of the emotional state or state of interpersonal contagion which underlay the act of setting fire to a person, but also an agreement about how these boys could make reparation to the man and to the community. Patterns of defensiveness had been generated between the legal authorities and the parents, but would undoubtedly be experienced in other parts of the system (e.g. boys and school mates, parents and neighbors), and these would lead to shame and ostracism. But if the family and legal system worked together, these defensive patterns would not be generated, because the family would be holding its children properly accountable.

Beyond Binary Decision Making

Although the three circumstances of child and family involvement with the legal system discussed in this chapter are quite different, mental health professionals' responses to the requests made of them to assist with evaluation and planning need to follow similar principles. First, the mental health professional should establish the broadest possible definition of who is his client. If the request comes from a correctional facility for evaluation of a youthful inmate, such as Walter, the professional needs to view those taking care of and concerned about Walter as the clients and as a significant part of the assessment. If the request comes from an attorney or one parent in a custody situation, the mental health professional will be able to act most effectively if she can arrange for the other attorney and parent to agree to her appointment as an expert for the case, or to have the court appoint her. If this is not possible, she should insist that all parties to the case be available for evaluation, and she should evaluate the children with each of the households and/or individuals with whom they will have significant interaction. Very often in custody cases this includes grandparents and new partners of the parents.

Second, having included a significant relationship system among those seen as her client, the mental health professional should evaluate significant patterns in which difficulties occur and enlist the involved individuals in an exploration of more competent patterns, always directing them to explore other resources they have for helping correct the situation. For Johnny this involved a variety of resources in the community where he lived as well as many members of his mother's large and sprawling family. For children in custody disputes this may involve teachers and playmates as well as the larger family group. Third, the mental health professional must always keep in mind the issue of accountability. And this is not just the accountability of the individual youth, in the case of delinquency, or the parents, in the cases of domestic violence or custody disputes. Parental accountability for expectations and consistency with their delinquent children must also be addressed. And children's roles in the patterns of violence or the heated escalation of a custody conflict must be carefully examined. When children are involved with the legal system, it seems particularly important to mitigate the binary system of decision making, because one side or another may win, but the child always loses.

CHAPTER 11

The Education System: Finding a Fit

The trap of Special Education was now open and waiting for the little boy. It is a beguiling trap. Children of Special Education are children of Small Expectations, not great ones. Little is expected and little is demanded. Gradually, these children—no matter their IQ level— learn to be cozy in the category of being "special." They learn to be less than they are.
—LORI GRANGER AND BILL GRANGER, *The Magic Feather,* 1986

The juvenile era, observed psychiatrist Harry Stack Sullivan, "is the first developmental stage in which the limitations and peculiarities of the home as a socializing influence begin to be open to remedy" (1953, 227). Erik Erikson described the primary school period as an occasion for a child to master the industry of his or her society. Other developmentalists elaborated further that there is a convergence of child developmental issues— such as the evolution of concrete operations, the entrance into the conventional stage of moral development, and "latency"—with the social opportunities provided by entrance into formal schooling. This step also brings expanded peer relationships, the critical evaluation of personal experience through the eyes of others, and the family's developmental move from centripetal to centrifugal organization, opening up and increasing circulation with systems outside its nucleus (Combrinck-Graham 1985). Going to school is a critical experience because the school provides a definition of personal role and social system second only to that provided in the family. In school the child's role as a member of a society is defined and shaped; in school the child's discovery of self through competence and perception of self as a member of society is initiated and stamped. A child's school and the educational system of which it is a part are central to the lives of schoolchildren and adolescents and their families, as the school experience shapes and reshapes the mental health of the children and the well-being of their families.

In order for a child to develop the self-evaluative skills that underlie other accomplishments in the school-aged period, there has to be a congenial pattern of fit between the child, family, and school. Development occurs more easily when consistency, mutual understanding, and cooperation exist between family and school in relation to culture, educational aims, and life goals. Beginning with the assumption that the basis of an individual's mental health is his experience of competence in relation to expectations in his societal context, this chapter further amplifies the importance of education to mental health. In order for a child's education to produce the outcome of mental health, there needs to be a fit between the child's abilities and aspirations, the expectations of those who influence the child (parents and teachers), and the school's ability to provide education that meets the particular child's capacities.

Once again, the four giant steps are essential to assist the professional in recognizing the contribution of schooling and the education system to a child and family's well-being and in aiding this process. Step 1 requires that in any consultation for a child of school age, the multiple perspectives of child, parents, and school authorities must be sought and appreciated. Input from children's peers is also important and can be gained without embarrassment to the child through classroom and playground observations at school and visits to the child's home when playmates are present. Patterns of fit between child, family, and school are discernible and crucial to the success—or lack of success—of the school experience. Assessment of the competence of each level of the system underlies the formation of patterns that enhance fit. And, finally, in school, where so many systems converge, the well-being of the various components (students, teachers, school administrators, and parents) establishes the mentally healthy environment.

Education and Mental Health

The education system has a major impact on modifying the view of self in the present and future that has been created by the child's experience prior to school entrance. Because the sense of self as a valuable, competent, and contributing individual is fundamental to mental health, education systems are fundamental to child mental health. But the compartmentalized systems in the United States from the federal level on down tend to separate the functions of mental health and education, so that teachers are encouraged to refer a child identified as emotionally disturbed to the treatment of another kind of professional, and mental health professionals tend to disregard the central role of education in their young clients' overall health. This separation has a variety of deleterious effects. One concerns funding streams and arguments about them. The Education for All Handicapped Children Act, Public Law (PL) 94-142 and its amendment, PL 99-457 (requiring appropriate education for handicapped infants and toddlers) include the emotionally disturbed as a class of "handicapped" persons. These laws, which extend to all children the constitutional entitlement of an education, place an enormous burden on educational systems. The services required under the laws differ according to interpretation, with some locales requiring the education system to provide necessary psychiatric and psychological services, and others limiting themselves simply to providing the therapeutic supports to a pedagogical environment, such as occupational, physical, and speech therapies, as well as remedial work in technical areas. Still others provide mental health services in the form of counselors or school social workers, who may do psychotherapy with individuals or groups of children. Some provide psychological and psychiatric evaluations, whereas others include psychiatrists and psychologists as a part of their consulting teams. Even in these most integrated settings, however, the turfs of the mental health professionals and those of the educational professionals are sharply demarcated. With extremely difficult children whose further treatment/education promises to be lengthy and expensive, educational authorities may seek to divest themselves of the responsibility for the great expense by declaring that the child could be educated in a less restrictive school setting but that his emotional needs require a more restrictive living situation. This demarcation, once again, is characteristic of a movement to shift into the mental health system those children whom other systems are unable or unwilling to serve. It clearly differentiates mental health and education—something I view as impossible.

Nevertheless, the demarcation is frequently attempted, and the implications of this demarcation vary with the relative strength of the professional group in a given setting. In one residential school, mental health personnel were ancillary, whereas education was central. Thus, therapy was an adjunctive modality, but it was hardly substantively connected to the educational curriculum. In another long-term psychiatric treatment center, which is typical of most hospitals and residential *treatment* settings, school was required for all children, but their psychotherapy came first. Any signs of disturbance in class were ascribed to the children's emotional problems and were referred to the child's therapist. Again, the therapy and the educational program were disconnected.

Some programs have been designed specifically to blend the objectives of education and mental health. The Intramural (inpatient/day treatment) program initiated in 1974 at the Philadelphia Child Guidance Clinic is an example of this. When consciously seeking the connection between educational adjustment and mental health, the staff found that a majority of children referred for behavior problems and emotional disturbances were academically failing, too. A curriculum developed for these children's educational experience focused on the children's personal accomplishments in the context of a group of peers working together. Each designed classroom activity permitted each child in the class to contribute to the project, gain something from her participation, and evaluate her experience and contribution. As an example, a group of children might set out on a nature walk in the fall. Collecting leaves, a child with few skills might sort the leaves according to shape and color; a more advanced child might name the leaves according to the type of tree from which they came; a still more advanced child might study the anatomy of the leaf and relate it to the physiology of trees. All three of these children would participate in the same activity.

This level of specificity to each child's abilities and needs for assistance within the classroom curriculum was developed through the shared commitment to the educational program as the primary treatment milieu for the children. Administratively, this involved differentiated, but equally important, contributions to the evaluation and treatment plan development from all of the professionals in the institution—educational, child life, and clinical services. Technically, it necessitated team meetings in which relevant individuals from each discipline were represented. Conceptually, it required that the implications of each of the children's problems with adjustment, orientation, and modulation of mood and behavior be understood as they affected his formal learning and were affected by learning experiences; and each child's progress had to be evaluated in these terms, as well. Furthermore, emotional and behavioral problems that erupted within the classroom had to be considered relevant to the content of the educational and social experience in which they appeared, and they had to be managed therein. We staff members learned that it was rarely necessary to remove a child from the direct experience of the classroom, since doing so usually reinforced the child's disruptive behavior as a way of avoiding difficult experiences. If a child needed to be separated from the group's activity, there were two possibilities: removal to a different part of the room, where the child could be present, but not a part; and removal to the observation room, where the child could be apart from the group, while still confronting the activity in which difficulties had arisen.

Mental Health Consultation in Schools

A practical example of education as mental health also appears in a model of mental health consultation to schools. Special education programs usually have psychiatric and/or psychological consultants. It is the usual practice to have these consultants evaluate children and recommend, in the case of psychiatrists, medication and/or psychotherapy, which will aid the child's ability to function in the classroom. These professionals are also asked to evaluate children for whom special education is being considered, and in many locales, the recommendation of a psychiatrist is necessary for the referral to special education services for the emotionally disturbed.

Consultation to the schools should be based on two principles of competence: (1) the acknowledgement that teachers have greater experience with the particular child and with children of that age group in general than does the consultant and (2) the recognition that the child's family members also have greater familiarity and experience with the child. Thus, the consultant approaches the questions about a particular child with a number of questions of his own. Addressed to the teacher, these questions will be the following: In what ways is this child different from the other children you have known or the others in this classroom? What have you tried; how does it usually work; how does it work here? What are your hypotheses about the problem? What are your ideas about what is needed? In what areas does the child demonstrate competence? For the classroom observation, the questions will include these: How different is this child from the others? Does the child have any friends or compatriots? How is the child treated by her peers? How is the child treated by the teacher? How does the child seem to feel about herself? For direct evaluation of the child, it is useful to have a parent or the whole family present and to ask the following: How do they view the child? Is it different from how the child is viewed in the school environment? Is the child's demeanor different with the family than in school? What is the child's level of competence? What is the child's attitude about her competence? How much does the child expect to be successful? How easily does a child give up rather than pursue mastery of something possible? The results of these separate areas of assessment are then related to one another along with data from report cards, teacher comments, and testing, with the objective of trying to figure out how the classroom can be an environment more conducive to successful adjustment for the child.

Impediments to Coordinated Approaches

A particular setting in which I practiced briefly serves as a good example of an education-oriented mental health program and of the disruption in this orientation by the finance-driven compartmentalization of professional inputs. The setting was an experimental classroom for kindergarteners through second-graders whose teachers had appreciated that these children had problems adjusting to school but had withheld special classification in favor of an enriched program and mainstreaming. Children spent half days in their regular classrooms and half days in the special class. Thus, the special class had a different group in the morning and in the afternoon. The group size was a maximum eight children, all between five and seven, and there was a teacher and an aide. Furthermore, it was a neighborhood school, so that all of the children lived within walking distance of the school. What an ideal arrangement! My approach was to spend two half days observing in the classrooms, meeting regularly with the teachers, and developing my hypotheses about the children through classroom work with them using materials the teachers recommended. For example, if a child was having trouble with puzzles, we worked with puzzles; if there was difficulty with recognizing letters, we worked with letters, and so on. My aim was to develop some working experience with the child and the given area of difficulty in order to develop with the teachers an intervention that was organic to the classroom and would foster the child's educational success.

In our early staff meetings the teachers would put forth hypotheses about the children's emotional status unconnected with their educational experiences (e.g., Lisa has experienced too many separations; Bonnie is suspicious about strangers; Kevin is unsocialized and has no remorse). The teachers felt that psychotherapy was necessary to help the children address their emotional problems. They tended, at first, to be in awe of what psychotherapy could accomplish and to diminish the importance of their own contributions to remediate the problems they identified. Furthermore, they identified these emotional problems through their assessment of the child's learning and adjustment problems in school. We needed to reverse the process that they had accomplished in an almost reflex fashion. How did Lisa's experience with separations translate into her learning and school behavior, I asked? How could their curriculum increase Bonnie's sense of evaluation of strange situations, so that she could be more comfortable with new people? How could they build on Kevin's reciprocal interactions with other children during play so that he could develop a better sense of empathy?

Gradually, the teachers began to use themselves as the primary units of intervention. This became the practice in the classroom and in the interaction with the children's regular classroom teachers: they were the experts. In addition, they were the ones with whom the parents and caretakers interacted (or didn't, as in the case of some children whose parents could never be located). They had their observations of the families, too, and these also became the focus for therapeutic interactions. Their formulations of the children's difficulties and their observations of the children's progress could be practically communicated to parents in such a way that parents could be asked to assist without being told to get into therapy or dismissed because they were hopeless. Parents were invited to observe their children in the classroom and to work with them in this context.

Problems followed quickly after the establishment of a working relationship with the teachers, in the form of business. A local hospital took over the mental health services to the program in hopes of turning a profit through the collection of medical assistance fees for partial hospitalization and psychotherapy. A psychologist and a social worker were hired, and each of us was instructed to prescribe a program of at least weekly individual psychotherapy, because the collectible fee for a psychotherapy hour was greater than that for half a day in the classroom. Once again the children's emotional lives were separated conceptually from their educational experiences, but this time because of finances. The families were once again seen as adjunctive to the central therapeutic issues for the children, and once again the possibility that the families would have a constructive influence was dismissed. The program was doomed within a year, because it had little redeeming value. It had been effectively dismantled as a public service with a sensibly integrated framework for service delivery, and it was found to lack the potential for turning a profit.

In many states the educational programs of psychiatric hospitals are adjunctive to the central treatment; and day treatment—which, for children, is primarily education—is not funded by mental health, because it is educational (despite being called day treatment and being placed within the continuum of systems of mental health care). These political realities foster dysfunction in the efforts to provide coordinated support for children's development, creating the possibilities of conflicts, dysfunctional triads between agencies and families, and, ultimately, poor fit—which has drastic consequences for the children.

Fit

Fit is the term that refers, first, to the suitability of a particular teacher, learning context, and approach to assessing learning style, given each student's needs; and, second, to the match between all of these factors and the available materials and information. These in-school accommodations are fostered by a good match between parents and the larger arenas of education and school reform. Even without the massive school reform that would be desirable and with the continuing segregation of children requiring specialized education, it is useful to provide school consultation on the basis of fit. As I have said, the fit of child, school, and family forms patterns that are related to the success of a child's education and that can be assessed and rearranged. What is the impact on the child and the family when the school culture is compatible and when it is not? What factors contribute to congenial fit? What are the consequences of poor fit? In regard to fit, I look more closely in this chapter at the circumstances of children with differences in physical, emotional, and cognitive development, in learning styles, and in sociocultural expectations. Several examples are cited to illustrate how some children's difficulties and apparent maladjustment are formulated through an understanding of the experiences in each of three interacting domains of childhood—the individual, the family, and the school—and how these formulations lead to proposed solutions that enhance the fit between the systems and thereby improve the conditions in which the child may master the society's technology. In order to begin to make sense of the important role of school and a child's overall adjustment, it is critical to contemplate this reciprocal or circular relationship: the school affecting the child's self-awareness, the family affecting the child's interpretation of experience, the child criticizing the family through the lenses of the school, and the school criticizing the family through the performance of the child.

Structural Issues

School environments vary in their obvious impact on children's adjustment, but it has been demonstrated that if schools are socioculturally similar to the students and their families, the children will have better adjustment and higher achievement scores. Furthermore, other studies have demonstrated the important influence of the school ethos on students' adjustment when achievement status upon entering school is controlled for (Rotheram 1989). Finally, a convincing argument has been made for learning difficulties experienced by an apparently otherwise capable child being related to misapperceptions between family and school rather than to actual impairment or handicap *in* the child (Coles 1987).

School environments can be described by organizational features, communication patterns, role differentiation between students and teachers, and the system of values and meanings. School–family interactions have been characterized variously according to theoretical framework and language. One way is to observe the isomorphism between family interactions and between school personnel–student interactions involving symptomatic behaviors. For example, parents of a youngster may disagree with each other about his school performance and may also disagree with school authorities about the child's school performance. At home the child finds himself to be the object of parental quarrels; in the family–school interface, he finds himself to be the object of quarrels between parents and school personnel. How these kinds of patterns tend to perpetuate themselves and how helping professionals can be coopted into these patterns—especially if the professional concentrates only on the dysfunctional child, without considering the symptomatic cycles—were described in chapter 4.

Families who function at extremes of interpersonal involvement (i.e., enmeshed or disengaged) tend to be negatively evaluated, but there is an added dimension in assessment when the degree of family involvement is paired with that of the school system. Rotheram (1989) proposed that a school system emphasizing an atmosphere of affection and empathy over hierarchy and structure will tend to get along poorly with families who don't share this style (who may be underinvolved) and will see such families as uncaring. In an underorganized school system, on the other hand, there are few ties, because there are no organizing traditions within the school. Thus, the child's experience is uneven, and this is likely to be reflected in the child's failure. Rotheram suggested that a very common dysfunctional interaction is between underinvolved families and underinvolved schools and that this interaction is almost invariably associated with multiple agency involvements with the family members, generating, at a metalevel, an underinvolved treatment system. In the consistency of the underinvolved structurelessness across subsystems, the deviance of the child and family is amplified. This means that the more helping systems are involved unsuccessfully, the more likely it is for both child and family to be evaluated as deviant; the more compartmentalized and isolated they become, the more idiosyncratic and out of the mainstream they become, being evaluated as needing more services, and involving more helpers, and so on. This is an example of deviance amplification, as described in chapter 4.

Another way of describing the system formed between family and school is a feedback loop—a self-modifying, recursive system. This system actively participates in the construction of a self-evaluation process within the child, but one that optimally also results in self-evaluation and modification within both family and school systems. A positive outcome is when a child is encouraged to make comparisons between family, self, and other people (particularly teachers, other children, and other children's parents). And this skill of thinking critically is encouraged by parents' receptiveness, which fosters the child's taking advantage of the opportunity provided by the school experience. Competence and industry, such essential achievements for the school-aged child, occur in similar recursive cycles. A child's industry is rewarded by increasing competence, which is greeted by teachers and parents in such a way that the child is encouraged to further industry and achievement of greater competence.

Most children, families, and school systems are in some kind of synchrony that allows the children to advance through school without major incident. When this fit is between middle-class, corporate model families and educational systems, children advance and are rewarded in the terms of this society. This synchrony is often misinterpreted as reflecting a good educational system, meaning that pedagogical methods and school environment (whether open classrooms or structured grade systems) are evaluated and proven to be effective. The fit between child, family, and school values is only discovered at a metalevel, not the level that evaluates the functioning of any one of the three systems.

Unhappily, there is another kind of fit between children from poor, disadvantaged families—racially and ethnically different from the prevailing ethos of the educational system, but fitting with the school systems' expectations of them, nevertheless. These children are often expected to be poor learners and to exhibit behavior problems. This kind of fit between family, children, and school system generates consistent failure, for which the blame is placed variously, but with equal vehemence and conviction, on the families, the school system, and the children.

Subsystem or Individual Issues

There are other kinds of situations when the fit doesn't seem to be so good, namely, when school and family share certain values and expectations, but the child does not conform. The child demonstrates nonconformity by not doing well, either by not behaving or not learning according to expectations. Then attention turns to the child. These situations occur in several ways. When the child, the school, and the family are consistent with their expectations that the child could conform, but she does not do so, she is typically called learning disabled. If they are consistent in expectations but also agree that the child cannot conform, the child is usually called handicapped, retarded, or developmentally disabled. In this case, both school and family lower their expectations of the child.

The consequences of poor fit and the likely focus on the child's deficits are the development of a skewed system. The family and the school authorities busy themselves with developing remedial and corrective programs for the child. These programs are usually so oriented to the child's deficits that the education of the child to become a contributing member of society is neglected. The skewed system, focusing as it does on the child's deviance, becomes a deviance-amplifying system. As the child grows older, the gaps widen between his functioning and both what is expected and the level of functioning of the child's peers. In another example of deviance amplification, the child becomes more singular and less like other children in all areas of functioning, a fact that may invite the helpers to intensify their efforts to help, which then, unfortunately, also amplify the child's deviance.

As already suggested, any child in a special education program is at risk to become a part of such a deviance-amplifying cycle, but some do not. Children who have other major strengths, such as athletic ability or social assets, may be included in other systems that correct for the differences in learning potential. What happens in these instances is that there is an essential fit between school, family, and child in most areas, and this fit tends to compensate for the deviance in expectations about learning. But the unfortunate youngster whose systems are seriously out of fit may never recover.

Factors Contributing to Poor Fit

The most obvious factor that makes for poor fit in the family–child–school system is a child who has some physical, emotional, or temperamental differences. There is a good understanding about how these kinds of differences interfere with an individual child's accumulation of experiences that shape into a consensual reality. Sensory abilities and motility have been described as primary ego functions; lacking a balance between these functions, it is more difficult to develop a healthy ego, healthy sense of self, and a healthy sense of one's self's place in a world peopled by "typical" people whose appreciation of the patterns of sensual, cognitive, motor, and social experiences dominates convention.

Families and children from racial and ethnic minorities are more likely to fit poorly with the school system, as I have described. But there is a particular population of children, many of whom are not from racial and ethnic minorities, who form a particularly vulnerable group. These are children who have obvious physical or cognitive differences, which are often referred to as handicaps or disabilities. In a study entitled *The Unexpected Minority,* Gliedman and Roth (1980) proposed that "handicap" is a social construction based on some consensual norms. When individuals with disabilities meet the able-bodied every day, they learn to experience themselves as inferior, as they are experienced as inferior by the able-bodied. It is a pattern of social interaction that occurs constantly, leading to the inescapable perception of oneself as defective and less valuable.

In chapter 8 I pointed out that the so-called talking cure excluded many children with developmental disabilities, handicaps, and mental retardation both because it was believed that they could not participate fully in the psychotherapeutic activity of play and interpretation, and because these youngsters were not seen as emotionally disturbed. Whatever disturbances they demonstrated could be explained by the facts of their disabilities. But when these children are examined in larger relationship contexts, the relevance of their emotional lives becomes apparent, not as separate from the other realms of behavior and experience but as a part of them. Then, the importance of aggressive and early intervention must be acknowledged. The most relevant contexts include, obviously, the child's family and extended family and friends, the system of special therapists for the handicapped, the educational system, the mental health system, the parents' work system, and the larger society's views about disability and wholeness. When the meaning and effects of disabilities are studied at each of these levels, and these meanings are integrated, one gets both a sad and hopeful picture of what it means to be disabled in this society. Sadness comes with the recognition of the pervasive prejudices our society has about the handicapped. Hopefulness comes from the recognition that every disabled person can do some things, has a personality, and can grow, even if slowly—an observation that inspires family members and educators who care for children with disabilities.

A major problem in referring to individuals who are different from the norm is what to call them. The popular terms *disabled, handicapped,* and *retarded* refer to a large, heterogeneous group of individuals whose common feature is that they are different from the group that any society calls normal. Defining *normal* appears to be more difficult than recognizing what is not normal. This is consistent with the deficit orientation of the medical model. Although it leads to specialized attention to those who deviate from the norm, it also leads to the creation of a class of individuals who are, to begin with, less like each other than like those who discriminate them. These phenomena can be understood best by examining them at several levels. At the level of the individual—the child, in this case—distinct patterns of development evolve in the context of the care that she receives. At the level of the family, the first level of care is provided both in response to the child's individual demands and also in response to a set of guidelines about child development and child rearing. When care provided within these guidelines is not adequate because the child's needs are different from those of others, parents may turn to specialists who will give another, special set of guidelines. At the level of parents seeking help and advice and professionals responding, all may be well, because the advice will be based on an evaluation of the child (perhaps in the presence of a parent, but usually not in interaction with the parent) and on the application of practical things to do, based on the professionals' experience with other children who are different. But at another level, it can be seen that the professionals' guidelines are for the development of a different child.

As soon as a family becomes involved with professionals beyond the routines of well-child care or brief contacts for childhood illnesses or even simple surgeries, the usual course of the family life spiral is altered. For in the usual life of the family with a young child, the internal culture of the family is relatively free of direct influence of outsiders (Combrinck-Graham 1983, 1985). This allows family members to evolve relationships built on the confidence of knowing one another and knowing what to do with one another, and this, in turn, seems to be a basis in family life for the development of intimate relating and basic trust (Combrinck-Graham and Kerns 1989). Enter the professionals with diagnostic labels and therapies and guidance, offered with the best of intentions: this delicate negotiation within the family is disrupted; the "family" expands to include the professionals, and the critical role that they play in helping; and the confidence system within the family may be irreparably damaged, at least with respect to the child with the difference.

These events can be seen as the beginning of a process of exclusion, which some have suggested is the most handicapping aspect of being different. The exclusion may begin at different times. It may begin when a child is born looking different, and the parents are uncomfortable showing off their new baby. Or it may begin later, when a teacher says, "I cannot manage this child in my class." At whatever point the exclusion begins, a new path is embarked on, and the child and his family are marked for a development differing from the mainstream. The consequences of segregation in special education are long-lasting, whether it be in special education classes, remedial programs, or bilingual programs. Young people in such programs have a higher drop out rate and lower high school graduation rate. These in such programs who do graduate are less likely to continue in higher education programs and less well prepared for employment. These facts in the lives of children with differences and their families lead to a lasting experience of difference and, ultimately unite the class of the different.

Consequences of Poor Fit

Although I have alluded to the negative outcomes and negative evaluations of children, families, and school systems when there is a poor fit between them, it is useful to look more particularly at the devastating consequences for the children. As a group, children and adolescents who enter the mental health system and the legal system are more likely than not to have failed in school. Thus, serious maladjustments in children are highly correlated with inadequate education. What does this mean? It means that some of these youngsters have not had sufficient opportunity to attend school. This is the case with Tyrone, whose history until age ten was characterized by his mother's multiple male friends, multiple children, and his own crucial role in helping to provide for the family. Tyrone had no time to go to school; it did not meet any of his personal needs. It is also the case with Eduardo who, at nine, became a street person and spent his life surviving. Both Tyrone and Eduardo were ashamed of their ignorance and described themselves as dumb.

Tyrone, who was twelve when I saw him, was described as hyperactive and impulsive. After Ritalin failed to increase his attention span, he was placed on Mellaril and, subsequently, Haldol. By interviewing Tyrone and giving him some drawing tasks, I found that he was able to concentrate, he had strategies, and he was able to implement these strategies thoughtfully and deliberately. In school, in a home economics class, Tyrone demonstrated extreme discomfort when confronted with a reading task, moving uncomfortably in his chair, jumping up and down, seeming to search out distractions or interruptions. Reading was very difficult for him, and he was clearly not getting any gratification from the painstaking process. Yet, when it came to carrying out some measuring tasks that he had just read about, he was a well-coordinated, goal-directed, focused, and organized machine, moving swiftly to get the needed equipment and quickly accomplishing the required tasks. Like most children, Tyrone was prepared to do almost anything to receive some approval from the system of adults that had formed around him. When he was young and lived with his family, it was to steal and roam the streets. When he was older and a ward of the state, it was to gain recognition in almost any way he could. Unfortunately, the system had designated Tyrone as a disturbed, incompetent person. Not recognizing the child's thirst for social approval and his acute embarrassment about his inability to read, the teachers and mental health professionals around him focused on his deficits, his hyperactivity, and what they saw as a kind of antisocial immorality. Tyrone's educational failure seemed to be crucial to his continuing failure in every other area of his life. To date, he has been in a mental health facility for more than three years.

Some children attend school but experience frustration in educational achievement either because school means nothing to them in relation to the rest of their lives (as it would to Tyrone, had he attended), or because they cannot keep up with their peers and get any approval from their teachers. For the child whose school failure is of no consequence to his family or peer group, there may be no strong conflict with poor performance in school. The youngster may be able to succeed in another area. If the child is not particularly smart, it is very likely that she may be exploited by others, sent as a front for deals, put up to dangerous stunts, or sexually or physically abused. If the child's school failure is of consequence to his family, his sense of accomplishment will be deeply affected by the school experience. There will be pressure to provide specialized education for the child, initiating the systems that have already been described, which progressively isolate and differentiate the child from the mainstream of peers and normalized activity and which ultimately relegate the child to the "unexpected minority" Gliedman and Roth described. Scott is an example of this.

Scott's neurological problems included clumsiness and a complex seizure disorder that produced intermittent *absences* with head nodding and a loss of continuity with what was going on. At nine, Scott demonstrated an understanding of the intricate working of transformers; a familiarity with the relationships between characters in TV series, such as "He-Man"; and knowledge of baseball players in both leagues, reflected in his extensive collection of baseball cards. Scott also tested in the bright average range of IQ. Yet Scott did not progress in school. Classroom observation found him to have no direct interaction with his classmates in a special education classroom. He did, however, engage in complicated maneuvers to get their attention. When they did notice him, it was to laugh at him. He was unwilling to work on his own, requiring the full attention of one of the teachers in order to accomplish anything. While he worked, as she pushed him to do what she knew he could do, he moaned, held his head, said it was too hard, and complained that it did not make him happy.

At home, Scott had no friends his age. He preferred to play with toddlers and preschoolers rather than his sister, three years younger. Scott's problems were very trying and were exacerbated by his father's frequent and prolonged absences for overseas duties, his mother's difficulties in taking over all the family responsibilities, and the extensive medical attention Scott required. Family life focused around Scott, emphasizing his incompetence and catapulting his sister into a position of caring for, protecting, and also despising her troubling brother. Scott seemed resigned to his difference while also expressing his distress at not having friends and his real pain at being laughed at.

Bobby is another child whose difference set him apart. Shortly after Bobby was born, the last of six children, his mother was told that he was retarded. On hearing this news, Bobby's father abandoned the family, and Bobby's mother devoted herself to caring for her special son. At two he was placed in an early intervention program, and when he entered kindergarten at five, he was referred to a trainable mentally retarded (TMR) class. Bobby's mother had her own faith in the child but depended on experts to tell her what kinds of services to get for him. Although Bobby was somewhat slow in developing motor milestones, his language development was very slow, so that he was not talking by age four and had very little receptive language as well. On the other hand, his mother observed, Bobby had early on shown a skill in drawing, and by the time he was six, she stated, he could draw all the cartoon characters from TV.

Someone in Bobby's kindergarten recognized that he was more capable than the TMR designation and referred him to a classroom for language impaired children. This program ended when Bobby was eight, but by this time many people had realized that he had at least average intellectual potential accompanied by what they described as serious learning disabilities. He was placed in a classroom for children with learning disabilities. It was in this classroom that Bobby's life of difference began to express itself in ways that alarmed his teachers. Bobby spent most of the day off in his own world, drawing in his special science fiction book, not seeming to connect with the activity in the classroom. He was seen to be talking to himself as he wended his way into school in the mornings. The school staff recognized that Bobby had constructed a private world. They felt that he was psychotic.

I evaluated Bobby first in the presence of his mother. His grasp and work with complex visual–motor tasks was impressive. He showed me his science fiction book, a book that told stories about people and other planetary beings. It also told that Bobby was observant and competent in the graphic world. Bobby's mother trod a thin line between the information she was given by educational experts and her own experience of her son. Throughout the conversation Bobby was content to draw. Even when he was directly addressed, he continued to draw, unless his mother turned his face toward her while she was talking. It became apparent that Bobby could not decode aural language that was not connected to visual cues. Although his audiometry showed normal hearing apparatus, both his speech and language teacher and his special education teacher confirmed that Bobby often appeared deaf to what was going on.

These three boys illustrate in very different ways poor fit between child/family and school, which resulted in failures to progress educationally and socially, and to increasing maladjustment of the child with resultant increased exclusion from the mainstream of education. In Tyrone's case, educational failure in the past contributed to his negative evaluation of himself and what I perceived to be efforts to minimize those situations in which he felt inadequate and maximize time in those situations in which he felt competent. These behaviors were labeled as disturbed, however, and he was given medication to correct his behavior. For Scott, neurological differences set him apart; and despite his adequate intellectual potential, he could not progress, this failure accentuating his difference and, ultimately, isolation from other youngsters in his class. Bobby, not being able to decode aural inputs, was liable to misinterpret what was going on. He developed his own occupations, which concerned observers interpreted as signs of his being psychotic.

How to Improve Fit

Clearly, I am presenting a specific approach to working with children with school problems when I suggest that the task is to improve the fit between the child, the family, and the school system. It is not unique. The individualized education plan (IEP) that is required for every child in special education is an effort to develop a proper fit between an education system and a child's special needs, with the parents involved to understand what is being undertaken so that they can support the effort. But the IEP is usually based on an assessment of the child, without an explicit assessment of the matrix of the child's lack of learning success, and I am advocating that this is necessary to develop a learning environment that is not further handicapping.

Evaluation of children who are not progressing in school must include a thorough assessment of the child, including her level of maturity and the integration of sensory, motor, and cognitive functions. Assessment of these and of social/adaptive functioning with a thorough developmental history comprise the usual evaluation of such a child. I advocate, in addition, an assessment of the child's, the family's, and the school's expectations of behavior—the child's in the family versus in the school; the school's with the child, with the family, and with the consultant; and the family's, when with the child and when with the school personnel. All of these observations must be considered in the context of the referral and of the person of the consultant. For example, as noted in chapter 5, if school personnel has requested the consultation, they are likely to be the prominent influence on the consultant, and the child's and family's response to the consultant may reflect that. If the family requests the consultation, however, the school personnel may feel somewhat defensive. These details, which will be evaluated in terms of differences in expectations, behaviors, and level of comfort will be the basis upon which the consultant evaluates fit.

Tyrone's mother had gone off somewhere, and he had been placed first in a group home and then, because of his uncontrollable and impulsive behavior, in a treatment facility. His aunt visited periodically, but from the perspective of the hospital staff, Tyrone had no family. He was a ward of the state. This was not at all how Tyrone saw it. He had his aunt and her children, who brought clothes, candy, and money when they visited. And he had a mother. She didn't write, but he guessed that she loved him. He also had a father and the comforting sense that his aunt knew where to find him. Thus, Tyrone's perception of his family did not fit with that of the agencies taking care of him.

Could there have been a better fit for Tyrone? Yes, very possibly. Had the teachers recognized that the hyperactivity was generated by embarrassment, offered him encouragement, and talked with him about what he might accomplish by learning how to read, he probably would have been able to endure the discomfort and evaluate his successes within his own framework. But for the teachers to have worked with Tyrone in this way, they would have had to hear from the treatment staff that Tyrone did not really have ADHD or some other disorder that needed to be controlled by medicine. They would have needed to hear that their management of Tyrone's feeling about his increasing academic skills was a valuable contribution to Tyrone's treatment. Overall, a better fit between the treatment "family" and the teachers was needed. In Tyrone, I deliberately picked an example of a child who did not have specific learning disabilities, to show how lack of fit tended to emphasize his pathology and what better fit might do.

Scott, whose situation was discussed earlier, had a complex seizure disorder. The seizure episodes interfered with the continuity of his experience, so that in the middle of a conversation he would have a moment of "absence," nod his head, and then struggle to reenter the stream of conversation. Scott suffered from an organic disruption in his processing of all experiences. The list of complaints about Scott's school performance was all about behavior. As noted earlier, Scott seemed to put little effort into his work, whined, and depended on the singular attention of his teacher or an aide to progress at all. Also, Scott had no relationships with his classmates. My observation was that he could not keep up with them; and a secondary cycle was established with the other kids teasing or laughing at him, and Scott alternately feeling hurt and thinking of antics to provoke this kind of attention. The upshot of the cycle was to amplify the differences between Scott and his age-mates. But Scott did enjoy being with much younger children, and he had even approached the principal with the request that he spend some time in the kindergarten.

Both the school personnel and Scott's family believed that his attraction to younger children was a sign of his immaturity, and they discouraged it. They expressed great disappointment that despite his ability, Scott failed to develop academically. In short, they shared the opinion that Scott could do better in both of the areas of his difficulty if he would only try. In this area there seemed to be a fit between the school's and family's expectations, but neither set of expectations fit with Scott's own beliefs in himself. On another level, however, although there was sympathy for the burdens of Scott's mother, school personnel felt that she was not doing as much as she could to involve Scott in after-school activities that would increase his social contacts and his sense of competence.

Was there a possibility of better fit? In this instance, it seemed that Scott was showing the way. Could the school capitalize on his strengths and his preferences? If he felt that he could benefit from spending time in the kindergarten, was there not a chance that he could accomplish something by doing so? That was one proposition that I, as the consultant, offered to the teachers and principal. Suppose that Scott were allowed to help out in the kindergarten? Suppose that after having established a "big brother" relationship with the youngsters in the kindergarten, Scott was given a regular role in the kindergarten for which he would have to earn the time by accomplishing specified academic tasks. Suppose that, by having earned this privilege, Scott gained some prestige and sense of his own important contribution to the younger children?

The built-in reward in this plan was designed by Scott, and because it was his choice, the efforts he would have to make to bridge the gaps in conscious continuity would be greater and more adaptive, and he would get more personal reward from it. Scott had defined an area where he thought he would feel competent. It really was up to the school and his family to take advantage of it. Scott's awareness of his difference from other children, of his failure to please his family, and of the unrewarding effort it took to have a coherent experience was enhanced by his bright average intellectual ability. With the exception of his seizure activity, Scott was as able as any other child in his class, but neither he nor his classmates thought so. A second area of work for Scott would be the difficult task of developing peer empathy and advocacy among his classmates. Each child in Scott's special class had personal reasons that presumably interfered with his ability to function in school. Since each child's situation was personal, however, the reasons for each being in special education were never officially discussed and mastered within the group. After Scott had achieved a sense of competence and status through his role in the kindergarten, it would have been valuable for him if the other boys had understood the disruptions in continuity imposed by his seizures. They could have then assisted him by waiting, filling him in, and standing up for him.

Bobby, in contrast to Scott, had a serious perceptual impairment that interfered consistently with his processing of social reality. Having formulated Bobby's problems in terms of his "deafness," Bobby's teacher, his speech therapist, his mother, and the consultant began to understand Bobby's behavior in these terms. Instead of defining Bobby as mentally ill and psychotic, they began to see that Bobby was often insufficiently oriented both to academic tasks and to his social role. Because of the class size in the learning disabled (LD) class, it was impossible for the teacher to do with Bobby what seemed to be the most useful, namely, orient him to each academic and social task, using kinesthetic and visual cues to augment auditory ones. Bobby was transferred to a classroom for the emotionally disturbed (ED), where the class size was smaller and the particular teacher placed a greater emphasis on just the issues of orientation everyone had agreed were important for Bobby. Tasks in the ED class were often interactional in nature, and each task was followed by a discussion period where the children reviewed the accomplishments, applauded each other's competence, and reflected on their own feelings about the task and the group. In this classroom it was possible for both the teacher and the other children to help Bobby remain in contact with the social grouping.

A hurdle to be overcome was the patterns Bobby had generated to make his own meaning—his preoccupation with science fiction and his tendency to lapse into his familiar world of drawing, much easier than to exert the effort that was being required to grasp and interpret the real interactions in his classroom. Furthermore, Bobby's mother was accustomed to interpreting and managing his world for him; and she would need to put more demands on him to make his own interpretations. Thus, treatment for Bobby was not a simple matter of developing better fit in his classroom in school, but also of addressing some of the adaptive patterns that had been generated but were no longer adaptive.

Giant Steps Revisited

I have taken the first giant step in discussing the education system by proposing that it is not just another compartmentalized domain of childhood. It is the system in which the developing child, after age six, spends most of her waking hours. It makes no sense to separate out the functions of education and mental health, for doing so creates the possibility that a child's education will be increasingly irrelevant to her overall development of competence and self-confidence. When education does not provide the sense of competence and self-confidence necessary for a person to feel effective, then there is little else that will. I have proposed that education be seen as a primary context for mental health, and I have described several programs in which mental health services were delivered through the medium of education by specially trained teachers. I have further proposed that the role of education is more than pedagogy around the technology of reading and mathematics; it provides a culture for learning to live in our civilization. In taking the second step, I have described several patterns of interaction between school, family, and child under the general category of fit, observing that when there is good fit, everyone is likely to feel successful; when there is bad fit, there is a likelihood of deviance amplification. The probable consequence of deviance amplification for the child is the development of emotional disturbance, which, getting back to my first point, may then direct attention away from the educational milieu to the mental health system, thus further amplifying deviance. The third step requires fitting the family competence together with that of the educators, recognizing the vital function of educators for schoolchildren and the important experience and skill they bring to their work, and helping them recognize the peculiar culture of each child's family. Finally, all the steps, beginning with reframing education as vital to mental health, lead directly to the fourth step—recognizing and supporting a healthy system organized for the benefit of all of its parts. Here, in addition to the children, the parts include their families and the school system. It is a paradox to exclude children from mainstream education because of their special needs (especially when these are thought to be due to emotional disturbances), because the exclusion and sequestering have such a devastating effect on the child's self-perception and view of himself as a whole and healthy person.

One large study of children described as severely emotionally disturbed found that 90 percent of them were more than two grades behind age level academically, thus confirming the close relationship of education and mental health (Friedman et al. 1989). But what is this relationship? In a few children emotional disturbances interfere with education. This is true of children with psychotic processes through which the learning process is distorted. It is true, periodically, with children who have severe anxiety or depression, and this group of children runs into a larger group of children whose preoccupation with events outside of school interferes with attention to school. The latter group is also mixed with those children, to whom I alluded in chapter 5, whose home culture and school culture make conflicting demands, resulting in a poor fit between family and school expectations. Then there is a substantial group of children whose failure in school is connected to poor self-esteem, depression, distractibility, and resignation. I have known many children who would rather appear either mad or bad than dumb.

Alan Gartner and Dorothy Kerzner Lipsky (1989), citing Thomas Kuhn's point about the necessity of a paradigm shift (a giant step) in scientific revolutions (see chapter 1), propose the following radical revisions of special education practice:

1. Rather than equate a child with his or her impairment and regard the child as handicapped, clarify the relationship between impairment and the social response to what is regarded as a handicap, and prepare the student to cope with the impairment and become an advocate for needed services.
2. Rather than accept IQ as a unidimensional view of intelligence and cognitive ability, reexamine the definition of intelligence, recognizing its multidimensional aspects.
3. Rather than attribute failures and difficulties to deficits in the students, reframe students' problems as the mismatch between learning needs and instructional systems.
4. Rather than regard the students as vessels that become containers for the information and skills taught, recognize a different role for students as participants in their learning and learning as an interactional experience.
5. Rather than provide special services for a heterogeneous group of children with special needs in a special setting, integrate all students so that special education services are delivered in the mainstream,

243

truly individualized to meet each student's needs. In this way differences among students are respected, and all students benefit.

6. Rather than treat parents as impaired and requiring professional help, involve them as partners.

7. Finally, these changes cannot be made in special education without being embedded in broader school reform, directed at more appropriate education for all students.

These proposed reforms capture all of the giant steps. They illustrate, further, how the mental health of children can and should be addressed within the broad arena of education and the specific experience of a child's school.

CHAPTER 12

The Health Care System: Ironies of Technology and Healing

Social reality is so organized that we do not routinely inquire into the meanings of illness. . . . Indeed, the everyday priority structure of medical training and of health care delivery, with its radically materialist pursuit of the biological mechanism of disease, precludes such inquiry. It turns the gaze of the clinician, along with the attention of patients and families, away from decoding the salient meanings of illness for them. . . . The biomedical system replaces this allegedly "soft," therefore devalued, psychosocial concern with meanings with the scientifically "hard," therefore overvalued, technical quest for the control of symptoms. This pernicious value transformation is a serious failing of modern medicine: it disables the healer and disempowers the chronically ill. Biomedicine must be indicted of this failure in order to provoke serious interest in reform, because a powerful therapeutic alternative is at hand.

— ARTHUR KLEINMAN, *The Illness Narratives*, 1988

Physical integrity is fundamental to mental health. By the same token, mental health also underscores physical integrity. Health care systems for children are increasingly prepared to guarantee a foundation of mental health by establishing and protecting physical integrity through developments in prenatal care, well-child care, and immunization against deadly or disabling childhood diseases. Ironically, with the increase in technology for protecting robust physical functioning, there is also an increase in the viability of compromised babies and an increase in the survival of youngsters with serious, chronic, and often disabling illnesses, thus producing new challenges to the quality of survival and the mental health of all of the survivors in the child's relationship system.

Overlooked Aspects of Health

Substantial accomplishments in identifying disease processes and mechanisms to fight disease have not been paralleled by progress in working with the emotional, psychological, and spiritual aspects of health. This is unfortunate, because emotional, psychological, and spiritual domains are the essence of the family system's contribution to health. It is vital for health providers to examine and acknowledge these functions of interpersonal systems, and to incorporate in the overall health care plan an understanding of a given family system's style of providing these elements of health. This will lead the committed health care provider to study methods of healing that reach beyond the limits of biomedical technology, activating healing responses in the patients' systems. Attention to healing and the function of attitudes and role assignment in the management of illness will also lead health care providers into the exploration, or at least recognition, of the meaningfulness of techniques of healing beyond the biomedical. Techniques such as hypnosis and imagery tap into the patient's and family's vernacular modes and images. Involvement of healers is a bolder step that must also be considered if such individuals or groups are seen by the patient system as significant.

The health care system for children has enlarged its conscious involvement of families in the care of sick children by providing rooming-in for parents of hospitalized children and recognizing the critical role of parent education and cooperation in compliance with medical regimens. These developments reflect the acknowledgement of the impact of family functioning on the overall health of children. There are two sides to the effects of involving families more, however. On the one hand, families are supported in carrying the now-recognized burdens they have for the care and maintenance of their children when they are ill, parents are engaged with the health care provider in helping their children, and pediatricians generally attempt to ally with parents. On the other hand, treatment failures, reflected in repeated relapses or repeated bouts or in a deteriorating course despite the best of medical care, are often blamed on the family—accusations that they did not adequately carry out medical orders or that they have psychologically undermined the child. Clearly, when the health care providers are critical of family members, there is a dysfunctional relationship at the interface of the family and health care systems, which is certainly reflected in the care the child receives.

I have noted that the health care system, in maintaining physical health, is essential to the well-being that underscores mental health. But as a social system led by physicians—perhaps the most influential professionals in American society—the health care system also has enormous influence on attitudes about child care and child rearing. This influence of experts is the force behind successful immunization and public health programs. Ironically, it is also a force behind a professionalism that undermines natural resources and competence.

Two areas of the health care system are examined in this chapter: health maintenance and management of illness. In each area advances in the technology of detecting and attacking disease tend to distract health care providers from healing. But preventing, detecting, and attacking disease should not be mutually exclusive. Proper attention to significant relationship systems provides the overarching connection between them. On the other hand, ignoring both relational resources and the interpersonal processes involved in managing health polarizes systems and militates against healing, well-being, and mental health, which recursively affects physical integrity.

Promising Developments

There has been significant progress in including and utilizing the energy of a child's family, even since the early 1960s when I entered medical school to work with children. In my early medical school experiences I found out two things: (1) Prevention and health maintenance were the underpinnings of general pediatric practice and the orientation of much pediatric research, and (2) professionals who focused on children were of two minds about the family—some said they loved the children but couldn't stand the family, whereas others said that caring for children required getting along with parents. Generally, however, in the late sixties and early seventies, even in a major children's hospital, care was focused on the child with little regard for the family unit as a potential source of expertise and assistance. If distress was manifested by another member of the family, individual services would be provided to that person, as well. The outcome was often the experience of protection of family members from others' fears and grief, with all of the accompanying isolation.

Two Cases of Family Involvement

Take, for example, Jonathan, eleven years old, the youngest of three children and only boy, who had acute lymphoblastic leukemia and was in his second relapse. Because of the relapses, his long-term prognosis was poor. He was in the hospital and was waiting for his white cells and platelets to come back after aggressive chemotherapy. Each night he received white cell and platelet transfusions, suffering the chills that were a part of his response to these treatments. Jonathan's leukemia had been diagnosed at a time when the child was protected from the knowledge of his illness and particularly from the idea that the illness might be terminal. The parents were encouraged to shield their child from this knowledge. In that period during the 1960s one could see parents perambulating their hairless, hollow-eyed, weeping children through the corridors, each isolated in personal grief.

Jonathan had bad dreams, and that is why I was asked to see him. I talked with his mother and with him and quickly realized that the two were protecting each other from what they each knew. Joining them together seemed the obvious solution but was not immediately possible because Jonathan's mother had grown accustomed to having her son's most serious needs attended to by doctors, and she did not have confidence in her own ability to provide necessary emotional support for him. She told me of her fears and wishes for her son. I tried to honor them in my dealings with Jonathan. I was a go-between.

We had about two months. Jonathan went into remission, was discharged, and gradually, tentatively, reentered his school life. Within a few weeks, he relapsed, developed sepsis, reentered the hospital, and died after about fifteen hours of heroic medical treatment. Those last hours were extraordinary. Jonathan, often delirious, would suddenly focus on his parents, as they stood by his bed, grasping their hands, and reporting his experiences from "the other side." He, at last, broke the barrier between them and gave them the last gift of the fullness of his experience of his impending death and the courage to deal with it. It was a privilege to observe the healing occurring in this family, even as the precious son was dying. Later that summer, I became the consultant to the oncology service, with opportunities to intervene earlier and with the oncology staff.

The contrasting tale to that of Jonathan was of Melanie, who, at six, had had acute lymphoblastic leukemia (ALL) since she was three. She had had so many relapses and remissions that her family began to feel the rhythm of her illness without fully accepting that it could ultimately be fatal. Early one July, she was admitted with meningitis. Her intracerebral pressure was so great that she had begun to show brainstem signs, coma, and spastic paralysis. Treatment was initiated quickly, and she recovered from the infection and went into remission, but remained spastic. She graduated from intravenous feedings to a gastrostomy, and her mother was taught how to feed her through this. She stayed with Melanie constantly and was finally able, by massaging her neck while having her suck on a washcloth, to get her to accept oral feedings. Finally, Melanie was ready to go home, everyone in the hospital feeling that there was no more that could be done for her there.

Melanie was the youngest of seven children, several of whom had not seen her since she had been admitted. I suggested that in preparation for her going home the entire family come in to talk with the doctors. They all came—six children, ranging in ages from nine to nineteen, and both parents. The oncologist explained Melanie's problem, about how something had interfered with the messages from her brain to her muscles and she couldn't walk or talk, and they wouldn't know if she could understand them. And no one knew how much better she would get. In fact, the oncologist said, "Melanie is like a baby in many ways. And one thing we know about babies is that they need lots of love." Everyone in the room was moved, tears glittered in the eyes of the older children and rolled down the cheeks of the nine-year-old sister. They took Melanie home that day, to feed her with a bottle and to love her. In a month Melanie was back to visit, walking with a slightly spastic gait and smiling the six-year-old's toothless smile as she anticipated her first day in first grade! We don't know what happened, but we were sure that her family's love had been a potent ingredient.

Melanie died when she was nine. Her parents wrote gratefully about the care that she and they had received, noting that her life and her death had brought the family together in a way that they could not have anticipated. They thus found healing in their struggle and loss.

These two stories illustrate the evolution of attitudes about the family's involvement in the care of sick children from advocating the isolation of family members and concealment of their feelings from each other (which prevailed even in the early 1970s) to providing opportunities for togetherness, mutual comfort, and mutual healing.

By the mid-1970s, parents were invited to stay with their children; to assist in difficult, painful, and scary procedures; to comfort their children in recovery rooms after surgery; and to become partners in medical care. We discovered that even squeamish, troublemaking, and challenging parents could become competent partners if we did three things: (1) give them adequate information in a vernacular they could understand, (2) solicit their input about major treatment decisions, and (3) make sure that all of the relevant adult caretakers in the family got information directly from the physicians (thus avoiding message transmission and distortion within the family).

Giant Steps in Health Care Delivery

It should be easy to see how the giant steps ought to affect the mental health consultant's involvement with the health care delivery system. First, the realities of illness must involve not just disease processes but also host factors, which include individual emotional status as well as interpersonal system functioning and response. The reactions of caretakers, from immediate family members to the medical staff, are among the many sides that have to be heard and integrated into the picture of the illness. In taking the second giant step it must be recognized that illnesses have roles in family life; families do become organized around management of illness, and these patterns and functions have an important reality beyond the disease process itself. There are important patterns established by all those involved with the illness—the patient, family members, and health care providers. As described later, these patterns can unwittingly interfere with healing. Third, patients and their families have competence and resources, and although they require attention and assistance from health care providers, most families bear the burden of keeping their children healthy and caring for them when they are sick. The means by which they do this are extraordinary as they involve extended family members, form support groups, and develop their own philosophies to guide them through the tough spots. The consultant to the health care system should learn from the uniquely elaborated ways that systems find to cope with illness, for what people confronting these complex challenges devise far exceeds what could be designed by the most imaginative clinician. Taking these three steps together, the health care professional must realize that many families with children who have serious or handicapping conditions are very healthy. They organize in such a way that the needs of each member are met while they cope with the extraordinary demands of the illness. Melanie and her family, just described, are fine examples of this.

Health Maintenance

Essential contributions of pediatrics to public health have been in the identification of and immunization against dangerous childhood diseases and the development of a schedule for well-child care. Both of these have evolved with the technology that first identified the bacteria causing diphtheria, tetanus, and whooping cough and later the viruses causing measles, rubella, mumps, and polio. After the organisms were specified, additional technology led to production of vaccines that protected the vulnerable from these illnesses and to a schedule of administration that maximized this protection. Well-child care evolved out of this technology but evolved into the inclusion of a much broader assessment of child health and family functioning. The schedule of well-child visits is set to accommodate the immunization schedule and also to track the child's developmental accomplishments. Motor, sensory, social, and adaptive functioning is assessed in the child, who is always accompanied to visits by a caretaker. It is impossible to do well-child care without a caretaking adult, be it a parent, grandparent, guardian, or baby-sitter. Thus, it would appear to be impossible to do a well-child assessment without observing the child in relationship to someone more familiar than the examiner.

Involving the Family in Well-Child Care

Even routine well-child care has an important influence on the family's experience of its ability to care for its children. From the prenatal visits to the visits during the first months of the baby's life, the interactions between the health care professional and family have significant impact. When the infant is evaluated by a health care professional, the various physiological systems of the child are investigated. Anyone observing the examination would note that the examiner has a routine and particular set of questions—a framework through which the examination is conducted, data about the child are gathered, and conclusions are drawn. If the child's parents are present in the examining room, additional data about both the child and the family are available. For example, if the child is frightened by the examination, the parents' handling of the child's fears becomes a part of the data. But if the examiner has been trained to use data only from the individual child, she will not integrate the data from the family.

This was the case with one pediatrician who videotaped a well-baby visit for supervision with me. He was accustomed to dealing with only the mother and the infant. But in this particular session the baby's father and eighteen-month-old sister also came, and the pediatrician boldly invited all of the family members into the examining room. Not knowing what to do with the other family members, he proceeded with his routine examination of the baby and questions for the mother. The father watched quietly, and the little girl played noisily with the contents of a toy box. After the physical examination, the mother sat down with her naked infant on her lap while the physician asked a few more questions about the pregnancy. The older child saw the opportunity to approach her mother and brought her a piece of foil she had found in the toy box. The mother, intent on her conversation with the doctor, ignored the child, who persisted, rattling the foil under her nose. Finally, she abstractedly took the foil and placed it on the floor. The child went back to the toy box. Neither the mother nor the pediatrician paused to consider these data from the family ecology of this mother and infant.

When I saw it on the videotape, I stopped it and looked at the pediatrician. "Yes, wasn't that interesting," he said. "She may have had a bit of blood pressure elevation." The pediatrician was locked into the verbal-information-recording mode. I replayed the segment. He commented that the mother most certainly did have preeclampsia. I replayed the segment without sound and asked him to describe what was going on. Only *then* did the little girl get his attention, and we could discuss the implications of this opportunity. If he had noticed the little girl's efforts to get her mother's attention, he could have promoted well-child interaction with the siblings, as well as involving both parents. He could, for example, have paused in his conversation with the mother, observing, "I think Gail has something she wants you to see"—a brief but important invitation to the parents to divide the attention between two small children. Doing this, however, requires attention to the opportunities presented by the relationship system and the professional's commitment to the importance of this system and the information its members generate. These data about relationships are always present in pediatrics, because a child is always brought by an adult caretaker. Thus, it is up to the health care professional to use this information.

The examiner's response and judgment about the child and family interaction have such a significant effect that they, too, must be considered part of the data. In many cases parents are very readily influenced by pediatricians or nurse practitioners. For example, if a physician observed the parents' handling of the child's fears and remarked on what he experienced as strictness and lack of understanding displayed by the parents, here is a pattern that could be established. He would convey disapproval of their handling of the child. He might then attempt to correct their behavior with the child by encouraging them to comfort her rather than demanding that she stop crying. The parents would then experience themselves in relationship to the physician's criticism, and they would have to reevaluate their attitudes and behavior in light of the physician's point of view. They might choose to disagree and possibly even to seek out another doctor. But they probably would assume that he is an expert, and they are not, so that they would try to correct their behavior.

Imagine that their approach to their child's fears was consistent with the sociocultural ethos in which they were raised—namely, that one learns to be stoic and to master one's fears. They were helping their child do that.

But the physician had another point of view; and the parents, feeling criticized, might have either objected and rejected the physician as a helper or questioned themselves, introducing doubt and uncertainty into their relationship with the child. These kinds of interactions can ripple through the ecosystem in both directions. The physician could shape the parents' views of their child, perhaps even defining the child as fearful or cautious. The child's tentative approach to new experiences might then be reinforced by the parents' uncertainty. The parents' uncertainty might then be amplified by the criticism they subsequently experienced from their own family and friends, who would observe that they have not been strict enough with the child. Further patterns could be elaborated that would give character to the child's school experience and relationships with peers and siblings, and to the parents' self-perceptions at work and in their peer groups. These are potential far-reaching consequences of a pediatrician's judgment, but they are not far-fetched. Routine well-child visits should, therefore, include a more conscious assessment, not just of the child's health and development and child–caretaker interaction, but also of the relationship between the family and the health care provider and the relevance of this to the family's own context.

In the situation where the pediatrician observes the parents being strict with a fearful infant, then, a more competent pattern might be evolved if the pediatrician were to say, "I notice that you don't like it when the baby cries when I touch her. Do you think she is shy or afraid of this situation?" Through a question about an observation, the parents are asked to consider what they do. Next, the pediatrician might ask, "You want her to be brave, don't you? Do you think she feels safer when you are firm with her like that? Do you think she would feel safer if you held her while I examine her, so she could get to know me a little?" In asking further questions, the pediatrician offers possibilities but has the parents be the final judge. If they decide that comfort is more effective than discipline, they decide it for themselves, they can explain it to doubting grandparents, and they expect to help their child be less fearful.

COORDINATING THE CARETAKERS' EFFORTS

A more complicated function of health care professional–family interaction during infancy is in the management of basically healthy but difficult babies, such as those with colic, irregularity, or sleep problems. Frequently the child's difficulties seem more severe in the context of parent anxiety about them. All of these problems are more easily approached when all of the adult caretakers are involved in the health care. The baby's difficulties readily become parts of recursive patterns within a concerned family. For example, irregularities in the baby's behavior are bound to cause consternation among the adults. Consternation tends to promote disagreements as the adults embark on a series of strategies to solve the problems.

It is easy to imagine, for instance, the cacophony in the home of a new baby whose grandparents have come to help out for the first few weeks. The baby cries frantically and inconsolably. Mother rushes in, tries to nurse, but the baby spits up. "Did you check his diaper?" the anxious father asks. "I just changed him," chimes in the grandmother. "He probably needs to burp, Mary. You never give him enough time to burp." "Okay, I'll try to burp him." The baby screams louder. "Don't jiggle him so much—you're upsetting him more." "Here, give him to me, I'll try to walk him. You always calmed down when I walked you." "Can't you get him to stop crying?" "How about some sugar water?" and so on. The strategies conflict, the fuses get short, pretty soon people start to blame each other, and the situation escalates. This is not a situation in which a baby could calm down, sleep, or settle his digestion. The professional who does not appreciate this scenario is more likely to contribute to the chaos with expert advice to provide a solution. This may then provide a new content around which to enact the same scheme. Now, when the baby screams or cries, someone adds, "Did you do what the doctor said?" And another says, "That's not when, what, or how you were supposed to do it." They're off and running again. Whatever medical solutions might be offered will be most successful if the caretakers can be transformed from a well-meaning but dysfunctional crowd into a coordinated team. For the professional to assist in this process, she must involve the caretakers in order to recruit them into the teamwork.

Illness and the Mind–Body Interface

The relationship between physical illness and psychological well-being has been broached many times throughout the book. I have argued that principles of defining disease and of locating the causes of disease, which apply in ordinary medical specialties, are oversimplified metaphors when applied to emotional well-being. I have also noted that there is a recursive interaction between emotional and physical integrity, so that it is inappropriate to locate difficulties solely in either the psychological or the physiological sphere. I have asserted that the total person, together with his most significant relationship, must be addressed.

As discussed in chapter 3, James Griffith and colleagues (1989) have proposed some principles of mind–body patterns that serve as a map for sorting through the maze of symptoms that can be presented, especially to a mental health consultant in a health care environment. They posit a hierarchy of functions from anatomical to physiological to psychological to social. Disturbances at any one of these levels can cause behavioral changes. They assert that there is a more profound effect from the lower to the higher levels in the hierarchy, although there is some effect in the other direction, as well. Furthermore, there are disturbances that are primarily located in each level. Thus, there are neurobehavioral problems due to disturbances in anatomy (e.g., Alzheimer's disease, brain tumors, brain infarcts) that may cause memory deficits or delirium. There are psychophysiological problems in which emotional stress affects physiology, as in peptic ulcers, asthma, or brittle diabetes. And there are psychological problems, such as reactive depression and anxiety. It is easy to comprehend the effects of changes in the lower levels on the higher ones of psychological and social functioning. The effects in the opposite direction are less obvious, but nevertheless important.

I have seen two adults who have become severely handicapped through what I have appreciated to be an escalating process of engagement rippling through the domains of childhood. In one instance, a nine-year-old's struggle with her parents over what and how much she should eat rapidly became a life-and-death ordeal. The family progressively recruited more health care and then legal power in their fight to save their daughter's life, while the girl recruited more serious life-threatening symptoms in her fight for personal authority. By nineteen she had lived for five years in a psychiatric hospital, was on several psychotropic medications, and was placed on continuous one-to-one observation to prevent her from purging. When she turned eighteen, the state had awarded guardianship to her parents, because she was deemed incompetent to protect her own interests. A second case involved a young woman, an only child, in her mid-twenties who was a juvenile diabetic. When she was diagnosed at age seven, her parents were devastated and took total charge of her care. Having assumed such complete responsibility for her care at first, they were not prepared to continue the management through her adolescence. Her diabetes went wildly out of control as she asserted her independence, eating what she pleased when she pleased and involving herself in drugs and drinking, as well. As with the girl with the eating disorder, health care professionals came to the rescue and took charge. She was hospitalized frequently; and when she was twenty, a public guardian took over her care, and she was confined to a state hospital to prevent her from killing herself.

In both cases, well-intentioned but misguided social interactions had devastating effects on health and well-being, as health care providers were recruited into a system that took over functions of both the individual and the family. How could this be avoided when a child seemed so intent on destroying herself? Another example illustrates how a pediatrician skillfully turned control back to a child and her family, even after a psychiatrist had diagnosed her eating disorder.

Isabelle was thirteen and had always been chunky. Her parents, both professionals, were divorced, and both were occupied with their professional and social relationships. Quite without them noticing it, Isabelle began to lose weight and to exercise more. Her mother noticed it first and talked to her father, and they agreed that all the changes in her life must be upsetting her. Perhaps she should talk to a psychiatrist. Isabelle began more compulsive restricting of food and exercise, and the concerned psychiatrist told her parents that she had anorexia nervosa. Isabelle's general appearance of ill health alarmed her mother, who made an appointment with the family pediatrician, Dr. Goldstein, who had known her since she was born. "My goodness, Isabelle," he said, "you look terrible! You used to be a little on the plump side, but now you are too thin!" He arranged for a meeting with both parents and spoke with her psychiatrist on the telephone. It was February, and Isabelle had a ski trip planned for the spring break in March. Dr. Goldstein asked Isabelle and her parents if they thought it made sense for her to go skiing when she was so weak and undernourished. Isabelle began to whine and pout, saying she felt fine. Her parents thought maybe they should consult the psychiatrist, since telling her she couldn't go on the trip might make her worse. "I've already talked with her about that," Dr. Goldstein said. "I expect that if Isabelle really wants to go on that trip, she can put on some weight by then." For another half hour both parents and Isabelle discussed what would be a reasonable weight gain for the ski trip. She met the goal, went on the trip, and had no further eating disorder symptoms.

Management of Illness

John Rolland (1984), founder of a center for families with chronic illness, developed a scheme for categorizing illness dimensions and families' management of illness. Major dimensions include onset (acute or gradual), course of illness (progressive, constant, or relapsing), outcome (fatal or nonfatal), and degree of incapacitation. These characteristics combine to form a profile of an illness, conveying some of the special demands made on a child and family. For example, a fatal, slowly progressive, gradually incapacitating illness such as cystic fibrosis would demand dramatically different responses from those surrounding an acute, progressive, and fatal condition such as Reyes syndrome. Judith Libow, a childrens' hospital based psychologist, (1989) points out that three other dimensions are particularly important in the management of pediatric illnesses: pain, deformity, and treatment ambiguity.

Pain and suffering of children is agonizing for parents, who feel shamed that they cannot protect their children. Physical deformity focuses public attention on the child and constantly reminds parents of their failures. Treatment ambiguity refers to those situations where parents have to make judgments about when or how much treatment should be administered to their child. Each of these characteristics is an emotional trigger for most parents (and, I might add, for other caretakers). Another important dimension is the timing of the illness onset, as well as of the chronic sequelae, for the individual child and in the family life cycle. In chapter 4 patterns of the family life cycle were described proposing that all family members are involved in emotional issues characteristic of a particular era in the family's life. A discussion of the Funicelli family will illustrate how the family's developmental themes interplayed with other patterns in shaping the early experiences of Paul's illness.

The Funicellis' Response to Illness

Paul was the youngest of six children in the blue-collar Italian family. Mr. Funicelli had been a successful small contractor in his own business but had decided to sell the business and move with his family to the mountains to live a simpler life, which they all agreed would be more fun. This decision was made when Paul was just six and scheduled to begin first grade. Paul's oldest siblings, Elena and Peter, were scheduled to begin junior high school in the same year. In the mountains, away from the sprawling extended families on both sides, they would enjoy their nuclear family. Who cared if the schools weren't so great? Mr. Funicelli sold his business, and the family packed up to move "forever" to the house they had joyfully selected. That first heady night, Paul awoke, gasping. His brother, Joey, just seven, called for his parents, "I think Paulie is dying." They rushed him to the hospital, where they learned that he had a large lymphoma pressing on his bronchial tree, obstructing his breathing. There were rocky days ahead for Paul, who had three cardiac arrests in the first two days. The parents drove back and forth to care for their children at home and to be at the hospital with their critically ill child. At one point Mrs. Funicelli was rear-ended by a jeep, sustained a whiplash, and ended up in the hospital.

With good care in the local hospital, Paul improved. His lymphoma regressed and converted to leukemia. It was clear that the family needed to move back to the city for the care that only a children's hospital could offer. The Funicelli family had suffered the acute onset of a life-threatening condition in their youngest child. This had occurred during a time of important transition of the family and in the face of the family's having made a deliberate move away from the diffusion facing them as the family, now, of school-aged children moving into early adolescence. Developmental forces would normally lead to the family coming apart, with the children becoming more involved with school, peers, and personal activities. Paul's illness changed that, at least for a time.

The Funicellis were referred to me for a consultation when Paul refused to go to school. His parents were outraged that he would not go, although they also wondered whether he was too sick to go or whether it was necessary for him to go to school, since he would surely die as a child. His siblings thought he wouldn't go because he was wearing a wig over the baldness caused by his treatment, and he was afraid another child would pull it off. But looking at the family situation, there were many anomalies in its organization, and these seemed to be related to Paul's refusal to attend school.

Mrs. Funicelli had not recovered from her accident and was often bed-ridden with persistent pain in her back and neck. Mr. Funicelli did all of the shopping and cooking. In his persistently indulgent style, he frequently prepared several different meals, so that each child would get what he or she wanted. Mr. Funicelli seemed to enjoy what he was doing, and on the surface it appeared to be important, since his wife was unable to perform these functions. Another point of view, however, was that since he performed all of her normal duties, Mrs. Funicelli had nothing to do but focus on her pain. And it was this hypothesis that I acted on first. I wondered why Mr. Funicelli didn't get a job. He pointed out that he had sold his business, and he had no health insurance. No insurance company would take him on with a son with leukemia, and if he earned more than a certain amount of money, he would jeopardize the family's eligibility for Medicaid.

The logic of this position was unarguable, but it still left us with a skewed family, a child refusing to go to school, and a mother upstairs in bed all day. Mr. Funicelli was willing to imagine what kind of work he would do, if he could. And it was a job of an entirely different sort than what he had been doing. He had always wanted to have his own fresh produce store. By some odd coincidence, he was able to get some work in the Italian market for a cousin who paid him under the table. Within a week his wife was up caring for the house and cooking for the boys, and Paul was back in school.

Paul's illness entered a chronic phase with periodic relapses and remissions. The family grew accustomed to the rhythm of his illness, and Mr. Funicelli became active with the oncology group at the hospital and with the other parents. He became an active fund-raiser. The family suffered no more serious crises requiring special interventions. Paul died quietly four years later, and the Funicellis received the sympathy and respect from the hospital staff and other families that they had offered to others during those four years.

Psychosomatic Illness and Chronic Handicapping Conditions

Two types of childhood illnesses or disabilities—psychosomatic illness and chronic handicapping conditions—illustrate the distinct advantages of understanding interpersonal patterns in illness and involving families in the management of sick and handicapped children.

PSYCHOSOMATIC ILLNESS

In the mid-1970s, researchers with Salvador Minuchin (Minuchin et al. 1978) began to work with brittle diabetics, children who, despite the most careful management, made repeated trips to the emergency ward in ketoacidosis. No one was really uncomfortable about the idea that there was an emotional component, but Minuchin's group went a step further to explore the family context of these youngsters.

They confirmed several hypotheses about patterns in the families of children with psychosomatic illnesses: (1) There needed to be a biological predisposition to the condition; (2) the families were enmeshed, overprotective, rigid; and (3) they had poor conflict resolution. In some classic studies they demonstrated that the families of brittle diabetic children were different from those of diabetic children with no problems in management (normal) or those with management problems (behavioral diabetics). They also demonstrated that when the family changed in a particular way, the child's condition improved. The same principles were investigated with children with steroid-dependent asthma. The findings of general family patterns were the same, and the children improved with family therapy aimed at increasing differentiation and flexibility, decreasing protectiveness, and improving conflict-resolving mechanisms. What has become apparent since that work was published in 1978 is that families form and maintain their structure, or patterns, in the larger contexts in which they survive. When a child has a medical condition, one of the most important larger contexts is the health care system. Once again, the relationships at the health care professional level tend to be very similar to those within the family. That is, there tends to be enmeshment, overprotectiveness, rigidity, and, most important, poor conflict resolution, often in a situation where conflict is not even acknowledged.

Karlotta Bartholemew (1986), a clinician at the Philadelphia Child Guidance Clinic, described the treatment of Chris, a fourteen-year-old boy with hard-to-control diabetes, who was first referred to the endocrinology clinic at Children's Hospital of Philadelphia. Because of psychological issues that needed attention, the family was referred to the Child Guidance Clinic's inpatient unit. The first signs of unacknowledged conflict at the health care level came when the attending pediatrician emphasized that in spite of the psychological treatment that had been recommended by her boss, everyone should remember that the child had a medical illness, thus underscoring ambivalence already troubling the system. When the therapist observed that the family was organized around Chris as if he were a dying child, the pediatrician was offended and came to the defense of the family. The pediatrician had been inducted into a protective stance toward Chris and his family and was therefore supporting the dysfunctional family structure. The treatment for the family was not effective until the pediatrician could also take a position that both held the family members—Chris, in particular—accountable for self-care and recognized their competence to do so.

CHRONIC ILLNESS OR HANDICAP

Those who have studied families with a chronically ill or handicapped child have also discerned some distinct organizational features that may be adaptive to the demands of the illness but limit the family in many ways that could jeopardize their overall well-being. These features include a cross-generational coalition, usually between the mother and the child; the possibility of frozen gender roles, with mothering and nurturing being so much in demand that the mother can do nothing else and the instrumental functions of breadwinning being locked in for the father, who often cannot change jobs because he must be able to get medical coverage for his child. The family may become bound in these arrangements as a defense against the unpredictable demands of the illness. Thus, they not only have little ability to adapt to changes required by circumstances, such as development, but they regard change with suspicion, because it threatens the very structure painstakingly arrived at.

In a study assessing the families of children with cognitive handicaps, Jeanette Beavers (1989) and colleagues described how families cope. What they found is that most families *do* cope. The percentage of families with adequate or better functioning was the same as that of families who do not have the special challenge of dealing with a handicapped child. This is important news for health care professionals. It means that most families find the means to manage these extraordinary circumstances. The Beavers group did something further. They made a list of the coping patterns of families who functioned well and of those who had difficulties. Those who functioned well demonstrated the following characteristics: contextual clarity about the handicap, modification of family composition and organization, high levels of activity and interaction, problem-solving orientation, self-consciousness as an element for reflection, conscious balancing between acceptance and pushing, protectiveness and toughness, expressiveness, reframing of the role of the handicapped child, and values. On the other hand, pitfalls for families included the reverse: confused context, parental coalition disturbances, boundary problems, problems for siblings, communication deficits, and vulnerability to additional stressors.

The Beavers group asked the families to tell them their secrets. This is what they learned from the families:

- Pay attention to the child. Be patient and let him know he is loved.
- Treat the child naturally and expect her to do what she can.
- As soon as you know your child has a problem, seek all the help available. Keep looking until you feel satisfied.
- Find things the child likes to do and work with him; the child's self-esteem grows with experience.
- Parents must help each other with feelings and responsibilities about their child.
- Don't neglect the other children; spend individual time with them, too.
- Talk about the disability naturally within the family and be open to each other's feelings about it.
- Have as many outside experiences as possible to enjoy your life.
- Find help and understanding wherever you can—talk to other parents, join an organization, get counseling.
- Don't rush things and don't give up. It takes time, and remember you and the child are learning.

This advice, given by families of children with cognitive handicaps, can be offered generally to families of children with other chronic conditions. The observations about healthy family functioning in the face of the stress of handicap or chronic illness are derived from personal experience. This advice illustrates another powerful force in caring for chronically ill children: families helping families. The Funicelli family's recovery from their own rocky beginning with Paul to become involved with families of other sick children left them, when Paul died, with a rich support system far beyond their own family and the hospital workers.

A major advance in the care of most chronically ill or disabled individuals has been the multiple family group. In many cases these are naturally occurring, and in many cases these naturally occurring groups function much better than those organized by professionals. I experienced one example of a self-organized group of bereaved parents. The head of the pediatric oncology service had wisely permitted them to use space in the hospital but otherwise let them organize and run their own group. Some mental health professionals associated with the service were very concerned about the consequences of these "amateurs" coming together to confront such painful losses. I found myself curious about what went on in the meetings, and to my great satisfaction, I was finally invited to a meeting by some parents who had brought a surviving sibling for consultation with me. I was clearly a guest and observer.

The parents were polite and occasionally asked me a question, but they generally got on about the business of the group. Different parents brought different agendas to the group. Often mothers had different agendas from fathers. Some came because the group represented a way to remain in touch with their child. One couple's child had died fifteen years earlier, and they attended Compassionate Friends (a nationally organized group) as well as this one. Another group came to deal with the raw pain of acute loss. These articulate, often young, parents discussed how they were avoided by their friends, as if they, themselves, were ill. They also reviewed the pain of the child's illness, particularly reflecting on the distress of not being able to protect their children from the pain and terror. They felt ashamed that they had not been able to do for their children what parents are supposed to do. These parents got confirmation, comfort, validation, and much-needed contact with others who had experienced similar feelings. Some people brought their spouse to the group to renew social involvement; some, to help them survive. Some of the parents would come once or twice. Some seemed to have accomplished what they came for in the group that I witnessed. Others would come regularly for years.

I came away feeling privileged to have been there and convinced that such a group tolerated and supported the agendas of all its members without professional guidance or intervention. To let the discussion ramble without goals or closure seemed most beneficial for those who needed something from the group. It was clear to me from this experience, as well as through all my dealings with handicapped and chronically ill children and their families, that the professionals must constantly be taught by the families. A symbiotic system must be developed that blends biomedical technical expertise with experience in adaptation and coping. Each system will have its own rhythms and patterns, and the professionals must be prepared to recognize them and join them, blending their own rhythms and patterns to form an effective caretaking and healing system.

Health Maintenance Revisited

Well-child practices in adolescence have not been as well thought through or as successful as those for young children. There are several observations about the adolescent dilemma that, when assembled, lead to certain conclusions. The first is that well-person visits drop off in frequency and focus when children grow older. Pediatricians know that the most important health issues are not common diseases of childhood or those that can be immunized against in a classical way. Major hazards for adolescents are accidents, substance use and abuse, and sexually transmitted diseases. Many pediatricians feel uncomfortable talking with a youngster about these personal (i.e., nonmedical) aspects of life. Hence the development of "adolescent medicine." A second observation about the adolescent dilemma is that the youngster's family becomes less involved in her formal health care. The professionals examine the youngster alone and talk to the youngster alone. If she can travel independently, the youngster may actually make appointments and come to them on her own. The third observation is that there appears to be an increasing prevalence of dangerous behaviors on the part of youth. There is the much-publicized escalation in the rate of teen suicide. And this, shocking as it is, is minor compared with the rates of substance abuse, aggression and antisocial behavior, running away, and teen pregnancy. These five self-destructive behaviors may be different manifestations of a common problem for adolescents: having been isolated from a relationship system, which then depletes their problem-solving resources.

Psychologist Alan Ward (1989) has proposed a state of "cognitive freeze" preceding a thoughtless, desperate act of an adolescent. In what context do youngsters find their own problem-solving mechanisms locking? To whom do adolescents turn when they have problems? Many must turn to each other, unless there is some reason not to, either because they are socially isolated or because they are socially aggrandized. Where are their families? Sociological observations offer to explain the lack of availability of family support to adolescents confronting difficulties. These include increases in the divorce rate, in the number of working mothers and dual-career families, and in the number of parents in the "me" generation. These are said to be to blame for the abandonment of youth. In responding to the perceived lack of parent availability, professionals offer themselves as substitutes. But a professional is an inadequate substitute, for professionals have their own families. Ultimately, they go home, and the youngster needs to do that, too.

In the normal course of pediatric care, health care professionals tend to involve the family heavily in caring for children under thirteen. But ambivalence sets in when children reach puberty. Shouldn't the system be supporting the individuation of the youngster, by relating directly to him and involving the family only with his consent? But if we accept that the family is the primary relationship system, this is true not only for children, but for adolescents and adults, as well. Thus, it should be up to the family to make decisions about how independently an adolescent should make decisions about his or her health. If health care providers arbitrarily separate youngster from parents, they risk alienating the youngster, placing her in a position of making decisions without the support of those closest. This also renders parents less able to support a youngster who is often faced with extremely critical decisions, whether about treatment, birth control, or some of the many life-style issues that affect adolescent health. But how do professionals, so confident about imparting valuable information and advice about development to parents of young children, continue in their roles of experts and advisors to families of adolescents without pressing for the youngsters' independence? This can only come about if the families are engaged in the enterprise of their own increasing differentiation.

Involving Jennifer's Parents: An Example

An example is Jennifer, a fourteen-year-old only child, who had finished her first year in boarding school. She reports that she had been lonely all her life, being an only child of professionally ambitious parents of modest means. They lived in a neighborhood where the children went to private school, whereas she attended public school. She was thrilled to get a special scholarship and to go away, and she went wild in the peer culture of her boarding school, one that was an easy distance from her home city. Going wild, it turned out, meant becoming involved with drugs and sex. The combination of drugs and the heady personal relationships seemed to have contributed to panic and hysteria, as well as a very poor school performance.

Her parents, however, did not know any of this until it came time for summer vacation. Jennifer's teachers and advisors knew that she was

264

under tremendous stress, that she often "lost it" and one time ended up in the infirmary for what might, in former times, have been called "the vapors." The parents had to know about the infirmary visit, but they were told it was flu. Jennifer's teachers assumed that her parents were not resources, a position that she cheerfully reinforced by denouncing them as uncaring and abusive. And her teachers reinforced the barrier between her and her parents by offering themselves as sympathetic substitutes. But then it was summer vacation. The teachers were going away, and it was time for Jennifer to go home. She had another collapse, her parents were called, and they brought their hysterical daughter home, utterly bewildered by the whole thing.

Jennifer pulled herself together sufficiently to go on her previously planned trip to the Tetons with trusted family friends. While she was away, her parents gradually uncovered the details of this horrendous year in school. They were furious with their daughter, who they felt had lied and betrayed them. It was fortunate that she was away. As we examined what had happened, they turned their anger to the school: How could the school allow these things to happen? Finally they turned their anger to the fact of the school personnel having substituted themselves as a resource system to Jennifer, instead of involving the parents. They did not want her to return for the next school year.

Upon her return from the summer trip and upon being confronted with her parents' knowledge of the experiences, Jennifer was sullen and demanded to return to the school. She protected herself from their anger; and she also protected herself from their efforts to engage her, to comfort her, and to support her. This was hardest, as both Jennifer and they were supersensitive to each other. Gradually she persuaded them to reconsider the school, and they decided that if the school personnel made a commitment to involve them if and when Jennifer experienced further difficulties, they would allow her to return. This is an example of the kind of adolescent–family system mutual isolation that can be fostered by professionals eager to promote highly touted adolescent individuation and independence. It is interesting that as a society we have chosen to foster adolescents' isolation in the name of healthy development, even when the most extensive studies of normal adolescents (Offer and Offer 1969) clearly demonstrate how embedded these youngsters are in their families.

Well-Adolescent Family Care

My proposal is, therefore, for well-adolescent family care. The purpose is for the professionals to promote family interaction at a level that will foster the more independent functioning of its adolescent youngsters without pulling the relational rug from under them. This is how a well-adolescent-family checkup might look. The family would be invited to attend a routine meeting at the time that each of the children showed signs of approaching adolescence. This could be defined by age but would then have to vary according to the children's rates of maturation. Thirteen seems to be an average time for the onset of psychological adolescence, manifested by a change in children's attitudes toward school, peers, and families. One could also define the time by physiologic criteria such as the Tanners stage of puberty, or set the timing by when family members begin to raise questions about adolescent matters.

Like the family life interview described in chapter 9, the meeting would include all those who live in the household and, if possible, those relatives or intimates who are influential in the child's life (e.g., grandparents, if they are close). The format of the meeting would be semistructured, with the interviewer asking questions that promote curiosity about salient aspects of the family's functioning. As with the family life interview, the family would be asked questions about membership, role functioning, decision making, communication, problem solving, resources, adaptability, cohesion, and general emotional tone. Instruments have been developed to ask family members how they rate themselves on these dimensions, but this interview would not be looking for "the answer," but rather for the family members' consideration of the questions. For example, the question about membership would be, "Who is considered family? Is there anyone you feel is family who is not here?" If obvious people are not included, like the absent father, a follow-up question might be, "If your father were a part of the family, how would that change things in regard to . . ." (something about the content of the discussion such as discipline, school performance, peers, or internal family relationships).

In addition to these generic questions about the family, questions specific to adolescent concerns would be raised. Again, the objective is not to get the family to settle on the answers but to anticipate how they are going to approach certain issues. These questions will be about dating, sex, birth control, pregnancy, abortion, sexually transmitted diseases, school performance and attendance, drug and alcohol use, smoking, gang membership, safety, rules and expectations, allowance, jobs, and other financial matters. The family may be reluctant to discuss many of these matters in detail, they may profess ignorance about some of the topics and request more information, and they may be encouraged by this opportunity to define certain structures for themselves. At any rate, the most important concerns of parents and adolescent children will have been broached, opening a window for the family.

The important outcome of these interviews would be to stimulate the family's process of interaction about these issues. It would be possible, however, for the interviewer to assess how well the family was doing and whether further intervention in some form would be useful, always keeping in mind that the objective is to stimulate natural resources and connect the youngster with those, rather than to connect the youngster with the health care professional as a primary source. Some follow-up measures might be a series of family sessions to work further on the difficult issues raised in the interview, referral of family members to groups for education, referral of family members to treatment programs for substance abuse, or referral of family members to programs in the community that offer something particular, such as recreational facilities or church groups.

The health care system has an important role in the establishment and maintenance of healthy relationship functions. Health care providers have authority in family lives. This affects basic health care of children, and it also sets important expectations for parent–child interactions. The authority of health care providers can be marshaled effectively to help families prepare for future changes in their lives that may be stressful, such as those of major developmental changes in their children or those posed by the challenges of major illnesses. This can best be done by engaging the family members to review the situations, so that they, as a group, can assess their own resources and plan accordingly. Mental health consultants' task for children and the health care system is to direct the provider's attention to the interpersonal system of the patient, so that the authority and technology become healing.

CHAPTER 13

Mental Health Is Not a Place

The professional who has taken the fourth giant step—always working with systems so that they are organized for the benefit of all of their members—is moving with each therapy case or consultation toward the goal of mental health. From the concentric circles representing the domains of childhood, detailed in chapter 3, it is clear that the systems in each of these domains must be organized for the benefit of their individual components in order for the whole to be mentally healthy. A mental health system, therefore, should be a metasystem ensuring that the agencies that serve children, adolescents, and their families are organized so that all of the parts will benefit. What this means is that the needs, aims, and goals of the systems have to be respected and made consistent with the needs of the society in raising healthy children. I have asserted that children's families are essential to this task. And I have asserted that child-serving institutions and agencies are also essential to this task. Furthermore, neither the families nor the child-serving agencies can function well when they are under criticism and adopting a conservative policy of self-preservation. The mental health system and agencies have a complex set of tasks in order to provide mental health services, because they must assist systems in each of a child's domains—sometimes different ones for different children, sometimes all at the same time. Thus, mental health professionals should evaluate and treat individual children in the contexts of their families and be mindful of each family's well-being within its community. To evaluate the fit between a child and a school, not only the child and family's needs but the resources of the school must be considered. And when the child welfare or the legal system is involved, the mental health professional must take these systems and their functional requirements into consideration as well. It is for this reason that some have suggested that a professional of the systems persuasion is not a family therapist, for she neither limits herself to the family or does therapy. Rather, the mental health professional is a consultant, involving herself with those domains of the child that seem most relevant to the solutions required.

A mental health system, as a concept or a governmental agency, should serve a particular locale, whether it be a neighborhood, district, city, county, state, or nation. Locales served by mental health systems should be hierarchically organized, like the domains of childhood. The system at the national level has to be general enough to accommodate special differences at the state level and all others on down to the particular communities and households in which there are children. Mental health systems don't work like this at all now. In fact, what is called mental health has already been described as a discordant collection of services representing conflicting and mutually exclusionary principles about child mental health and boiling down to the four remedial practices of diagnosis, containment, psychotherapy, and medication. Many have confirmed that there has been an undue emphasis on containment of children in hospitals or residential treatment, a practice that has consumed most of the mental health dollars in the treatment of a few children, leaving without mental health services at least two-thirds of the children who have been estimated to require them. The alternative to containment has ordinarily been psychotherapy or medication management in an outpatient clinic, either of which succeeds only if people show up for appointments and have some meaningful continuity in their lives into which therapeutic experiences might be integrated. In the 1980s considerable enthusiasm arose for developing services between these two extremes of intensity, such as various outpatient services in home, school, and community; day treatment; and various family substitute services on a temporary or long-term basis.

Developments in Child and Adolescent Mental Health

In the early 1980s very few states in the United States had a component of their public mental health systems specifically designated to address the child and adolescent population differentiated from adults. At that time there were only about 10,000 beds for adolescents in freestanding private psychiatric hospitals, and it is estimated that there were more in general hospitals (Weithorn 1988). By the end of the 1980s there were 300 percent to 400 percent more psychiatric beds for adolescents in the private freestanding and general hospitals, whereas the number of beds in state hospitals remained fairly stable. Children's service analyst Jane Knitzer's *Unclaimed Children* (1982) documented the lack of specific attention to child and adolescent mental health, the scarcity of resources applied to prevention and treatment, and the unbalanced services that emphasized expensive out-of-home care. This monograph became the published spearhead for initiatives for children and adolescents in the public sector.

A System of Care

In 1983, the National Institute of Mental Health (NIMH) sponsored the Child and Adolescent Service System Programs (CASSP), and several state mental health departments were awarded grants to develop a system of services. Technical assistance centers to support the CASSP awards developed conceptual approaches to systems of care that emphasized the necessity of having an array of services in a continuum, which would make it possible for any child to receive services at the level he might require (Stroul and Friedman 1986). Stroul and Friedman proposed two core values: (1) the system should be child centered, with the needs of child and family dictating the type of services provided; and (2) the system should be community based, with the locus of service as well as management and decision making resting at that level (17).

They further outlined a framework of seven dimensions, including mental health, social, educational, health, vocational, recreational, and operational services. Within each dimension of the system of care, specific functions are detailed. For example, mental health services include the two categories of residential and nonresidential services. Under the first are therapeutic foster care, group care, and camping; independent living, residential treatment, crisis residential care, and hospitalization. Under the nonresidential category are included prevention, early intervention, assessment, outpatient services, home-based care, day treatment, and emergency services. Social services include protective, shelter, foster care, and adoption, as well as financial assistance, home aid, and respite care. Operational services include case management, self-help and support groups, advocacy, transportation, legal services, and volunteer programs. By specifically addressing the components of each of the seven dimensions, the system of care concept expanded the arenas of attention to children and families that are necessary for mental health. The proposal was also realistic in assigning services to particular agencies, but in doing so, it sustained the compartmentalized nature of the system which poses so many barriers.

Family Preservation

As noted earlier, family preservation was developed to serve families identified because they were at risk for having a child removed, and family preservation programs have typically belonged in social services. They have been successful in supporting the integrity of as many as 80 percent of the families in this system (Knitzer and Cole 1989a, b). In Illinois a family preservation act requiring that all such services be available to eligible families by the end of 1990 assigns the responsibility to the Department of Children and Family Services. Family preservation has also been found to be successful in keeping emotionally disturbed children at home (Knitzer and Cole 1989a, b; Gutstein et al. 1988). Thus, some mental health systems have adopted family preservation as a component of their systems of care and have classified these as home-based services. During the 1980s with the support of CASSP, many more states formed offices of children and adolescents in their mental health or human services departments. Models of community responsiveness and means to assist with keeping troubled children functioning in their communities were represented by such examples as Chicago's Kaleidoscope program, which combined respite care, specialized foster care, and youth workers who were extensively connected to children and families in their homes.

Interagency Coordination

Progress has been made in some areas to coordinate services from different child-serving agencies. In some states, such as Ohio, there are "clusters" that involve representatives of education, child welfare, mental health, and juvenile justice at both state and local levels. The clusters, which pool funds and expertise, were originally created to deal with the most difficult children, particularly the ones who tended to circulate from one agency to another. Other states have different structures to accomplish the same aims. In Illinois the coordinating body is called the Residential Services Authority. Like most of the interagency coordinating structures, it was established to mediate disputes between child-serving agencies about who should pay for residential treatment. Through these meta-agency structures, the costs were shared, and slowly these groups have been able to develop alternatives to residential services for some of the children who come to their attention. One mechanism for following through on a coordinated service plan is through the assignment of a case manager who is responsible to the aggregate committee, or cluster.

Case Management

Case management is in a primitive stage of development. The concept appears to be straightforward, and ideally, the case manager would be the kind of mental health professional who has taken the four giant steps. But there are many realistic bureaucratic problems to be tackled first. For example, since the agencies are still compartmentalized at the level of service delivery to children and families, from which agency should the case manager come? Who is responsible, and to whom should she report? In some programs agencies are designated as lead agencies—the case manager comes from those agencies, and the agency is responsible to whatever higher authority (the federal government, in implementing PL 99-457; the funding source, in grants and contracts). Case managers do not truly have the authority that permits them the metaposition ideal for the function.

Another area where case management is still undeveloped is in the clarification of the functions. Does the case manager do shirts and windows, if necessary, like the family preservation workers? Is the case manager just a kind of switchboard operator, facilitating connections? What kind of professional background and specific training should case managers have? Who should be their supervisors? It should be clear that I think case managers should be prepared to do what is necessary—to enter a system at whatever level is most appropriate to facilitate the changes in patterns that are thought to be beneficial. The case manager has to have an understanding and respect for the function, rules, and regulations of each involved agency; a knowledge of the skills of the workers; a familiarity with the settings in which services are delivered; and personal contact with the children and families. Furthermore, along with this knowledge, the case manager has to have authority to deploy staff and funds; to have this, the case manager has to have the confidence of those whom he serves. No doubt, because I am a psychiatrist, I believe that the training of psychiatrists is ideally suited to this role. Through medical school and postgraduate training, child psychiatrists combine biopsychological and psychosocial experience with the authority vested in physicians in this society. Yet there are not many child psychiatrists who are fully prepared for this role because they, as much as any professional group, have been coopted by the dichotomous structure of mental health technology. Social workers have done more shirts and windows than any other mental health professionals. Social workers have more often been on the line in the midst of all of the mental health experiments performed in the public sector. Nurses, too, as they redefine nursing, are comfortable in people's homes and see this kind of personalized contact as a part of their professional function. Psychiatrists having been coopted, much of the leadership in mental health systems has been provided by psychologists. At this point it must be concluded that no professional group could make an exclusive claim on the case manager role, and none should be excluded. What needs to take place, however, is construction of models of case management, curricula for training case managers, and ongoing supervisory groups to assess the appropriateness of the training and continue the evolution of the model.

Individualized Service

The core values of Stroul and Friedman's system of care were that the system be child and family centered and community based. In describing the components of a system and recommending implementation strategies, however, Stroul and Friedman implied that each community should either develop the components of the system or arrange access. The system of care concept became a kind of slogan for CASSP directors and state child and adolescent program directors. It was interpreted to mean an array of services into which children can be plugged, for this is the clearest way to influence legislators. Tell them that X number of hospital beds, X number of residential beds, X number of slots in day treatment, and so on through each component of the system are needed, at what cost and at what anticipated impact, and they will allocate a portion of the money needed to develop those services. This approach may work well in densely populated areas where statistical and real numbers for utilization may converge. It does not work well in sparsely populated rural areas where the number of children requiring any particular service component could be none or only a few.

Other approaches have developed, leading to a new slogan: have the dollars follow the child. In sparsely populated Alaska most of the emotionally disturbed youngsters had been sent to treatment programs out of state. Within the state there was no community large enough to justify the development of a community-based residential treatment center or many of the elements of the community-based service system. In such situations the notion of having an array of services developed on the basis of some formula of child needs is giving way to the notion of going to the community to invent the services for a particular child at a particular time. This approach has been developed in Alaska, where emotionally disturbed children live in far-flung communities. Now, all of Alaska's children formerly placed out of state have returned to their home communities. Monies saved from the residential treatment have been used to provide special workers, tutors, respite services, homemakers, and whatever else was necessary to sustain the youngsters and their communities. These "wraparound" services are tailored to the particular child and family.

Turning to the community in this way requires more than just infusing money into the area as a kind of payoff for keeping a difficult child. It requires activating the community to claim responsibility for its members and then providing the resources to meet these responsibilities, again, not according to a formula or a program that has been tested successfully in another setting, but according to the requirements of the specific child and family and the values of the community. This approach obviously benefits the community, too.

Baby Steps

These have been important steps to improve child and adolescent mental health systems since the beginning of the decade of the 80s. But in the game of "Mother, May I?" these are like baby steps—progress is slow, but perceptible. And also like the game, many of these steps can be undone. The ultimate goal of the game has not been clearly defined. The system of care is a step, but it is not the end. Adopted as is, it is unwieldy and compartmentalized. The principles have expanded the overall mission of mental health care for children, but they are based on underlying assumptions rooted in the biopsychological model of childhood disturbance and in the sensibility of the separation of service functions. None of the giant steps has been taken in the system of care proposal.

System planners are family oriented because they have realized that it is more efficacious to involve the families; the public system cannot assume responsibility for all of these children. Lacking a fundamental understanding of patterns and a fundamental belief in competence, most system planners who advocate family-centered treatment find themselves in the conundrum of the welfare system: When is the family safe enough, and When do we protect by removing? In almost every instance where a father is suspected of being a threat to his children, even in family-centered programs, the father is sacrificed, although the family is declared to have remained "intact." This family orientation does not include a belief that families have the basic competence to care for their children, nor does it utilize assessment of patterns or modification of those in assisting families.

Parent advocacy, which is one of the components of the operational services dimension of the system of care, presents an ambivalent view of parents and their central role in the care of their children. On the one hand, through the parent advocacy movement, parents of emotionally disturbed children may have been more effective at moving legislators and getting programs established than public-serving professionals. But these expediencies have not changed the prevailing orientation of mental health professionals and system planners to individual children, the concept of psychopathology, and a persistent belief in a theory of causality in which unhealthy environments and harmful family relationships play a strong part. A backlash from the families in some instances has stimulated a withdrawal to a position of biological causality in which both the child and her family are victims. This places activist families in a more effective position to advocate for their children, but it sidesteps the issues of the family patterns that may maintain or accentuate dysfunction. It is much more difficult to collaborate with such families in the review and revision of patterns that will help them effectively adapt to life with difficult children and cope with the crises that inevitably arise.

It has become routine at national meetings of mental health program planners to have parents in the audience and among the panelists. Parents always present moving stories of despair and courage. A typical story of a parent begins with the parent being stumped by some aspect of their child's behavior. Perhaps the parent notices that the child was different as an infant; or the child was more difficult than most to discipline, more reckless, more aggressive, slower in talking, or more moody than they expected. Typically, the parent consults with the pediatrician and gets a temporizing response, such as, "Let's wait and see. This is just a stage; he'll grow out of it." The parent's concerns are brushed aside until the child enters school. At this point the child's difficulties in keeping up and getting along with other children are targeted as problems, and the parents are told that there is something wrong with the child. Finally, their earlier concerns are being confirmed, but often this is communicated in a patronizing and discouraging way, such as, "I'm sorry, but we cannot keep your child in this school. You will have to get help for him." The parents inevitably feel shamed and helpless, usually not knowing where to turn.

Going to the local mental health center often results in insufficient response, because there are so few professionals particularly trained to evaluate and treat young children. Frequently, the professionals who do the children's services are ones who have been trained in family therapy, and these have little specific training in child development and emotional problems. Thus, these professionals focus on working with the parents, which intensifies their sense of responsibility and concern for their child but does not answer their questions about what to do with him. Often a working mother has to leave her job to care for the youngster at home, or she has to postpone plans to return to work for the same reason. Other children in the family may be neglected when the disturbed child occupies so much time and emotional energy. Child psychiatrists may be involved as consultants or, if the family is well off, may be consulted privately. They tend to make diagnoses, prescribe medication, and recommend hospital or residential treatment, but they usually don't assist parents with finding the recommended services, unless it is a hospital in which they work. Thus, the burden of the search for residential treatment, day treatment programs, or special schools, as well as the search for funding for these programs, falls on the parents. They then must thread their way through a morass of social services, each of which tends to have only partial responses, to be responsible for only a piece of the system, and to be unable to pull things together as a program.

One parent of preschool twins with severe but different developmental disabilities described the complicated treatment programs for her children, which included medical treatments; physical, occupational, and speech therapies; and a schedule of exercises to be administered by caregivers between therapy sessions. Medical treatments involved shunt revisions, orthopedic procedures, and abdominal surgery at different times on one or the other of the twins, and these procedures were followed by a regimen of medicines and attention to the wound sites, and so on. To coordinate these treatments, the parent had put the regimens on her computer. But finally she realized that the various helpers were operating out of their own compartments, making their absolute demands for what should be done for each child, based on their expertise, and the demands were excessive and conflicting. She reported calling a meeting with all of the involved professionals and caregivers. Many of them had neither met each other nor even known of the others' involvement with the twins. As they began to look at the programs for the children and the demands placed on the family, several of them began to cry in sympathy. They could then begin to work on a coordinated plan that addressed the children's needs.

As in this case and most others that parents present, they are told what their children need and are expected to get these services or perform the required regimens, get the required equipment, and give the required medications. An explanation for the child's difficulties, especially if there are no obvious physical problems, remains in the form of a mysterious and ominous form of "mental illness" or "emotional disturbance." Sometimes parents are told specifically that their child is depressed or autistic or psychotic or hyperactive. They may be given advice about the day-to-day management of the child, but persistent difficulties or new crises with the child are then seen as the parents' failures. Many of these parents have

276

energetically joined with those system planners who explain their frustrations on the basis of lack of funding to provide necessary services. They attack the problems at the legislative level, making further sacrifices to organize to do this, and they remain unaware of how they are placed in a one-down position vis à vis those who are evaluating and prescribing for their children. Thus, families are getting only partial and ambivalent recognition. In large measure this adds to their emotional burdens as well as to the number of tasks required both to care for their children and to advocate for more support for the system. But there is usually not a systemic approach that involves families in assessment and planning for their own situations as the case managers for their own children, nor as caregivers and experts in their own right. Without this, the families continue to have a precarious grasp of their disturbed child, to be dependent on professionals, and to feel angry and ripped off.

The promise of case management will not be fulfilled until compartmentalization of child-serving agencies is addressed through establishing a true meta-authority. As for the individualized wrap-around services for children in their own communities, these often partake of invention inspired by necessity. At this level, true mental health, in the sense I have defined it, can take place. But invention is often not fostered at the next levels of supervision in the mental health bureaucracy, charged with developing a system, defining a technology, and following standards. Thus, for example, an exchange of services between a county mental health association and a native American reservation could not be condoned, since they illegally mix jurisdictional and legally incompatible functions. Many professionals operating at this level just went about their business, trusting their superiors to look only at the ends, not the means.

These baby steps in mental health are taken with recognition of the political and economic realities that shape service development. Politically minded mental health planners have to keep a finger to the wind to catch the shifting breezes that have focused alternatively on the homeless, drug abusers, the poor, the abused, then the depressed and suicidal, and so on. Having done so, they can go to their state and federal legislators with their portfolio of needs for the target population in vogue. These same planners, however, seem quite oblivious to how these forces become the frames through which service systems are designed and beliefs in service efficacy are maintained. These baby steps in mental health lack an overall vision or goal. What should a mental health system be? What, in fact, is mental health? I have offered a definition in presenting the fourth giant step. Mental health is a state of systems. The mental health system cannot be effective without the corresponding effectiveness of other systems serving children and their families, in the innermost domains, and the other child-serving agencies, in those domains shared by the mental health system.

Square Pegs

A particular population of children found in mental health settings poses a specific challenge to the way mental health care is usually conceived and delivered. I call them square pegs who do not fit into the round holes of the mental health system. They are discussed here because their numbers are increasing, and they can serve as a rallying point for some of the change that must be made to resolve the crisis in child mental health. Estimates of the proportion of these youngsters in the mental health system vary. In one state hospital, 6 out of 80 adolescents were described to be in this special treatment category; in another, the conservative estimate was 16 out of 100.

Square pegs are a special distillate of the 60 percent of severely emotionally disturbed children and adolescents who could be classified as bad. They have been consumers and survivors of many of the services in the large network of usually public institutions for children—special education, children and family services, and juvenile justice. They have all been charged with multiple counts of psychopathology and have had a series of tours in hospitals and treatment centers. They are persistently challenging to their caretakers because they fail to respond to standard treatments. They are often extremely aggressive and personally self-destructive, but engaging and unforgettable. Their names: Arlene, Joe, Beatrice, Tyrone, Andrew, Peter, Eduardo, Charles, Sharon—regular sorts of names. Their family stories are almost mythical, with as many versions as there are people to tell the story (and with these children, there are many people).

Characteristics of Square Pegs

Many children admitted to a mental health facility readily accommodate to the institutional culture and progress in a sad, but reasonably uncomplicated, fashion. A few youngsters do not accommodate. They do not respond to medication and psychotherapy, and they treat the child-care and professional staff in the same arms-length way that they have learned to treat others in their lives. These children have come from young parents; parents with many children; and families in which there have been losses, poverty, exploitation, substance abuse, and crimes of one sort or another.

Usually, because of these circumstances, even though the youngsters have a sense of connection to their families, the families have been discarded by various levels of the system. When the families are discarded, they don't show up when asked to attend a conference about their child, thus confirming from the professionals' point of view that they don't care about their children and arranging for further dismissal by the system. It is believed that the youngsters should be helped in psychotherapy to deal with the rejection and loss, even while they maintain connections with these same families through their own networks, by which they can often give vivid details of siblings' activities that can only come through direct and immediate communication. They are often loyal to their parents, even while confused, not so much by the staff's rejection of them, but by the staff's insistence on helping them cope with a loss they're not sure they have. One youngster said, "I don't know where my mother is. My aunt says she's in Minnesota. I know she loves me. I have a father. He's somewhere in Chicago."

Most of these adolescents do not fit clearly into any diagnostic category. If the diagnostic manual included relationship disturbances, most of these youngsters could be seen to have come from, and to somehow generate in their current contexts, relational systems characterized by disorders in status, membership, and proximity. Their status has been and is continuously ambiguous. In institutions these youngsters often achieve "special patient" status, which makes them an exception to rules that govern other patients and makes them subject to confused responses from the staff. Frequently, different staff members accord them different status. Staff members call this "splitting." Membership problems also clearly begin early in these young people's family lives. They are complicated in the institutional setting by the multiple placements and the beneficent intention to discharge to a "less restrictive" environment, thus making most institutional placements temporary and keeping the issue of membership unresolved. Disorders of proximity in relationships are complex. On the surface, most of these adolescents maintain distant and unconnected relationships. They would prefer to go away rather than remain involved in difficult interpersonal situations. If they are prevented from leaving, they may resort to desperate acts, inflicting harm to themselves or others. Yet most of these children are charming and engaging, and their charm is often quite seductive, drawing people close to them. Most of them are educationally compromised, many by realistic cognitive limitations and learning difficulties, all by sparse education.

Eduardo, for example, reported himself to be dumb. At age sixteen he had been living on the street since he was nine, until he was picked up by the police and began a circular course through correctional and mental health institutions, all the while being a ward of child welfare. Eduardo's life-style had contributed to his abilities to defend himself and to avoid coercion into interpersonal situations that made him uncomfortable. For example, he had worked for several weeks to contrive a weapon from some hospital furniture. When the weapon was finished, he had a standoff with the staff, during which one person was injured. The response was to send him to the maximum security hospital, where he behaved well and was shortly returned to the Department of Corrections. Here he soon claimed to have a relationship with little green men who were telling him to eat light bulbs. Within a year, much to the terror of the hospital staff, he had been returned to their unit.

Eduardo's dream was to have a family. He imagined that a family was where someone would give him food. He had a relative, an aunt, who was interested in him, but no one thought she could actually have Eduardo live with her. After two more years, a stay in a residential center, and the remaining time in prison, Eduardo graduated from youth institutions and was sent off to fend for himself. He had grown wiser in the face of his upcoming freedom, and when he left, he was able to reflect on his need to acquire more useful skills in order to survive as an adult. On his first visit back to the prison, Eduardo was described by those who knew him as having lost that "crazy look."

Most of these youngsters, like Eduardo, have survived extraordinary circumstances. Eduardo's survival on the streets for six years is an example. Beatrice survived the sexual abuse by her uncle and the nomadic wanderings with her teenaged mother. Arlene's brother was killed in a fire that burned out the family apartment; her single mother, who was overwhelmed with many children, blamed Arlene for the fire and continuously rejected her. Sexual abuse and substance abuse were also part of Arlene's family life. Joe's father died in prison, where he was serving a life term for murder. His youthful mother had multiple unsuccessful relationships and was recurrently charged with child abuse and neglect. From the age of four, Joe was alternately placed in foster homes and returned to his mother. By seventeen he had been in fifteen different foster homes, and his mother had died. Many of his foster home changes had taken place because he reported physical and sexual abuse. Psychiatric hospitals began to be included in the sequence when Joe, at eleven, stole a motorcycle from one of his foster fathers and went on a joy ride. At seventeen he had returned for a third stay at a state hospital after he had physically assaulted staff members in his residential treatment center. Tyrone's mother had a succession of men who physically abused her and physically and sexually abused her children. Tyrone, the oldest of the children, spent his days, not in school, but on the street snatching purses and shoplifting to provide for his family. He was hospitalized at age ten after a month in a group home, because he constantly picked fights with other children and stole money and candy whenever he had the opportunity.

Square pegs distinguish themselves because they don't go along with most of the programs in which they are placed. They refuse to accommodate themselves to the round holes. There appear to be a number of explanations for this. One explanation is that the system is unsuitable for these youngsters. The system is geared to treat problems these youngsters don't have (e.g., biopsychological) and not at all prepared to treat problems they do have. When we get to this level, we ask What problems do they have, and how does the system fail them? Again, we have already suggested some answers. The system treats them as if they are ill and incompetent, abandoned and dysfunctional, when in fact they are not ill. They are competent survivors and in this framework may be seen as quite functional. Many efforts to assist them actually undermine their competence and cause confusion and humiliation. One area for which this is true, as I have already mentioned, is in the treatment of families. A second, and no less significant, area is in the lack of respect given to these youngsters. Although many children in the mental health system accept that they are deficient and possibly ill, square pegs do not.

Arlene was going on twenty-one years old when I first met her, and she had been in institutions since age seven. She had received multiple diagnoses, including various forms of schizophrenia, affective disorders, and personality disorders. She set fires, ingested objects like razor blades, and carved her forearms with anything sharp she could find—and she could do this even when on one-to-one observation! This *behavior* made it clear to the staff that Arlene could not survive outside the institution; but the only acceptable definition of her that permitted a continued stay was that she was ill and needed treatment. Yet what treatment?

Arlene vehemently disagreed. She could see that there was nothing for her in the hospital except gestures at education and rehabilitation. She observed that the name of the school program was "special education," which she interpreted to mean "education to be special." She wanted to be regular, to get her GED and then training for a decent job. Fortunately for my formulation of the situation, Arlene had spent a few months outside of the hospital within the past year. This occurred after she had set a fire, was charged with arson and admitted to the county jail, and was subsequently released. She had found herself a place to live, had gotten a job, and had enrolled in school. Then, when things had begun to break down in her interpersonal relationships, she had tried to return to the hospital.

I asked the staff how long they could continue to take responsibility for Arlene's life by treating her like a mentally ill person. Shortly after this, they began to treat her like a young person who needed to leave home, which by now was the hospital. They discharged her with an invitation to return whenever she wanted—to be readmitted, to visit, or just to keep in touch. In four months' time she had been readmitted three times, for short periods of one to two weeks. She moved into the community where the hospital is. She went for several months to Virginia, where her family had lived before moving. When she came back, she was pregnant. She returned to the hospital until delivery. Her behavior was generally much better, but occasional bouts of the old self-destructive routines flared up. Careful examination of the timing of these episodes connected them with ambiguity about what would happen with the baby. Arlene both wanted the baby and knew that she couldn't care for it, and she appeared to be willing to sort through this herself. When the hospital authorities indicated that the Department of Child and Family Services (DCFS) would take the baby—that is, take over Arlene's decision-making function—then she would become upset and lapse into symptomatic behavior. Nevertheless, shortly after she delivered a healthy daughter, who was placed with DCFS, Arlene again left the hospital, by mutual agreement. She continues to reside in the community around the hospital, and she continues to be welcome to return when she wishes. All of her self-destructive behavior had been connected with the hospital. It was both her ticket of admission and her mark of familiarity to her long-time caretakers. When the hospital staff accepted her on different terms, the self-destructive behavior, previously thought to be symptomatic of her illness, abated.

To summarize the distinguishing characteristics of this growing group of youngsters: They are special, because they do not have readily identified biopsychological conditions. Their multiple diagnoses reflect the consternation of a system in which one remediation response is diagnosis. They do not assimilate to the institutions in which they are contained. Having fought their ways out of family homes, foster homes, group homes, and correctional facilities, they refuse to be contained in mental health centers, as well. Within the institution there are fairly typical patterns of staff response to these children, and there are rifts among the staff about issues from diagnosis to treatment to discharge planning. Regarding diagnosis, the critical issues are how much control the youngster has over her behavior and how accountable she can be. Arguments over treatment focus on psychodynamic issues, expectations for participation in the community, decisions about involving the family, the role of medication, and the consequences for both "good" and "bad" behavior. With discharge planning, disagreements occur over the degree of restriction and containment that needs to be sustained, and these conflicts often extend to the other systems, such as education, corrections, and welfare, with whom these children are also involved. Staff arguments are often described as "splitting" and are ascribed to the "borderline" conditions of the children.

Treatment of Square Pegs: Modifying the Round Holes

The treatment of this population of adolescents requires substantial modification and elaboration of the standard remedial practices available in the mental health system. The round holes need to be reshaped to accommodate these square pegs—but how?

First, it is important to recognize that *these children are resilient* and that the most difficult aspects of their management may result, not from their psychopathology, but from their resilience. This is not a simple reframing but a recognition of considerable resourcefulness and personal solidity that these individuals bring with them into the system. When they are being most difficult, they are being most unyielding of their personal integrity.

Second, *these children need to be accorded respect.* This attitude evolves from acknowledgement that the child's position is one that has been painfully evolved as a means of survival and, if it is consistently displayed, will assist in clarifying the status of the child as well as of the other members of the system. Whatever the youngster brings has to be respected. For Beatrice, a fourteen-year-old who was so combative that she was spending all of her time in restraints, the respect began with the staff's acknowledgement of their fear that she would hurt them. Then Beatrice chose to try to assure the staff that she would not hurt them. Respect for survival in unspeakable situations, for the youngsters' loyalties, for the youngsters' future, for the youngsters' efforts to please, to accomplish, to find a place for themselves—all this needs to be expressed consistently.

These children have to be assisted in making a realistic assessment of their family relationships, beginning with a position of respect for the key family members and the youngster's attachment to them. For Tyrone, whose mother disappeared to somewhere in Minnesota after the series of abusive men friends: "I'm sure your mother does love you. It sounds as if she has a lot on her mind—too much to be able to take care of you right now. I imagine she will be proud of you if you can make something of yourself." Trust cannot be confused with respect and should not be assumed or expected. These children have not experienced others as trustworthy and are not trustworthy themselves. Thus, it is respectful to be realistic about how trustworthy to an institutionalized child is a staff member who has a life outside the institution, who works shifts, and who might leave to take another job? And how trustworthy is a youth whose major lesson in life is that other people are inconstant and exploitative? Respect should be present in all interactions and can be institutionalized by including the youngster in the decision-making process about treatment, consequences, placement, family visits, and discharge plans.

Third, following close upon respect, *accountability should be conveyed to these young people*—they are responsible for what they do. Remember, this is not the message that is sent to the mentally ill. If they hurt or frighten other people, or themselves, they need to be called to account. It is not an accident that Arlene's life course changed following her short jail stay for arson or that Eduardo lost that "crazy look" when he was released into the adult world. These kids' actions need to be taken seriously, and this includes serious consequences for actions against which there are social sanctions. If they are excused on any grounds, such as they don't know any better or they're so ill or deprived, they are not being respected or taken seriously. Accountability must extend, too, to the mental health professionals through their being consistent and through their not promising more than is reasonable or than they can deliver. Because there are ordinarily so many people involved with these youngsters, accountability of personnel to one another is of major importance.

Fourth, it is necessary to *move slowly for relationship changes to take place.* It is often advisable for these youngsters to settle into a stable residential setting for a long period (often as many as three years). The relationships the youngsters value need to be respected, and those values need to be preserved. Connections need to be made, and the children need to learn how to care for people while accepting their limitations and how to find a realistic place in their relationship systems for them. In many cases this may not mean living with them, but somehow sustaining connections. Involving the child as a partner in the evolving treatment includes joining with him in recognizing and accepting things over which neither child nor staff has control and reviewing the status of treatment on a regular basis.

Fifth, one should *be future oriented and help the youngsters visualize and prepare for a future that is different in mutually defined ways from their past.* This is the most constructive way to review past experiences without judging them. The youngsters can be helped to contrast past experience with how they would like things to be in the future and to evaluate self, personal abilities, and progress toward future goals.

These efforts represent a modification of the mental health response according to the giant steps, with the first three steps being (1) to recognize and integrate multiple points of view, in this case that of the child and her family as well as the staff, who often hold multiple opinions; (2) to identify patterns in the current situation and throughout the child's life that account for the difficulties; and (3) to recognize the competence, resilience, and integrity of the child through respect. Of course, the fourth step remains.

Giant Step 4

Mental health is a state of almost infinite variety that is characterized by adaptation and fit within and between systems, and a sense of value and well-being experienced by the individuals at each level of the system. A sense of belonging and loyalty delineates members of healthy subsystems, and the identities of individuals, subsystems, and systems are mutually accepted. Mental health cannot, therefore, be a service delivered in a place, as state departments of mental health deliver services in state hospitals and mental health clinics. Mental health must be a collaborative enterprise of all those who are involved with raising children. For those children who are at particular risk, mental health services should be offered within the most familiar environments. A system of care must include welfare, health, education, and justice; thus, mental health is a fundamental aspect of each of these systems. Mental health professionals should be able to assess systems at each level and be able to offer consultation at each level that helps the systems organize in a way that will address the welfare of all members. Parents shouldn't be sacrificed for their children; teachers shouldn't be sacrificed for their students; welfare departments and workers shouldn't be sacrificed for their wards. And children should not be sacrificed to maintain systems that are traditional but ultimately do not contribute to their future ability to become functioning and contributing members of any and all of their own domains.

Ideally, mental health departments would provide metaservices—consultations to child-caring systems. Child-caring systems include those agencies designed to address the primary realms of child functioning: shelter and safety, health and nutrition, education, recreation, vocation, family, legal issues, and psychological processes. Thus, welfare departments focus on safe places to live; health care systems on health and nutrition; school systems on education and sometimes vocation; recreation departments and programs on recreation, leisure time, and social relationships; justice systems on legal matters; and families on family life. The psychological realm, expressed in affect, cognition, and behavior, will re-flect the successful interplay between the child and competence in the other fundamental areas. I propose that all institutions for children should have strong educational, medical, and treatment programs, and that a thoughtful approach to social and legal accountability should be built into these programs, which would not be categorically "child welfare" or "mental health" or a "residential school." Typical children would go to regular schools, get treatment in regular health centers, and, I hope, have their welfare looked after by families and communities. But special chil-dren would enter programs where all of these essential programming needs would be coordinated.

Of course, I'm not naive enough to believe that the system would ever achieve this level of collaboration and coordination. But it is necessary for mental health professionals to offer services by identifying belief systems and frames, identifying patterns, activating resources, and responding in a multilateral way. Mental health professionals can take these giant steps. When one mental health professional takes these steps in only one case, a system is transformed.

Approaching Tameka's Situation

Take, for example, the case of Tameka Samson, a nine-year-old girl who had been hospitalized in a state hospital for a year. The hospital personnel had been trying to discharge her since two months after she was admitted, but her mother claimed that she was not well enough to be safe at home. She was concerned about her destructive and dangerous behavior, which consisted of stealing food and hiding it under rugs and mattresses and surreptitiously setting small fires. She claimed that Tameka did these things on all of her visits home, so that she was unwilling even to take her home. When the hospital staff attempted to discharge her, the mother hired attorneys for help in her suit for more definitive treatment of Tameka. When the attorneys appeared on the scene, the hospital staff backed down and recommended residential treatment for the child, a posi-tion that was crazily inconsistent with their previous efforts to send her home. What had developed was a deadlock between mother and hospital staff, exacerbated by the entrance of lawyers and the mental health depart-ment's sensitivity to lawsuits.

As I read the history of this conflict, it appeared to me that there was a basic misunderstanding between the mother and the hospital staff, with each side believing that the other was irresponsible and uncaring about Tameka and neither recognizing the merit in the other's position. I proposed a meeting of all the involved individuals to talk this over in a two-hour session. Included were Tameka, her mother, the hospital unit director and therapist, Ms. Samson's attorney, Tameka's occupational therapist from the school she had attended before entering the hospital, two family systems experts, and two child and adolescent coordinators from the mental health department who would be responsible for finding a placement for Tameka, if residential treatment was ultimately sought.

I began by asking Ms. Samson what she felt Tameka needed. She presented a theory of Tameka's emotional disturbance based on a troubled history and allegations of abuse. Ms. Samson recounted that she was undergoing some hard times and "had to get myself together" when Tameka was about nine months old. At that point she asked Tameka's father to take care of the girl. When she was ready to get her back, she found that the father had absconded with Tameka. She searched for several years and then took several more years to go through the legal red tape to get custody of Tameka. After only a few months of living with her mother, Tameka was hospitalized. The mother claimed that Tameka had been abused by her father and that she had emotional scars from this early experience that would take years of therapy to sort out. She thought her daughter's destructiveness was a manifestation of bottled-up anger and frustration that needed treatment to be resolved.

As she was talking, she was asked to talk with Tameka, who often refused to respond, staring stubbornly at the floor. She would then turn to us and say, "She's very upset. You see what I mean?" In doing this, she would not persist in her expectation that Tameka would respond to her questions. I wondered if that might also apply to her destructive behaviors, and she confirmed that she did not want to interfere with Tameka's emotional expression. Involving some of the others who worked closely with Tameka, we discovered that Tameka was a mild, likable child in the hospital. She was not destructive or aggressive. She had a severe stutter and seemed to have significant learning disabilities. Ms. Samson suggested that Tameka's emotional expression was suppressed in the hospital. She restated that she did not want to interfere with the necessary emotional outlets, and that perhaps Tameka felt free to be destructive at home, because she trusted her as a mother. Tameka's teacher from before she went to the hospital also stated that she had not been destructive or aggressive at school. I told Ms. Samson that I'd be pretty angry if my daughter chose to be on her best behavior with everyone else but really gave me a hard time. She maintained that she obviously needed the outlet. I asked her if she felt that Tameka was emotionally compelled to be destructive, and if so, how she could control herself most of the time, as when in the hospital and, previously, all day in school.

Up to this point, I had elicited Ms. Samson's theories about Tameka's problems and their solutions. This was her frame of reference, and within it her actions were sensible. I was beginning, now, to explore the frame and offer a reframing. The frame was, Tameka has been emotionally traumatized, and she is out of control of these things. The new frame was, Tameka chooses when to be destructive; she seems to choose to do these things only when she's with you. To press the point about Tameka's accountability, I asked Ms. Samson to ask Tameka why she was on good behavior with others but was destructive with her. Tameka refused to answer. I encouraged Ms. Samson to insist on a response from her, but she persisted in excusing her. Finally, just as her mother had declared that she would not embarrass her in front of all these people, Tameka muttered, "I do those things on purpose." We all barely heard her, so we asked her to repeat it. She did.

Ms. Samson wasn't the only one whose views of the problems in this situation were changing. All of the hospital staff had seen Ms. Samson as erratic and exploitative. In struggling with her refusal to take her daughter home, they had overlooked the meaning of her faithful visits to her. They had seen Ms. Samson as ambivalently committed to Tameka. Now she had her back; now she was prepared to send her away for a long time to get her fixed. As she struggled with her frame of Tameka's problems, the staff struggled with their view of her as an uncommitted, uncaring mother. They could not ignore her tenderness and protectiveness toward her daughter. And when Tameka admitted that she chose when to be destructive and when not, everyone began to appreciate Tameka's manipulative contributions to the situation.

By the end of the session both Ms. Samson and the hospital staff were feeling appropriately outraged by Tameka's cool operation and realized that they were dealing with more than just an emotionally disabled youngster. New directions for treatment were established that led the staff to consider how to hold Tameka accountable for her behavior at home and how to ally more effectively with the mother, having seen and accepted her side. More energy was also put into Tameka's education, as it was appreciated that she had greater ability than she had previously demonstrated. The treatment plan changed, and the adversarial atmosphere shifted to one of cooperation. Tameka remained in the hospital, but now everyone had a plan. The hospital staff had to work with Tameka on her passive "I'm a disabled child" routine, and they had to work with Tameka's mother on reaching a common understanding, supporting her experience, and leveling the appropriate sanctions when Tameka misbehaved on her visits. Ms. Samson had to set appropriate expectations and consequences for Tameka. Tameka's problems were not solved by this intervention. But what did happen is that the pieces of the picture of her situation, which had formed a pattern of symmetrical struggle between Ms. Samson and the mental health staff (and before that, between Ms. Samson and Tameka's father), now cascaded into a different pattern, a shaky pattern of alliance and cooperation that needed to be strengthened. And it would be through the feedback of Tameka's improvement and the general sense of competence to be experienced by all who were working with her.

In the end, Tameka did not return to live with her mother. Ms. Samson finally acknowledged that she could not cope with another child, and Tameka expressed that she did not want to live with her. She became reinvolved with her father. Tameka learned to read, and her stutter disappeared. She expressed herself more directly and confidently, and when she went to live in a residential home with connections to both of her parents, everyone (including Tameka, who was now eleven) felt that this was a good next step.

Acting Like a Mental Health Professional

Mental health is not a place and it is not a service. Accepting the financial and political realities and scientific frameworks that dominate mental health approaches as the 1990s begin, it is not likely that systems oriented to mental health will be formed soon. So it will be incumbent on individuals and groups of professionals to take the giant steps, offer mental health services, and in each individual instance in which they work, gradually resolve the crisis in child mental health.

Daniel, Revisited

Daniel and his family, who began this book, were waiting amid the crisis for a residential placement. Daniel was like a square peg in that he didn't fit well into any of several diagnostic categories that had been tried, he didn't respond well to a variety of medications or to behavior management and counseling, and a stay in the hospital had not ameliorated his condition. What else was there to do? More containment, structure, trials of medication, and psychotherapy for this child who has been designated as severely emotionally disturbed—but there is no room in a program that might provide these. Furthermore, his parents visited several residential treatment centers, and they believed such a setting would be more harmful than good. They did not accept that containment would be remedial for him. On the other hand, what could they do? At home Daniel was driving them all to distraction with his seemingly continuous contrariness and devilment. His mother needed only to ask him to do something, and he would decide to do the opposite. The local school district provided some respite when the homebound teacher showed up a couple of hours a day during the week. Of course, the school personnel were just meeting their obligations; no one expected Daniel to make any academic progress, and the school people were waiting for his placement, too.

In view of the paucity of conventional options for Daniel, I took giant steps. First, I convened a meeting of all family members at their home. We wanted to hear everyone's story, and we wanted to experience the context in which they were living. From this I learned several things: that there was an important moral commitment to this child, and that the moral commitment, shared by all of the family members, including the children, tended to override personal discomforts. Specifically, there were several children who, when encouraged to speak out, managed to tell their parents that they were sad to have Daniel at home, because he occupied so much of their time that they had little access to their parents. Second, together with the family members I identified some patterns. Generally, people treated Daniel as if he were an incompetent, sick little boy who couldn't help himself. The family members and I made a map of his problematic behaviors by identifying them as acceptable or unacceptable. Under the unacceptable category we listed disobedience, consisting of refusals to do what was asked and insistence on doing what he was told not to, and antisocial behavior, consisting of hitting, name-calling, swearing, and destroying property (his own or others'). Acceptable behaviors to be fostered or developed included paying attention, finishing tasks, reflecting on and evaluating his own performance in a positive light, asking appropriate questions, negotiating, and showing appropriately timed generosity and concern for others' comfort and safety. With this organization of experiences it was then possible for the family members to develop specific responses to Daniel.

Finally, I placed before the family the question of whether Daniel could and should remain in the family, suggesting the option either of residential treatment or of actually having him permanently placed outside the family. I did this to address the issue of mental health in the family. As we saw it, almost everyone was sacrificing for Daniel. We could certainly not make the best decision about how the family balanced the interests of the various family members. We could simply elicit the points of view, articulate the options, and help the family members become multilateral in the process of reestablishing a healthy environment for them all.

Mental Health Professionals

Currently, so-called mental health professionals and departments serve the mentally and developmentally disabled. They are therapists for those who require remediation of their situations. They are mental illness professionals. Mental health, as I have defined it and described it throughout this book, is an approach to the domains in which children live and grow. A mental health professional may be consulted only about people who are suffering, but this professional will differ from a mental illness professional by broadening his perspective and taking four giant steps. Those steps involve appreciating different frames of definition of the distress and its causes; assessing the patterns in which difficulties are experienced at as many levels as possible; elucidating strengths and resources; and, finally, respecting the role of each part of the system, so that the system can function for the benefit of all of its members.

A mental health professional cannot function by hearing a story from only one person. The story must be heard from as many involved people as possible, preferably at the same time so that their differences can be experienced by them as well as the professional. Thus, a mental health professional should always assemble as many involved people as possible. Mental health professionals are not interested simply in establishing a diagnosis; a diagnosis does not provide an explanation or a map for mental health professionals. A formulation of problems lies in apprehending patterns; a formulation of solutions lies in apprehending how patterns can change. Mental health professionals do not limit themselves to a particular arena. They do not stay in an office or a hospital. They go where there is the most salient experience of the children's lives. This may be more than one place for some children in order to get the flavor of different contexts. Mental health professionals are always looking for competence and resources. Thus, they do not rely solely on their own experience or knowledge to assess, advise, or prescribe. Instead, they solicit from the involved systems input and suggestions that more immediately tap into what the system members can and would be willing to do. Mental health professionals are not solo players or prima donnas. When involved, they are team members. And when taking a metaperspective, they are directing in the best tradition of a play director, one who lets the talented players make the script come to life.

REFERENCES

AICHORN, A. [1925] 1935. *Wayward youth.* Trans. New York: Viking.

―――. [1923] 1964. On education in training schools. Reprinted in *Delinquency and child guidance: Selected papers by August Aichorn,* ed. O. Fleischmann, P. Kramer, and H. Ross, New York: International Universities Press.

―――. [1934] 1964. The Juvenile Court: Is it a solution? Reprinted in *Delinquency and child guidance: Selected papers by August Aichorn,* ed. O. Fleischmann, P. Kramer, and H. Ross, New York: International Universities Press.

AMERICAN ACADEMY OF CHILD PSYCHIATRY. 1983. *Child psychiatry: A plan for the coming decades.* Washington, D.C.: AACP.

AMERICAN PSYCHIATRIC ASSOCIATION. 1987. *Diagnostic and statistical manual of mental disorders,* 3rd ed. revised (DSM-III-R). Washington, D.C.: APA.

ANDERSON, H., H. A. GOOLISHIAN, AND L. WINDERMAN. 1986. Problem determined systems. *Journal of Strategic and Systemic Therapies* 5:1–13.

ANTHONY, E. J. 1987. Risk, vulnerability, and resilience: An overview. In *The invulnerable child,* ed. E. J. Anthony and B. J. Cohler, 3–48. New York: Guilford.

ARIÈS, P. 1962. *Centuries of childhood.* Trans. R. Baldick. New York: Random House.

BARTHOLEMEW, K. 1986. Family therapy for children with chronic illness. In *Treating young children in family therapy,* ed. L. Combrinck-Graham, 43–51. Rockville, Md.: Aspen.

BATESON, G. 1958. *Naven.* Stanford, Calif.: Stanford University Press.

―――. 1972. *Steps to an ecology of mind.* New York: Ballantine.

―――. 1979. *Mind and nature: A necessary unity.* New York: Bantam.

BEAVERS, J. 1989. Physical and cognitive handicaps. In *Children in family contexts,* ed. L. Combrinck-Graham, 193–212. New York: Guilford.

BERNE, E. 1964. *Games people play.* New York: Grove.

BIRD, H. R., G. CANINO, M. RUBIO-STIPEC, M.S. GOULD, J. RIBERA, M. SESMAN, M. WOODBURY, S. HUERTAS-GOLDMAN, A. PAGAN, A. SANCHEZ-LACAY, AND M. MOSCOSO.

1988. Estimates of the prevalence of childhood maladjustment in a community survey in Puerto Rico. *Archives of General Psychiatry* 45:1120–26.

BOSZORMENYI-NAGY, I., AND G. SPARKS. 1973. *Invisible loyalties.* New York: Harper and Row.

BOSZORMENYI-NAGY, I., AND B. KRASNER. 1986. *Between give and take.* New York: Brunner/Mazel.

BOWEN, M. 1978. *Family therapy in clinical practice.* New York: Jason Aronson.

BREUNLIN, D.C. 1988. Oscillation theory and family development. In *Family transitions,* ed. C.J. Falicov, 113–55. New York: Guilford.

BREUNLIN, D., AND R. SCHWARTZ. 1986. Sequences: Toward a common denominator of family therapy. *Family Process* 25:67–87.

BRONFENBRENNER, U. 1979. *The ecology of human development: experiments by nature and design.* Cambridge, Mass: Harvard University Press.

BYNG-HALL, J. 1980. Symptom bearer as marital distance regulator: Clinical implications. *Family Process* 19:355–65.

CAPLOW, T. 1968. *Two against one.* Englewood Cliffs, N.J.: Prentice-Hall.

COLES, G. 1987. *The learning mystique.* New York: Pantheon.

COMBRINCK-GRAHAM, L. 1983. The family life cycle and families with young children. In *Clinical implications of the family life cycle,* ed. H. Liddle, Rockville, Md.: Aspen.

———. 1985. A model for family development. *Family Process* 24:139–50.

———. 1987. Invitation to a kiss: Diagnosing ecosystemically. *Psychotherapy*

COMBRINCK-GRAHAM, L., AND L. KERNS. 1989. Intimacy and identity in families with young children. In *Intimate environments,* ed. B. Okun and D. Kantor, 74–92. New York: Guilford.

CONRAD, P. 1980. On the medicalization of deviance and social control. In *Critical psychiatry,* ed. D. Ingleby, 102–19. New York: Pantheon.

COSTELLO, E.J., A.J. COSTELLO, C. EDELBROCK, B.J. BURNS, M.K. DULCAN, D. BRENT, AND S. JANSIZEWSKI. 1988. Psychiatric disorders in pediatric primary care: Prevalence and risk factors. *Archives of General Psychiatry* 45:1107–16.

CRAINE, L., C.E. HENSON, J.A. COLLIVER, AND D.G. MACLEAN. 1988. Prevalence of a history of sexual abuse among female psychiatric patients in a state hospital system. *Hospital and Community Psychiatry* 39, 3:300–304.

DELGADO, J.M.R. 1969. *Physical control of the mind.* New York: Harper & Row.

DELL, P.F. 1980. Researching the family theories of schizophrenia: An exercise in epistemological confusion. *Family Process* 19:321–35.

———. 1982. Beyond homeostasis: Toward a concept of coherence. *Family Process* 21:21–41.

DOSTOYEVSKY, F. [1880] 1950. *The brothers Karamazov.* Trans. C. Garnett. New York: Random House.

ELKIND, D. 1981. *Hurried children: Growing up too fast too soon.* Reading, Mass.: Addison-Wesley.

———. 1984. *All grown up and no place to go: Teenagers in crisis.* Reading, Mass.: Addison-Wesley.

ENGEL, G.L. 1977. The need for a new medical model: A challenge for biomedicine. *Science* 196:129–36.

FOUCAULT, M. 1965. *Madness and civilization: A history of insanity in the age of reason.* New York: Random House.

FRIEDAN, B. 1963. *The feminine mystique.* New York: Norton.

FRIEDMAN, R.M., S.E. SILVER, A.J. DUCHINOWSKI, K. KUTASH, M. EISEN, N.A. BRANDENBURG, AND PRANGE, M. 1989. Characteristics of children with serious emotional disturbances identified by public systems as requiring services. Tampa, Fla.: Research and Training Center for Children's Mental Health, University of South Florida. Monograph.

GARBORINO, J. 1982. *Children and families in the social environment.* New York: Aldine.

GARDNER, R. 1982. *Family evaluation in child custody litigation.* Cresskill, N.J.: Creative Therapeutics.

GARTNER, A., AND D.K. LIPSKY. 1989. *The yoke of special education: How to break it.* New York: National Center on Education and the Economy. Working Paper.

GLEICK, J. 1987. *Chaos: The making of a new science.* New York: Viking.

GLIEDMAN, J., AND W. ROTH. 1980. *The unexpected minority: Handicapped children in America.* New York: Harcourt, Brace, & Jovanovich.

GRANGER, L., AND B. GRANGER. 1986. *The magic feather.* New York: E. P. Dutton.

GREENWALD, D. 1989. Nuclear-age children & families. In *Children in family contexts,* ed. L. Combrinck-Graham, 502–525. New York: Guilford.

GRIFFITH, J. L., M. E. GRIFFITH, AND L. S. SLOVIK. 1989. Mind-body patterns of symptom generation. *Family Process* 28, 2:137–52.

GUTSTEIN, S.E., M.D. RUDD, J.C. GRAHAM, AND L.L. RAYHA. 1988. Systemic crisis intervention as a response to adolescent crises. *Family Process* 27:201–11.

HAFNER, H. 1987. The concept of disease in psychiatry. *Psychological Medicine* 17:11–14.

HALEY, J. 1973. *Uncommon therapy.* New York: Norton.

HARRISON, S.I., AND J.F. McDERMOTT, JR. 1972. *Childhood psychopathology: An anthology of basic readings.* New York: International Universities Press.

HASKINS, R. 1989. Beyond metaphor: The efficacy of early childhood education. *American Psychologist* 44, 2:274–82.

HEATHERINGTON, E.M., M. STANLEY-HAGAN, AND E.R. ANDERSON. 1989. Marital transitions: A child's perspective. *American Psychologist* 44:303–12.

HOFFMAN, L. 1981. *Foundations of family therapy.* New York: Basic Books.

IMBER-BLACK, E. 1988. *Families and larger systems.* New York: Guilford.

IMBER COPPERSMITH, E. 1985. Teaching trainees to think in triads. *Journal of Marital and Family Therapy* 11:61–66.

JACKSON, D.D. 1957. The question of family homeostasis. *Psychiatric Quarterly Supplement* 31:79–90.

KAGAN, J. 1984. *The nature of the child.* New York: Basic Books.

KAGAN, J., AND R.E. KLEIN. 1973. Cross-cultural perspectives on early development. *American Psychologist* 28:947–61.

KAZDIN, A.E. 1989. Developmental psychopathology: Current research, issues, and directions. *American Psychologist* 44:180–87.

KEITH, D. 1989. The family's own system: The symbolic context of health. In *Children in family contexts,* ed. L. Combrinck-Graham, 327–46. New York: Guilford.

KINNEY, J., AND D. HAAPALA. 1978. *Homebuilders resource guide.* Federal Way, Wash.: Behavioral Sciences Institute.

KLEINMAN, A. 1988. *The illness narratives.* New York: Basic Books.

KNITZER, J. 1982. *Unclaimed children: The failure of public responsibility to children and adolescents in need of mental health services.* Washington, D.C.: Children's Defense Fund.

KNITZER, J., AND E.S. COLE. 1989a. *Family preservation services: The program challenge for child welfare and child mental health agencies.* New York: Bank Street College of Education. Monograph.

———. 1989b. *Family preservation services: The policy challenge to state child welfare and child mental health systems.* New York: Bank Street College of Education. Monograph.

KRAUS, M.A., AND E.S. REDMAN. 1986. Postpartum depression: An interactional view. *Journal of Marital and Family Therapy* 12:63–74.

KUHN, T.S. 1970. *The structure of scientific revolutions.* 2d ed. Chicago: University of Chicago Press.

LEUPNITZ, D.A. 1988. *The family interpreted.* New York: Basic Books.

LEVENSON, E. 1973. *The fallacy of understanding.* New York: Basic Books.

———. 1983. *The ambiguity of change.* New York: Basic Books.

LIBOW, J. 1989. Chronic illness and family coping. In *Children in family contexts,* ed. L. Combrinck-Graham, 213–30. New York: Guilford.

LIEBMAN, R. 1973. *Constructing a workable reality,* ed. B. Montalvo. Philadelphia: Philadelphia Child Guidance Clinic. Videotape.

MACGREGOR, R., A.M. RITCHIE, A.C. SERRANO, F.P. SCHUSTER, E.C. McDONALD, AND H.A. GOOLISHIAN. 1964. *Multiple impact therapy with families.* New York: McGraw-Hill.

MADANES, C. 1985. *Behind the one way mirror.* San Francisco: Jossey-Bass.

MANDELL, A.J. 1986. From molecular biological simplification to more realistic central nervous system dynamics: An opinion. In *Psychobiological foundations of clinical psychiatry,* ed. L.L. Judd and P.M. Groves, 361–66. New York: Basic Books.

MANSHEIM, P. 1989. The family in the legal system: The family turned against itself. In *Children in family contexts,* ed. L. Combrinck-Graham, 369–90. New York: Guilford.

MASSON, J.M. 1984. *The assault on truth.* New York: Farrar, Straus & Giroux.

McDERMOTT, J.F., AND W. CHAR. 1974. The undeclared war between child and family therapy. *Journal of the American Academy of Child Psychiatry* 13:422–36.

MESIC, P. 1987. Little people, big thoughts. *Chicago Magazine,* Feb., 120–23, 135.

MILLER, A. 1984. *Thou shalt not be aware: Society's betrayal of the child.* New York: Farrar, Straus & Giroux.

MILLER, D. 1989. Family violence and the helping system. In *Children in family contexts,* ed. L. Combrinck-Graham, 413–34. New York: Guilford.

MINUCHIN, S. 1969. Family therapy: Technique or theory? *Science and Psychoanalysis* 14:179–87.

————. 1974. *Families and family therapy.* Cambridge, Mass.: Harvard University Press.

MINUCHIN, S., AND H.C. FISHMAN. 1981. *Family therapy techniques.* Cambridge, Mass.: Harvard University Press.

MINUCHIN, S., B. MONTALVO, B. ROSMAN, AND B. GUERNEY. 1967. *Families of the slums.* New York: Basic Books.

MINUCHIN, S., B.L. ROSMAN, L. BAKER, AND R. LIEBMAN. 1978. *Psychosomatic families.* Cambridge, Mass.: Harvard University Press.

MONTALVO, B., ed. 1972. *Between you and me.* S. Minuchin, therapist. Philadelphia: Philadelphia Child Guidance Clinic. Videotape.

OFFER, D., AND J. OFFER. 1969. *The psychological world of the teenager: A study of normal adolescent boys.* New York: Basic Books.

PAPP, P. 1980. The Greek chorus and other techniques of family therapy. *Family Process* 19:45–57.

PHINNEY, J., AND M.J. ROTHERAM. 1986. *Children's ethnic socialization: Pluralism and development.* New York: Sage.

PITTMAN, F.S. III. 1984. Wet cocker spaniel therapy: An essay on technique in family therapy. *Family Process* 23:1–9.

PRUETT, K.D. 1983. Infants of primary nurturing fathers. *Psychoanalytic Study of the Child* 38:257–77.

————. 1985. Oedipal configurations in young father-raised children. *Psychoanalytic Study of the Child* 40:435–56.

ROLLAND, J. 1984. A psychosocial typology of chronic illness. *Family Systems Medicine* 2:2–25.

ROTHERAM, M.J. 1989. The family and the school. In *Children in family contexts,* ed. L. Combrinck-Graham, 347–68. New York: Guilford.

RUTTER, M. 1986. Meyerian psychobiology, personality development, and the role of life experiences. *American Journal of Psychiatry* 143:1077–87.

SCHEFLIN, A. 1980. Changing one's own epistemology (lecture). Cancer and the Family (conference), New York, N.Y. (April)

————. 1981. *Levels of schizophrenia.* New York: Brunner/Mazel.

SCHWAB, G. 1950. *Gods and heroes.* New York: Pantheon.

SELVINI PALAZZOLI, M., G. CECCHIN, G. PRATA, AND L. BOSCOLO. 1978. *Paradox and counterparadox.* New York: Jason Aronson.

STEINGLASS, P. 1981. The alcoholic family at home. *Archives of General Psychiatry* 38:578–84.

STERN, D.N. 1985. *The interpersonal world of the infant.* New York: Basic Books.

STROUL, B., AND R. FRIEDMAN. 1986. *A system of care for severely emotionally disturbed children and youth.* Washington, D.C.: CASSP Technical Assistance Center, Georgetown University.

SULLIVAN, H.S. 1953. *The interpersonal theory of psychiatry,* ed. S. Perry and M.L. Gawel. New York: Norton.

SZASZ, T. 1961. *The myth of mental illness: Foundations of a theory of personal conduct.* New York: Hoeber-Harper.

References

WALLERSTEIN, J.S., AND S. BLAKESLEE. 1989. *Second chances: Men, women, and children a decade after divorce.* New York: Ticknor & Fields.

WARD, A. J. 1989. Adolescent suicide and other self-destructive behaviors: Illinois survey data and interpretation. Presented at the 33rd annual meeting of the American Association of Children's Residential Centers, Phoenix, Arizona, October.

WATZLAWICK, P., J.H. BEAVIN, AND D.D. JACKSON. 1967. *Pragmatics of human communication.* New York: Norton.

WEAKLAND, J., R. FISCH, P. WATZLAWICK, AND A.M. BODIN. 1974. Brief therapy: Focused problem resolution. *Family Process* 13:141–68.

WEITHORN, L.A. 1988. Mental hospitalization of troublesome youth: An analysis of skyrocketing admission rates. *Stanford Law Review* 40:773–838.

WHITAKER, C. 1967. The growing edge. In *Techniques of family therapy,* ed. J. Haley and L. Hoffman, 265–360. New York: Basic Books.

WHITE, R.W. 1959. Motivation reconsidered: The concept of competence. *Psychological Review* 66:297–333.

WOLFENSTEIN, M. 1972. Trends in infant care. Reprinted in *Childhood psychopathology: An anthology of basic readings,* ed. Harrison and McDermott, 176–88. New York: International Universities Press.

WOOD, B. 1985. Proximity and hierarchy: Orthogonal dimensions of family interconnectedness. *Family Process* 24:487–507.

WOOD, B., AND M. TALMON. 1983. Family boundaries in transition: A search for alternatives. *Family Process* 22:347–58.

ZUK, G.H. 1971. *Family therapy: A triadic-based approach.* New York: Behavioral Publications.

INDEX

299